THE HANGOVER

THE HANGOVER

A Literary and Cultural History

JONATHON SHEARS

KEELE UNIVERSITY

First published 2020 by
Liverpool University Press
4 Cambridge Street
Liverpool
L69 7ZU

British Library Cataloguing-in-Publication data
A British Library CIP record is available

ISBN 978-1-78962-119-8

Typeset by Carnegie Book Production, Lancaster
Printed and bound by CPI Group (UK) Ltd, Croydon CR0 4YY

Contents

Figures

Acknowledgements

This book has been a long time in preparation, and I would first like to thank the staff at Liverpool University Press for their patience in allowing me extra time to complete it and the extremely helpful feedback from two anonymous readers. I believe that the book is stronger for this.

I also thank my colleagues at Keele and other universities who have generously given their time to read drafts of the chapters and provide advice and suggestions: Rachel Adcock, David Amigoni, Bernard Beatty, Nick Bentley, Michael Davies, David Fallon, Jordan Kistler, James Peacock, Amber Regis, Nick Seager and John Wrighton. I am indebted to Richard Stephens for telling me about the field of hangover studies in Psychology and inviting me to a meeting of the Alcohol Hangover Research Group and to Andy Pickard for advice on pharmaceuticals. Thanks also go to David Wright and others who have suffered a 'bastard behind the eyes', for informal advice along the way. They helped me avoid some errors and misjudgements. Any that remain are my own.

As always, my family have provided me with ceaseless support, particularly Gill and Jessica, which has helped me to keep going, even when the going got tough.

The question I have been asked more than any other in writing the book is does it involve personal research? Alas, I was unable to secure funding for this and so my ambition to recreate Rochester's hangover in Tunbridge Wells remains unfulfilled. I have received many suggestions of examples of hangovers from friends and colleagues; please accept my apologies if I was unable to fit them in. Readers should also note that I took a decision to exclude the study of hangovers in film and television: it became clear to me that this required a book of its own and I would not have the space here to do the subject justice.

Introduction

Alcohol is a perennially fascinating topic of study for researchers in a variety of different fields. Its intoxicating effects on the mind have long been linked in popular culture with creativity and have been explored at length by scholars of literature and the arts. Conversely, its addictive qualities, that have been shown to do damage to both the body and mind of habitual drinkers, often place it at the centre of debates about public health. Alcohol brings people together, but it can also isolate them: it has consequently been an important subject for social anthropologists due to its central place in customs and rituals and also to psychologists for its impact on mental health. Its legislation tells us much about a society's values and economic status – about the relationship between individual responsibility and state control – and so it has preoccupied social and legal historians as well as economists.

In recent times there has been a growing interest in the representation of drinking and drinking cultures across disciplines in the humanities and social sciences, which has led to the emergence of a new field of drinking studies that has recognisable concerns and, in some cases, methodologies. Foremost in this regard are the long-historical accounts of alcohol production, consumption and addiction by James Nicholls and Virginia Berridge. Nicholls explores the reasons why excessive consumption of alcohol often creates alarm in capitalist societies; Berridge demonstrates how social anxieties about alcohol and other addictive substances shift as a consequence of increased medical understanding of addiction and changing levels of moral sensitivity.[1]

---

1   James Nicholls, *The Politics of Alcohol: A History of the Drink Question in England* (Manchester and New York: Manchester University Press, 2009); Virginia Berridge, *Demons: Our Changing Attitudes to Alcohol, Tobacco, and Drugs* (Oxford: Oxford University Press, 2013). There are more populist overviews of alcohol consumption

The physiological and social condition of intoxication has also received much attention as part of the modern development of drinking studies. Roy Porter and Stuart Walton have explored alcohol use through what Phil Withington in *Cultures of Intoxication* (2014) calls political, moral and medical 'epistemological frameworks', whilst Herring *et al* aim to foster an 'inclusive dialogue, regarding the causes, characteristics and consequences of intoxicant use in modern societies' through combining attention to the subjective experience of intoxication, captured in literature and the arts, with essays explaining the physiological and neurological impacts of alcohol.[2] As with Nicholls and Berridge, their ultimate aim is to contribute to the ongoing discussion about how the ability to control the use of alcohol – along with other intoxicants – has been governed not only by physiology but by 'cultural beliefs and social practices'.[3] The impact of this research is growing, and some largely scientific studies have begun to incorporate contributions that focus on socio-cultural and historical dimensions of alcohol consumption.[4] This research has helped us to understand more clearly that the decision to drink alcohol, what sort, how frequently and how much, is influenced by physiological concerns, but also by issues of class and gender, age, levels of education, ethnicity, belief and cultural background. It has also demonstrated that studying alcohol and drinking habits offers an insight into the way in which individuals, but also societies more generally, fashion their identity.

What has so far been missing from this revived interest in the representation of all things alcoholic is a key component of the drinking experience: that is the physical and emotional strains, the spiritual and social consequences of – usually heavy – drinking commonly known as a hangover. The hangover is the aftermath of drinking, ordinarily a period associated with the morning after a night of overindulgence. It is a by-product of the experience of intoxication and not a part of

available including: Rod Phillips, *Alcohol: A History* (Chapel Hill: University of North Carolina Press, 2014); Iain Gately, *Drink: A Cultural History of Alcohol* (London: Penguin, 2008).

2   Phil Withington, 'Introduction', *Cultures of Intoxication, Past & Present*, 222, suppl_9 (2014), pp. 9–33; Jonathan Herring *et al* (eds), *Intoxication and Society: Problematic Pleasures of Drugs and Alcohol* (London: Palgrave Macmillan, 2012), pp. 1–2. See also: Roy Porter and Mikuláš Teich, *Drugs and Narcotics in History* (Cambridge: Cambridge University Press, 1995); Stuart Walton, *Out Of It: A Cultural History of Intoxication* (London: Penguin, 2001).

3   Herring *et al* (eds), *Intoxication and Society*, p. 2.

4   See, for example, Peter Boyle *et al* (eds), *Alcohol: Science, Policy, and Public Health* (Oxford: Oxford University Press, 2013).

intoxication itself, which may explain its general neglect other than in passing reference. It is true that hangovers have begun to take a more central role in investigations into habits of alcohol misuse in the hard and soft sciences, particularly in medicine and psychology, and the Alcohol Hangover Research Group was formed in 2010 by Joris Verster, Richard Stephens, Renske Penning and Mark Young to explore the 'socioeconomic consequence and health risks' and to refine the scientific pathology of the hangover. However, literary and cultural studies are yet to make a contribution to this debate.[5]

This is a pity, because many of the issues given prominence in other discussions of alcohol in the humanities, particularly the relationship between an individual and their environment, the politics of controlling alcohol consumption, the complex ways in which alcohol affects our perception of body and mind and the clash of cultural values that often arises from overlapping epistemological frameworks, are central to studying hangovers. It is also a pity because, as this book will establish, the hangover is a larger topic than has yet been acknowledged by the sciences, which have tended to focus mostly on collecting quantitative data concerning the somatic effects of hangovers or investigating their impact on performance at work and on the economy.[6]

In a memorable essay on the subject, published in his 1972 volume *On Drink*, Kingsley Amis notes the hangover's multifaceted nature when he calls it a 'unique route to self-knowledge'. In reviewing the kind of light-hearted self-help literature that appeared, and still appears, regularly in the press at key points of the calendar, particularly New Year, Amis observes the preponderance of cures and remedies that target physical symptoms alone: 'They omit the psychological, moral, emotional, spiritual aspects: all that vast, vague, awful, shimmering metaphysical superstructure', which Amis argues constitutes a 'Metaphysical Hangover'.[7] He was thinking primarily about the emotional content of a hangover that might include anxiety, guilt, embarrassment, humiliation and self-disgust, although that does not rule out less self-lacerating responses such as

5   See Joris Verster *et al*, 'The Alcohol Hangover Research Group Consensus Statement on Best Practice in Alcohol Hangover Research', *Current Drug Abuse Reviews*, 3.2 (June 2010), pp. 116–26.

6   Verster *et al*, 'Consensus Statement', pp. 116–26.

7   Kingsley Amis, 'The Hangover', in *Everyday Drinking: The Distilled Kingsley Amis*, intro. Christopher Hitchens (London: Bloomsbury, 2010), p. 79. The list of books of hangover remedies are too numerous to mention here. The most significant recent publication on this subject is Shaughnessy Bishop-Stall's journalistic account of his attempts to find the perfect cure, *Hungover: The Morning After and One Man's Quest for a Cure* (New York: Penguin, 2018).

lighter self-deprecation, pride or defiance. Amis differentiates to amuse. In Canto II of his mock-epic poem *Don Juan* (1819), Lord Byron does likewise when he pithily bisects the hangover:

> Few things surpass old wine; and they may preach
> Who please – the more because they preach in vain –
> Let us have wine and women, mirth and laughter,
> Sermons and soda-water the day after. (II, 178)[8]

On one side lie the demands of the body, on the other the spirit. But Byron is being deliberately disingenuous. As we will discover, the hangover is too complex a coaction of body and mind to be remedied in such a bifurcated manner and Byron knew this just as did Amis. This book will show that the hangover is a complicated, often messy, troubling, though sometimes enlightening, richly subjective experience that we learn most about in the analysis of literature and other related cultural productions that expose, with a different kind of precision to science, the ramifications of the after-effects of consuming alcohol.

What self-help literature and scientific research also leave out of their investigations into the hangover is how culturally enlightening they can be. Although negative 'affect' – the term usually employed by science to refer to feeling[9] – may be compounded by the stresses put upon the body, and while science tells us these arise in disruptions to the body's system of neurocognition, this book will show that it is in literary representation that we will most readily see how they belong to a complicated psychosocial habitus. Many of the features of a hangover are generic – particularly somatic symptoms – yet they are also context specific and my approach demonstrates the ways in which drinking unsettles ideological restraints that belong to cultural moments. Michel Foucault believed the individual to be regulated by 'systems of thoughts composed of ideas, attitudes, courses of action, beliefs and practices' and, if drunkenness often does damage to those ideological workings, it is the hangover that discloses most apparently the social values that drunkenness is perceived to upset.[10] It does this in numerous ways, including variations on what psychologists have

8   Lord Byron, *The Complete Poetical Works*, ed. Jerome J. McGann, 7 vols (Oxford: Clarendon Press, 1980–93), V.

9   See Lisa Feldman Barrett, *How Emotions are Made: The Secret Life of the Brain* (New York: Macmillan, 2017), p. 72.

10   Iara Lessa, 'Discursive Struggles Within Social Welfare: Restaging Teen Motherhood', *British Journal of Social Work*, 36.2 (2006), p. 285 (pp. 283–98).

called the 'Traditional-Punishment' or 'Withdrawal-Relief' methods of hangover recovery.[11] These are useful yardsticks in measuring hangover reaction, broadly indicating acceptance or defiance of social values or restraints, and I will explain their pertinence to the study of hangover literature in Chapter 1.

Drunkenness is celebrated and censured to different degrees at different periods of history, but this book's contribution to drinking studies is to show that hangovers are one of the clearest indicators of not just the full physical impact of alcohol on the body and mind but also of the kind of cultural values that police drinkers, which critics like Nicholls, Withington and Herring have sought to define. The word 'hangover' is not applied to the after-effects of alcohol consumption until 1904 (*OED*) – and I will trace the word's etymology in Chapter 1 – but what connects hangovers of different periods is their ability to force a reappraisal of cultural norms and requirements on an individual. The hangover might at first seem a niche or quirky subject for a book, but when we begin to see them as more than just an unpleasant by-product of the drinking experience, as more than a cluster of physiological symptoms, we can appreciate their larger significance to the study of alcohol. To do this we need to turn from quantitative surveys to the play of meanings that literature permits, where the ability to express how one feels – the full range of sensations, thoughts and emotions belonging to a hangover – is paramount. It is this factor that motivates this literary-cultural study of the hangover.

While much of the hangover literature discussed in this book that comes prior to the twentieth century focuses on male drinking behaviour and habits, unlike literature about drunkenness *per se*, one of its intriguing features is that it is quite often framed by concerns about masculine excess expressed by women. However, it is important to note that the hangovers of women are often obscured in literary representation prior to the twentieth century. The hysteria that surrounds the gin craze in the first half of the eighteenth century is attributable, at least in part, to the widespread view that more women were drinking heavily than before, but there are very few examples in literature of women with hangovers from the nineteenth century through to the end of the prohibition era. One reason for this is that women's drinking is often a taboo subject.[12] Another is that it lacks the Bacchic or binging associations of male camaraderie in Western literature and culture, at

---

11   See p. 30 below.

11   See p. 30 below.

12   For a general discussion of this subject, see Moira Plant, *Women and Alcohol: Contemporary and Historical Perspectives* (London: Free Association Books, 1997).

least until the emergence of the 'ladettes' in the late twentieth century, who are often considered to ape and infiltrate male drinking rituals and spaces. Rather than draw conclusions from scattered evidence, I therefore offer analysis of drinking and femininity in Chapters 3 and 6 – most extensively in the latter, where my discussion of figures like Christopher Isherwood's Sally Bowles and Jean Rhys's Sasha Jensen, forbears in some respects of the ladettes, allows me to explore ways in which the hangovers of women drinkers are differentiated from those of men, particularly regarding judgements about sexual impropriety.

The book is divided into six chapters. Some overlap occurs in the chronology, particularly around the transition between eighteenth and nineteenth centuries. I also take the liberty of skipping forwards and backwards in time within chapter subdivisions as the thematic links direct me. In a potentially broad subject some selection is also necessary, so the book focuses on Western literary and cultural traditions, primarily Britain and, in the twentieth century, the United States. Some readers may object that this approach elides the differences in the alco-literary traditions of the two nations, but each chapter groups together texts under themes that I have found sufficiently prevalent across different periods and places to justify their being considered together.

The book begins with a chapter that recounts in more detail some of what science has told us about the physiological features of a hangover and shows, through some initial close analysis of famous hangover descriptions in novels by Amis, Tom Wolfe and F. Scott Fitzgerald, how literature enables writers to express the often opaque territory between mind and body, intellect, sensations and feelings that makes up the experience of a hangover. This chapter establishes my methodology of literary critical analysis, sets out the etymology of the word 'hangover' and introduces the Traditional-Punishment and Withdrawal-Relief recovery methods which form the backbone of the book's themes.

Chapter 2 begins the work of showing how hangovers disclose values that belong to different cultural contexts. This commences in the early modern period, broadly speaking the seventeenth century, because I argue that, following the rise of stern forms of Protestantism in England, drinking became associated with sin and shamefulness and hangovers regularly loaded with moral judgement. The chapter shows that the cultural coding of the hangover developed partly in reaction to male rituals of sociability and examines some of the vernacular of the hangover – tracing words such as 'qualms' and 'crop-sick' – that features both in sermons and bawdy verse and drama.

The state of the nation is paramount in hangover literature of the Georgian period or the long eighteenth century. Chapter 3 enters the terrain of Nicholls to show how hangovers revealed cultural and political tensions in Britain, arguing that they were a particularly conspicuous example of the idleness that was perceived as a threat to the economy. Hangovers feature prominently during the gin craze, but also in writing about the household, domestic life and the figure of the bachelor and the socialite.

Chapter 4 is about hangovers in literature of the Romantic period, focusing on what I call 'Odes' to the hangover by poets like Robert Burns, Samuel Taylor Coleridge and Lord Byron that sustained feelings of the insoluble, vague and shimmering variety. The hangover provided the Romantics with an opportunity to explore the creative mind under duress. Romantic-period poetry makes the individual, and their particular psychological make-up, a fit subject of study in a way that had not been the case in the earlier eighteenth century. My account of hangovers accordingly shifts from this point towards exploring in more detail what literature tells us about 'hangover consciousness': the subjective response of the drinker to the cultural judgements passed upon drinking and the other vices that it is often alleged to promote.

Chapter 5 turns to the nineteenth-century novel, which became the vehicle for writers such as Charles Dickens, Anne Brontë and Thomas Hardy to mine what Thomas Gilmore calls 'the complex humanity of the drunkard'.[13] Victorian novelists showed new interest in the effects of alcohol on the mind and, drawing on pathologies of addiction in medical texts, gave greater psychological precision to hangover descriptions, even as they retained a sense of the hangover's inscrutable elements.

In Chapter 6, I discuss how the hangover disrupts self-image and alternately stages shame-proneness and defiance in literature of the twentieth century and in some more recent texts from the twenty-first century. I explore the ways in which hangovers of habitual drinkers in novels by Jack London, Patrick Hamilton, Charles Bukowski and A. L. Kennedy, amongst others play host to a variety of cultural, social, gendered and intergenerational clashes. This is the longest chapter of the book, partly because of the psychological differentiation we find in drinkers, but also because the word 'hangover' is in use, unlike earlier periods. Prompted by the recent work of Steven Earnshaw, I place at the centre of my analysis the figure of the Romantic outsider or outcast, male and female, who typically fashions an identity through heavy alcohol consumption, and who seems initially less concerned with the need to reconnect with social values than drinkers in earlier periods.

---

13 Thomas B. Gilmore, *Equivocal Spirits: Alcoholism and Drinking in Twentieth-Century Literature* (Chapel Hill: University of North Carolina Press, 1987), p. 8.

Finally, I consider the common motif of memory loss, exploring the role it plays in impeding the outsider's realisation of self-knowledge through drunkenness.

Taken together, the chapters demonstrate that the hangover, just as much as drunkenness or intoxication, has a literary and cultural history that necessitates understanding continuities and changes in beliefs and social practices. Although I will not neglect descriptions of the physical hangover symptoms that have formerly occupied science, this book goes further in explaining the fluctuating psychosocial reasons for the formation of negative affect – guilt, shame, anxiety, humiliation – in sufferers and the reasons why drinkers might accept or resist the judgements passed upon alcohol use. The aftermath of drinking is often messy, but also personally and culturally illuminating.

Chapter 1

Isolating, Placing and Contextualising the Hangover

The telephone blasted Peter Fallow awake inside an egg with the shell peeled away and only the membranous sac holding it intact. Ah! The membranous sac was his head, and the right side of his head was on the pillow, and the yolk was as heavy as mercury, and it rolled like mercury, and it was pressing down on his right temple and his right eye and his right ear. If he tried to get up to answer the telephone, the yolk, the mercury, the poisoned mass, would shift and roll and rupture the sac, and his brains would fall out.

The telephone was on the floor, in the corner, near the window, on the brown carpet. The carpet was disgusting. Synthetic; the Americans manufactured filthy carpet; Metalon, Streptolon, deep, shaggy, with a feel that made his flesh crawl. Another explosion; he was looking straight at it, a white telephone and a slimy white cord lying there in a filthy shaggy brown nest of Streptolon. Behind the Venetian blinds the sun was so bright it hurt his eyes.[1]

Through this rather ugly yet compelling description, readers are first introduced to the journalist Peter Fallow in Tom Wolfe's novel of New York hedonism, *The Bonfire of the Vanities* (1987). There is little doubt about what is occurring as we immediately recognise a rather visceral description of a man with a hangover. Acute physical distress is registered by brain, ears, eyes and mouth making the victim hyper-aware of the damage that alcohol has done to his system. It is not just the physical impact of a hangover, but body consciousness that takes centre stage as

---

1   Tom Wolfe, *The Bonfire of the Vanities* (London: Vintage, 2010), p. 170.

Fallow attempts to process a situation that initially overwhelms to the extent that he does not recognise his head as his own.

So what is happening? How do we find some sense of order within this apparent chaos? The easiest way to approach the situation is to focus first on what is known about the effects of alcohol on the body. Were Fallow to be approached by a psychologist interested in gathering data about hangovers then he might well be invited to fill out a survey to record his symptoms. Psychobiological studies of the hangover have usually employed the Acute Hangover Scale (Fig. 1.1) first adopted by experimental psychology in cohort tests by Damaris Rohsenow. The scale consists of nine categories: Hangover, Thirsty, Tired, Headache, Dizziness or faintness, Nausea, Stomach ache, Heart-racing and Loss of appetite.[2]

	None (0)	Mild (1)	Moderate (4)	Incapacitating (7)
Hangover				
Thirsty				
Tired				
Headache				
Dizziness or faintness				
Nausea				
Stomach ache				
Heart-racing				
Loss of appetite				

Fig. 1.1 Damaris Rohsenow, Acute Hangover Scale (AHS) (2007)

2   D. J. Rohsenow *et al*, 'The Acute Hangover Scale: A New Measurement of Immediate Hangover Symptoms', *Addictive Behaviors*, 32.6 (June 2007), pp. 1314–20.

Symptom	Reported %	Symptom	Reported %
Fatigue	95.5	Audio-sensitivity	33.3
Thirst	89.1	Photo-sensitivity	33.1
Drowsiness	88.3	Blunted affect	29.9
Sleepiness	87.7	Muscle pain	29.4
Headache	87.2	Loss of taste	28.0
Dry mouth	83.0	Regret	27.1
Nausea	81.4	Confusion	25.8
Weakness	79.9	Guilt	25.2
Reduced alertness	78.5	Gastritis	23.4
Concentration problems	77.6	Impulsivity	22.7
Apathy	74.0	Hot/cold flushes	21.4
Increased reaction time	74.0	Vomiting	20.8
Reduced appetite	61.9	Heart pounding	19.4
Clumsiness	51.4	Depression	18.9
Agitation	49.5	Palpitations	17.0
Vertigo	48.0	Tinnitus	16.8
Memory problems	47.6	Nystagmus	16.1
Gastrointestinal complaints	46.7	Anger	10.1
Dizziness	46.0	Respiratory problems	9.7
Stomach pain	44.7	Anxiety	7.4
Tremor	38.9	Suicidal thoughts	1.8
Balance problems	38.6		
Restlessness	36.8		
Shivering	34.4		
Sweating	33.9		
Disorientation	33.8		

Fig. 1.2 Penning, McKinney and Verster, Alcohol Hangover Symptoms (including results) (2012)

Respondents are required to record their symptoms on a scale of one to seven, through four anchors ranging from 'None' to 'Incapacitating'. Although these symptoms are subjectively interpreted, it should be noted that the categories assess the physical effects of a hangover, suggesting science's longstanding privileging of the somatic over the psychological. In more recent years, a movement from a biomedical to a biopsychosocial model of understanding the hangover has developed and, in 2012, Penning, McKinney and Verster presented a more comprehensive, 47-item scale, based on a survey of Dutch students (Fig. 1.2).[3] The scale acknowledges greater complexity, although the small number of categories indicating, and low proportion of drinkers reporting, negative affect means the hangover still appears to be a largely physical phenomenon. Some of the symptoms we can see in our brief encounter with Peter Fallow. They include Nausea, Headache, Audio-sensitivity, Photo-sensitivity, Concentration problems, Agitation, Blunted affect and Balance problems. Others, including Dry Mouth, Hot and Cold flushes, Memory problems and Fatigue can be inferred, while Vomiting seems the logical next step.

The causes of the physical symptoms of a hangover are more complex than the ways in which they are measured in controlled research, but can be partly explained by the way in which the human body metabolises ethanol present in the bloodstream after drinking. According to a classic study of hangovers in Finland in the 1970s, symptoms first appear when the blood concentration of ethanol starts to decrease and peak once blood alcohol level reaches zero.[4] Alcohol is widely known to be a diuretic, explaining dehydration. It is also a vasodilator and hangover headaches are partly a response to the subsequent contraction of the blood vessels. Metabolites of ethanol include acetaldehyde, which is sometimes considered to be the toxic endpoint of drinking. Both are less reliable indicators in laboratory studies of the amount of alcohol consumed by an individual than biomarkers such as fatty acid ethyl esters and ethyl glucuronide – readily detectable in hair and widely used in alcohol and drug testing – and phosphatidylethanol, a blood marker useful for its long detection period.

Different types of alcoholic beverage contain active ingredients other than pure ethanol, which also have an impact on hangovers and can be recorded in urine and blood samples. The most significant of these

---

3   R. Penning, A. McKinney and J. Verster, 'Alcohol Hangover Symptoms and Their Contribution to the Overall Hangover Severity', *Alcohol and Alcoholism*, 47.3 (May–June 2012), pp. 248–52.

4   R. H. Ylikhari *et al*, 'Metabolic Studies on the Pathogenesis of Hangover', *European Journal of Clinical Investigation*, 4.2 (April 1974), pp. 93–100.

are congeners, present as flavourings, which are known to contribute to dehydration and headache. Congeners are produced during the process of fermentation and are responsible for the signature aroma and flavour of a drink, most notably in the tannins present in red wine. The greater the number of congeners the more severe the symptoms of hangover, with studies showing that darker drinks such as whisky, red wine and port are more likely to result in a hangover than clearer beverages such as white wine, gin or vodka.[5] Congeners are metabolised as methanol, from which toxins poisonous to the central nervous system such as formaldehyde and formic acid are also produced.

Other ways in which natural sciences measure the effects of hangovers can often sound cryptic or hermetic to the lay reader: these include hormonal alterations, disturbance in prostaglandin synthesis (control of muscle movement), deregulated cytokine pathways (interruption to the functioning of the immune system), hypoglycaemic symptoms (deficiency of glucose in the bloodstream) and an increase in pathogenic bacteria (harmful bacteria responsible for a number of diseases including tuberculosis).

We now know a little more about the physics of a hangover, and I will draw on this knowledge as we proceed, but my primary focus lies elsewhere. We need other types of knowledge to unravel hangovers. The advantage in attending to literature in researching the subject is that, unlike the gathering of quantitative data in experimental science, valuable though that is, we get a greater degree of subjective interpretation for which scientific studies are now looking, but which they find hard to reach.[6] Not just physics, or the body, but what I just called the body 'consciousness' of a hangover, along with other types of consciousness or perception. The most recent neurological research, such as that conducted by Lisa Feldman Barrett, has posited that emotions arise when the brain attempts to interpret the meaning of bodily sensations, but hangover literature is ahead of science in this regard, as we see in the example of Peter Fallow.[7] Wolfe uses

5   D. J. Rohsenow *et al*, 'Intoxication With Bourbon Versus Vodka: Effects on Hangover, Sleep, and Next-Day Neurocognitive Performance in Young Adults', *Alcoholism, Clinical and Medical Research*, 34.3 (March 2010), pp. 509–18.

6   For example, the 'naturalistic' approach, involving interviewing subjects with hangovers, is adopted by Beth Marsh in her recent research into the emotional dimensions of hangovers in 'Shyness, alcohol use disorders and "hangxiety": A naturalistic study of social drinkers', *Personality and Individual Difference*, 139.3 (2019), pp. 13–18.

7   Lisa Feldman Barrett, *How Emotions are Made: The Secret Life of the Brain* (New York: Macmillan, 2017).

an omniscient narrator, but through indirect discourse takes us into the mind of Fallow and his first stumbling attempts to process the hangover. Knowing about acetaldehyde, congeners and deregulated cytokine pathways is unlikely to help him. In order to deal with the hangover, we need to explain how it makes us feel, and literature is an outlet for feeling.

Let us now extrapolate a little more detail about Fallow from the description of his hangover. It appears to be everywhere, inside and out, a feature of the body but also of the mind and the spirit and increasing our awareness of their interconnection. Wolfe relays this intensely subjective experience in a kind of dual movement of assignment and disassociation that involves his use of the physical world. The image of the mercury egg magnifies the twin sense of fragility and weight: this physical precarity – the potential for Fallow's brains to fall out – is symbolic of Fallow's intellectual, professional and moral jeopardy at this point in the novel. Images of disgust are projected onto the furnishings ('Synthetic' is a judgement not just on Fallow but also on the values of 1980s neo-liberalism more generally), but they quite clearly belong to Fallow. They cannot immediately be owned, but neither can they be written off as a larger social failure. They hover somewhere between the two. Fallow's crawling flesh is both a product of self-disgust and physical sickness, of course. Inarticulacy on the subject of what exactly is wrong here – personally, socially and culturally – oscillates between the language of the body and of something more ontological, as the rapid use of conjunctions in the second sentence – 'and ... and ... and ... and' – gives the impression of language's failure to cope. 'Ah!' is simultaneously an indication of recognition – of the severity of the hangover, if not of what occurred to lead to it (Fallow suffers from memory loss) – and of physical pain.

In the hands of Wolfe, the hangover is a compelling topic. Once literature becomes the medium of communication and our primary focus, the subject also seems much larger than an account of what is physically occurring. The description makes us aware of the rhythms of consciousness encountering a surfeit of unpleasant physical sensations and Wolfe gives some indication of how these might settle down into explicable feelings of guilt, self-disgust or, perhaps, defiance. Those feelings disclose details about the individual and his environment. It is this opportunity to extrapolate larger conclusions about the hangover's multifaceted nature, drawn from close attention to literature, that underpins my approach to the subject and indicates how it might enrich the field of drinking studies.

Another example, this time from F. Scott Fitzgerald's *Tender Is the Night* (1934), further illustrates what I mean. Few writers have captured the exhilarating experience of getting drunk like Fitzgerald, but his contribution to the literary history of the hangover, which has so far passed unremarked, is just as significant. The novel recounts the fashionable 1920s world of Dick and Nicole Diver as witnessed by impressionable film star Rosemary Hoyt. The setting of the French Riviera lends more glamour to the drinking than does the apartment of Peter Fallow; here alcohol is part of the experience of a more sophisticated culture. For Olivia Laing, who explores the question 'why writers drink', drinking of this sort 'is not about anything so vulgar as gratifying an appetite, but rather part of an elaborate social code, in which the right thing done at the right time conveys a near-magical sense of belonging'.[8] Wolfe puts emphasis on the vulgarity of drinking, but the contrasting sophistication does not make Fitzgerald's characters immune to alcohol's consequences. In fact, quite the opposite is true. He constructs an ironic frame around the group's libations through Dick's reckless wish to organise a 'really *bad* party ... where there's a brawl and seductions and people going home with their feelings hurt and women passed out in the cabinet de toilette'.[9] These wry prognostications turn sour when Violet McKisco encounters Nicole – a character that Fitzgerald based on his wife Zelda, who had been diagnosed with schizophrenia in 1930 – having a fit in the bathroom. Warmth turns quickly into the heat of anger when Tommy Barban defends the Divers against the accusations of the McKiscos, leading Barban to challenge Albert McKisco to a duel.

The feminised space of 'erotic darkness' in which Rosemary wakes the following morning, still thrilling to the inhalation of the 'rare atmosphere' of the Divers' party, and unaware of what has occurred, yields to the remnants of masculine, alcohol-fuelled aggression that are visited upon the unfortunate McKisco:

> McKisco was sitting on his bed with his alcoholic combativeness vanished, in spite of the glass of champagne in his hand. He seemed very puny and cross and white. Evidently he had been writing and drinking all night. He stared confusedly at Abe and Rosemary and asked:
> 'Is it time?'

8 Olivia Laing, *The Trip to Echo Spring: Why Writers Drink* (Edinburgh and London: Canongate, 2013), p. 57.

9 F. Scott Fitzgerald, *Tender is the Night* (London: Harper Collins, 2011), pp. 47–48.

'No, not for half an hour.'

The table was covered with papers which he assembled with some difficulty into a long letter; the writing on the last pages was very large and illegible. In the delicate light of electric lamps fading, he scrawled his name at the bottom, crammed it into an envelope and handed it to Abe. 'For my wife.'

'You better souse your head in cold water,' Abe suggested.[10]

McKisco is not the first combatant to enter battle with his faculties impaired by alcohol. In *Vanity Fair* (1847), Thackeray's hussars march to face Napoleon at Waterloo nursing hangovers, and one tradition has it that William I conquered at Hastings because the Saxons were incapacitated through drink.[11] McKisco is comically unsuited to the role of soldier; and, of course, most people do not awake after an evening's overindulgence to discover their life is imperilled. Yet, his sense of impending doom presents an opportunity to do further work in isolating and placing some of the hangover's features.

Fitzgerald begins by recording loss, or the sense of an absence. McKisco is bereft of the spirit and pluck fuelled by drink – 'combativeness vanished' – lamely clutching onto the symbol of his ruin as the returns of increased inebriety (he has continued drinking throughout the night) begin to diminish. Hangovers are a consequence of the consumption of alcohol and the obverse side of its enrichment: as everything was amplified in the evening, so morning sees it correspondingly dwindle. McKisco's posture, perched on the edge of the bed looking cold and pale, captures the somatic symptoms of nausea and fatigue and the emotional ones of vulnerability and doubt. Cognitive impairment and delayed reactions are implied by his confused stare and failure to respond to Abe North's promptings, and his executive functioning is evidently compromised: a liminal seated position conveys indecisiveness and perplexity. He suffers from a headache, which is indicated by the electric light: increased photo-sensitivity registered by the transferred epithet 'delicate'. Disorganised papers and illegible handwriting indicate impaired fine motor skills, although it is the hangover's capacity to evoke 'pity and repugnance'[12] – the twin responses of Rosemary, which

---

10   Fitzgerald, *Tender*, pp. 54, 61.

11   See: William Makepeace Thackeray, *Vanity Fair*, ed. Peter Shillingsburg (New York and London: Norton, 1994), p. 301; BBC, 'Drinking Problem: What Did You do Last Night?' <http://news.bbc.co.uk/1/hi/programmes/the_westminster_hour/4109735.stm.> Accessed 22/11/2018.

12   Fitzgerald, *Tender*, p. 61.

Fitzgerald invites the reader to share – which is encapsulated by the clumsy note of farewell written for the hard-nosed Violet.

Returning from his dousing, McKisco, like a ham actor, descends into a maudlin reverie on his larger personal and professional failings. 'I never have finished my novel', he discloses to Rosemary, before recalling his deceased daughter and the mutual infidelities that subsequently scarred his marriage.[13] His chilly laugh, as with soaking hair and tears in his eyes he 'raised the cold cigarette butt toward his mouth', reflects his traumatised inner life. 'His breathing quickened'. His hand trembles. Speech comes thickly and with difficulty. Eyes and head ache. Hangover consciousness is not just about remembering the night before. It prompts immediate regret for his affront – 'I've let myself be drawn into something that I had no right to be'[14] – but it is also an occasion for a more extensive self-inspection as the sufferer modulates between acceptance and deflection, guilt and excuse, for the whole gamut of prior actions. Fitzgerald shows McKisco oscillating between clarity and denial – themes that correspond to the novel's larger concerns with the mysteries of the Divers' marriage – presenting the hangover as a period of unsteady, melodramatic, personal reflection.

As with Peter Fallow, the hangover provides a vantage point on both personal and social consequences. It is not the Divers' party but the *dissonance* between the sophisticated night on the Riviera and the more vulgar aftermath that sets the real tone of *Tender is the Night*, which is that of a 'lost generation' mourning the passing of a golden age of hedonism. The severity of that era's consequences is best expressed through the motif of the hangover. In another context, that of 1950s England, a similar motif presents itself, which is the 'Saturday Night and Sunday Morning' topos. The reference is to Alan Sillitoe's 1958 novel of that name, in which the angry young man Arthur Seaton gradually grows from a hard-drinking, reckless womaniser into a more responsible adult with plans to marry. Seaton's assimilation into conventional, working-class British life should be distinguished from the precise cultural configurations of the 'lost generation', but the idea that the language of the hangover can provide a way of viewing generational decline, as well as individual suffering, is something they share. In his 1972 essay on the hangover, Kingsley Amis warns that novels about it can too quickly run into such generational motifs – 'making it the whole of the novel',[15] as he puts it – losing focus

---

13   Fitzgerald, *Tender*, p. 62.
14   Fitzgerald, *Tender*, p. 62.
15   Kingsley Amis, 'The Hangover', in *Everyday Drinking: The Distilled Kingsley Amis*, intro. Christopher Hitchens (London: Bloomsbury, 2010), p. 79.

on the specific subject by adopting the form. But the regularity with which hangovers mark, and are used as a metaphor for, personal and cultural change at different periods means that some awareness of this is needed.

Even so, we should take heed of Amis's caution and not underplay the complex set of ingredients that go to make up the hangover experience in individuals. McKisco's tragedy is narrowly averted and, having subsequently survived the duel with Barban on the golf course above Juan les Pins, the episode is punctuated with a full stop of sorts, as he is sick into some bushes. Fitzgerald is arch enough to demonstrate that McKisco overrates his importance amongst the Divers' crowd, but through this sequence of events he allows him his moment of pathos. I commented above that perception is all-important, and here we find a man gaining personal insight, but simultaneously losing his perspective under the combined duress of sensory and emotional pressure. Drunkenness is well known to disturb rational thought – and has been advocated by some writers and musicians precisely because of this[16] – but the notion that the hangover brings a return to clarity is complicated by all the emotional melodrama of McKisco's experience. The potential for introspection to turn into egotism is something that Fitzgerald had earlier explored through a hangover experienced by his first hero, Amory Blain, in *This Side of Paradise* (1920), who indulges his misery at losing his lover: 'Purposely he called up into his mind little incidents of the vanished spring, phrased to himself emotions that would make him react even more strongly to sorrow.' His 'spasm of grief' is also 'an ecstasy of sentiment'.[17] There is catharsis in the hangover, but coupled to the kind of irrationality of Charles Jackson's alcoholic, Don Birnam, who, in *The Lost Weekend* (1944), senses, despite being an educated man, that the world is a cosmic joke played out personally against him.

There is also, as in the case of Fallow, the problem of finding a balance between expressiveness and redundancy to consider. McKisco struggles to articulate what is really wrong: '"I've made a lot of mistakes in my life – many of them. But I've been one of the most prominent – in some ways –" He gave this up and puffed at a dead cigarette.'[18] Wolfe tells us that 'These days [Fallow] often woke up like this, poisonously hung over, afraid to move an inch and filled with an *abstract* feeling of despair

16   See Marty Roth, *Drunk the Night Before: An Anatomy of Intoxication* (Minneapolis and London: University of Minnesota Press, 2005), pp. 100–101.

17   F. Scott Fitzgerald, *This Side of Paradise*, ed. James L. W. West III (Cambridge: Cambridge University Press, 1995), p. 188.

18   Fitzgerald, *Tender*, p. 62.

and shame' [my emphasis].[19] Chiming with Feldman Barrett's theory of constructed emotion, 'abstract' suggests feelings of apprehension, dread or anxiety that have not yet consciously registered as shame or guilt. Similarly, Birnam feels, when reflecting on the reasons for his drinking problem, 'you lived always in a state of mortal apprehension of some dreadful deed committed for which, though you were called to account, you could never bear witness'.[20] They all experience a 'deep sense of breakage',[21] to use Laing's wonderful expression, whereby the hangover leaves them exposed, vulnerable and struggling to account for their actions.

Each example shows that the nebulous feelings of dread commonly experienced during hangovers – recently termed 'hangxiety' by the British media[22] – are not always immediately intelligible. Examining such hangover literature has the potential to take us beyond previous studies of intoxication by inviting readers to grasp complexity by entering the subjectivity of another. Are Don Birnam's drinking problems ever resolved? The clouds of his hangovers gradually disperse to disclose a variety of issues, such as repressed homosexuality, family trauma and creative failure, that appear to combine to induce his destructive drinking habits, but we can never be sure. Examining hangover literature like this does not necessarily produce solutions, but it does contribute to our understanding of how alcohol use in individuals might come to be regulated. Concurrently, it gives space to explore the human condition at a time that usually involves some sort of process of reflection, however problematic the accompanying sensations may make this. In that regard, hangovers remind us that negative affect comes in different forms and that feelings of shame and guilt can alternate with expressions of defiance or resignation. Whilst it would be an oversimplification to say, as did Emile Durkheim,[23] that, in the West, shaming cultures give way to cultures of guilt, it is also true that hangover literature, as it moves from the early modern period to the present day, develops more sustained interest in the Birnamesque experience of free-floating 'hangxiety' that is less easily quantified than shame, which generally involves the fear of social exposure. It is not part of my concern to make hard and fast distinctions between what constitutes guilt or shame, which social historians David

19 Wolfe, *Bonfire*, p. 171.
20 Charles Jackson, *The Lost Weekend* (London: Penguin, 1989), p. 162.
21 Laing, *Echo Spring*, p. 88.
22 Recorded in the *Urban Dictionary* <https://www.urbandictionary.com/define.php?term=Hangxiety> Accessed 24/5/2019.
23 See Emile Durkheim, *Sociology and Philosophy*, trans. D. F. Pocock ([1953] London: Taylor and Francis, 2009).

Nash and Anne Marie Kilday have shown to be notoriously difficult,[24] but, as the chapters of this study progress, one thing I do want to do is recognise that hangovers confront sufferers with negative affect that can be causally determined as well as feelings that seem less immediately a response to specific drunken actions. In so doing, hangover literature of the sort analysed above enables us to focus on some of the inconsistent and, perhaps, irreconcilable aspects of human nature, after the highs of intoxication have dispersed, in ways that prior drinking studies have not.

***

So far, we have seen some examples of hangover literature that indicate the multifaceted nature of the topic. If we were in any doubt that literary language enables the articulation of what hangovers feel like without sacrificing their complexity, then attention to some of the semantics of hangovers removes this. One particularly fertile period for linguistic invention was the 1940s, when, in search of neologisms, the misery of the hangover was treated with a kind of relish. If there are many words for getting drunk, the hangover is shown to have its own ludic aspects.

In P. G. Wodehouse's *The Mating Season* (1949), for instance, Bertie Wooster records 'I am told by those who know that there are six varieties of hangover – the Broken Compass, the Sewing Machine, the Comet, the Atomic, the Cement Mixer and the Gremlin Boogie.'[25] A lot of fun can be had in listing and categorising, particularly the way that the physical and moral dimensions of the hangover, but equally the degrees of severity or size, are imagined by Wodehouse through knowing images of sensory – particularly auditory – discordance: not onomatopoeia as such, but drawn from a similar linguistic field. A noticeable verbal modishness – a contemporary vernacular or low diction of the hangover – matches its general unpleasantness. Such language attempts to meet the hangover on the terms of its physical and moral vulgarity. A 'gremlin' was a slang term first used in the RAF, deriving from the word 'goblin', to refer to a 'lowly or despised person; a menial, a dogsbody' (*OED*), although it was also applied to unspecified engine trouble in the Second World War. Wodehouse's use of the word in the genteel context of the English upper classes suggests

---

24   See David Nash and Anne Marie Kilday, *Cultures of Shame: Exploring Crime and Morality in Britain, 1600–1900* (London: Palgrave Macmillan, 2010).

25   P. G. Wodehouse, *The Mating Season* (London: Penguin, 1999), p. 23.

the kind of loss of status that we will see becomes a particularly identifiable component of hangovers in the nineteenth century. By the time Roald Dahl wrote *The Gremlins*, six years prior to *The Mating Season*, the word had also taken on its meaning of a creature of mischance. By 1917, boogie evoked jazz: inharmony is surely again implied in Wodehouse's reference to the music that dominated his middle years. The clatter of a sewing machine makes sense; so too does the greater din of a cement mixer. Atomic indicates an explosion, but also a more general impression of magnitude, and Comet suggests velocity. The Broken Compass undoubtedly connotes moral failure.

Jackson supplies a similar list in *The Lost Weekend*. For Birnam the following phrases are drawn, like those of Wodehouse, from a comic lexicon, but, despite being equally evocative, they indicate to the alcoholic that the hangover is a more serious business. In fact, in this case language and metaphor miss the melancholy essence at the hangover's core:

> The humour of the hangover: the hilarious vocabulary: the things other drinkers call what they suffer then – the things *they* can call it who endure the normal reaction, merely, of a few hours of headache, butterfly-stomach and (crowning irony!) nausea at the thought of another drink. The jitters, the ginters, the booze-blues, the hooch-humps, the katzenjammers; the beezy-weezies, screaming meemies, snozzle-wobbles, bottle-ache, ork-orks, woefits, the moaning after.[26]

It is a suggestive inventory. There is more alliteration, assonance and repetition – 'hooch-humps ... ork-orks' – which maximises the non-signifying properties of language. Jackson's list gestures more comprehensively towards a discourse of anxiety and nervousness than does Wodehouse's in the choice of 'jitters', while 'blues' and 'humps' signify depression, along with 'woefits'. Most of the expressions are not Jackson's own coinages and again have a vernacular contemporaneity. The word 'jitters' was first used in 1929; woefits or 'woofits' in 1918. 'Screaming meemies' implies hysteria, originally meaning 'a state of drunkenness, delirium tremens', as included in a list of terms denoting drunkenness common in the United States in *New Republic* magazine in 1927 (*OED*). Interestingly, and evoking Wodehouse's use of explosive images, the *Infantry Journal* of 1944 – the year of *The Lost Weekend*'s publication – includes the 'Nebelwerfer mortar, nicknamed

---

26 Jackson, *Lost Weekend*, p. 175.

the "woof-woof" or "screaming mimi"' (*OED*). Fredric Brown's novel, *The Screaming Mimi*, which commences with a hangover scene, was published in 1949. 'Ginters' is evidently a nonce word, and 'snozzle-wobbles' was a slang expression, recorded in the *Urban Dictionary*. 'Hooch' carries a sense of the illicit. 'Katzenjammer', again picking up on audio-sensitivity, translates from the German as 'screaming cats' and finds an equivalent in the English 'caterwaul' (the sound sometimes attributed to the groans of the sufferer). In the context of an alcoholic's confessional, these expressions are, however, alienating: they belong to 'other drinkers'. Such hangover jargon is, for Birnam, a sign of his essential difference from the crowd of occasional drinkers. His hangovers – stifled only by more alcohol – are a badge of authenticity.

It is just a brief review of hangover semantics, but what is interesting is that it tallies with my observations made in reading the hangovers of Fallow and McKisco about the complicated overlaps of body, mind and social judgement that quantitative surveys tend to miss. The hangover makes legible some of the cultural factors that make one feel guilt or shame. Nevertheless, disclosure is accompanied by displacement: an evident difficulty in expressing or perhaps admitting how one feels. The hangover prompts utterance, but also inhibits its denotation; slang terms are often evocative, sometimes amusing, but nevertheless somewhat elusive. Euphemism draws attention to language choice and the fact that culturally specific assumptions are generally encoded in such choices, which might point us towards body or mind, or help us frame the kind of problems of perception, cognition or vaguer impressions of misery that we have so far encountered.

Language choice is also key to my study because of the etymology of the word 'hangover'. Not until surprisingly late – the early twentieth century – is hangover first applied to 'the unpleasant after-effects of (esp. alcoholic) dissipation' (*OED*) and, suitably, given its other associations with the history of slang, this first recorded appearance is in a lexicon of contemporary vernacular, the *Foolish Dictionary* (1904) by the American humourist Charles Wayland Towne, masquerading as Gideon Wurdz. It features under the definition of 'Brain', which is 'usually occupied by the Intellect Bros., – Thoughts and Ideas – as an Intelligence Office, but sometimes sub-let to Jag, Hang-Over & Co.' Here, the word hangover connotes doltishness, opposed to sharp cognition, but also weariness: and jag refers specifically to an emotional burden, 'From the Spanish word zaga, meaning a load packed on the outside of a van. In America the load is packed on the inside of a man.' (The use of jag as a literal burden has a much older derivation in late sixteenth-century English.)

Wurdz's definition of 'Absinthe' also contains the adage 'Absinthe makes the jag last longer.'[27]

The notion that a hangover is more generally 'A thing or person remaining or left over; a remainder or survival, an after-effect' (*OED*) – the 'Saturday Night and Sunday Morning' or 'lost generation' topos – does not actually arrive much earlier, with the *OED* recording the first usage of the word in this sense in the magazine *Outing* in 1894. Medical research avoids consideration of the hangover as metaphor for other types of loss, as is only right. Psychology does likewise, using the expression 'alcohol hangover' to make this distinction absolutely clear, but as the etymology of the word 'hangover' incorporates other types of aftermath, I have taken the decision to periodically do so too. However – and it is an important caveat, as parameters are necessary to prevent the subject becoming too broad – when, in the ensuing chapters, I depart from the hangover as literal subject and acknowledge it as a marker for change or metaphor for other experience – for instance, sinfulness considered in the early modern sermon, or the loss of feelings of pleasure in Romantic verse by poets like Lord Byron and John Keats – I only do so when the language still tells us something about attitudes to the alcohol hangover proper.[28]

There are multiple ingredients in hangovers, of the kind we find Wodehouse and Jackson grappling with, and so 'hangover' is a hard-working word: we now know it draws together numerous thoughts, sensations and emotions whenever it is applied to the after-effects of drinking. It also has a metaphorical life. One final point about language is necessary here because it affects my methodology: the fact that the word 'hangover' is unavailable to a student of the subject prior to the twentieth century is something of a hindrance, but it is also an opportunity. I have begun by isolating and placing the hangover through examining a couple of notable examples from twentieth-century novels, but as I step into my long historical literary study, I will keep attention on the way that the language through which hangovers are expressed changes, demanding some flexibility in approach. If, in the absence of the word 'hangover', I cannot always guarantee that the figures I focus on are not still partly

27   Text available at <http://www.fullbooks.com/The-Foolish-Dictionary.html.> Accessed 11/8/2018. Jag does have another history in relation to drinking in signifying capacity: the amount of liquor 'a man can carry' or the duration of a drinking bout (*OED*), but its application to the emotional aspect of the hangover does not occur until the early twentieth century.

28   It is for this reason that I overlook some examples of hangovers in literature where, as Amis put it, the metaphor is the only real point of interest, such as Washington Irving's *Rip Van Winkle* (1819) or Thomas Hardy's *The Mayor of Casterbridge* (1886).

drunk, I sometimes take it that if enough common factors are present, including somatic symptoms of the sort listed by Penning, McKinney and Verster, then they can reasonably constitute the after-effects of drinking that we customarily call a hangover. Shared vocabularies act as a guide, and words such as 'headache', 'feverishness' and 'nausea' are reliable markers from the period of the earliest texts I look at, which derive from the turn of the seventeenth century, right up until the present day. If a man was 'sottish' in the seventeenth century, then he was possibly still inebriated, though the word could just as easily indicate a sore head. Expressions such as 'hair of the dog' have a long history;[29] references to the 'morning after' do not really enter popular usage until the late nineteenth century, the first recorded instance applying the phrase to a hangover appearing in *Punch* in 1884.[30] A lot of my material concerns the morning, but not to the exclusion of sickness and spinning rooms that usually belong to an evening or night. Science measures hangovers only from the point at which blood alcohol level returns to zero: imposing such tight parameters would prove unhelpful to my literary and cultural study and, as my account of hangover etymology demonstrates, I range a little more freely in that regard. Words set limits, but they also provide analytical opportunities in demonstrating how attempts to express and account for the hangover reveal the ways that drinkers respond to a society's attitudes to alcohol use.

***

Science has told us that there are a lot of reasons to feel rough on the morning after a night's overindulgence, but it should now be evident that my study will show that confining hangovers to physical or neurological pathologies misses much of their rich subjectivity and cultural significance. Much more is occurring in Fitzgerald's depiction

---

29   The earliest record of 'hair of the dog' cited by the *OED* is in John Heywood's
       A Dialogue Conteinyng the Number in Effect of all the Proverbes in the Englishe Tongue
       (1546), where a hungover drinker pleads: 'I praie the leat me an my felowe haue
       / A heare of the dog that bote us last night.' The etymology of the expression lies
       in a 'remedy formerly recommended as a cure for the bite of a mad dog' (*OED*): a
       hair of the rabid dog that gave the wound was placed in it to prevent rabies. The
       earlier phrase to 'drive out wine with wine' is attributed to the Greek playwright
       Antiphanes, and is the forerunner of the Latin expression *similia similibus curantur*,
       often applied in homeopathy.
30   'Bow Wow', *Punch* (31 May 1884), p. 264.

of Albert McKisco's hangover, for example, than can be ascribed to the body. His combined feelings of regret and resolution, the pitch of his self-evaluation and his mixture of insight and nescience that all enrich and round out the human experience of suffering from a hangover fall outside the normal remit of scientific enquiry.

To help with clarity, I will on occasion label physical symptoms, or even generic feelings such as guilt and shame, 'assignable', but we need to know that the way they are perceived and interpreted depends on how the individual responds to their environment. One example that underlines this fact is the famous hangover sequence in Amis's *Lucky Jim* (1953). Jim Dixon is a reluctant and inept lecturer in medieval history in a precarious state of employment, who finds himself with a lot to explain, and many reasons to feel melancholy, on waking with a painful hangover at the country house of his eccentric superior, Professor Welch, on the occasion of a weekend social. Dixon's bender included 'seven or eight' pints of beer and at least half a bottle of port. His hangover ticks many of the boxes on the more extensive list of symptoms that we have seen in Fig. 1.2 and would no doubt leave those responsible for tallying the returns of the None-to-Moderate range of the Acute Alcohol Hangover Scale (Fig. 1.1) largely untroubled:

> Dixon was alive again. Consciousness was upon him before he could get out of the way; not for him the slow, gracious wandering from the halls of sleep, but a summary, forcible ejection. He lay sprawled, too wicked to move, spewed up like a broken spider-crab on the tarry shingle of the morning. The light did him harm, but not as much as looking at things did; he resolved, having done it once, never to move his eye-balls again. A dusty thudding in his head made the scene before him beat like a pulse. His mouth had been used as a latrine by some small creature of the night, and then as its mausoleum. During the night, too, he'd somehow been on a cross-country run and then been expertly beaten up by secret police. He felt bad.[31]

Alcohol taken in large quantities is well known to disturb healthful sleep as it accelerates the body's production of glutamine. Amis expertly captures what I have referred to as 'hangover consciousness' in Dixon's abrupt feeling of collision with the morning, rattling through a series of physical symptoms including dryness and thirst, photo- and audio-sensitivity and aching limbs. The awareness of consciousness is rarely so

---

31 Kingsley Amis, *Lucky Jim* (Harmondsworth: Penguin, 1961), p. 61.

pronounced as during a hangover where thought itself seems to come as pain: Dixon's pulsing head makes the smallest vibrations in the room sound like a cacophony.

This is a description of a hangover that represents physical symptoms in detail, but it is not just that. It is also an account of an emotional and social crisis. Dixon is 'spewed up' – a physical purgation – while illogical combinations of stickiness – 'tar' – and dryness – 'shingle' and 'dusty' – aid the impression of his confusion before the sequence reaches the grotesque image of the mouth used as a lavatory.[32] Nausea, as Sartre affirmed, is both a somatic and an existential category.[33] Something undeniably comic informs the narrator's underwhelming conclusion, focalised through his protagonist, that Dixon 'felt bad'. In keeping with my theme of disclosure and denial, Amis's expressiveness leaves space within the passage to register the personal inadequacy of these – or possibly any – words to administer balm to Dixon's hungover body and mind.

Physical factors are noticeably paramount – as they press most urgently upon Dixon – but perception is as important. The hungover body signifies as much in a moral as somatic capacity. The use of words such as 'bad' and 'wicked' tell us this much, pointing to the numerous social reasons for Dixon to also feel ghastly. These include insulting, and narrowly avoiding a skirmish with, his host's son Bertrand, skulking off to a local pub, an inappropriate sexual entanglement with Margaret (an emotionally vulnerable female colleague), and a reckless nocturnal raid on Welch's drink's cabinet. None of this can yet be admitted of course: the body cushions the impact of Dixon's nocturnal misdemeanours, absorbing, though nonetheless registering at a non-cognitive level, information before the mind has had an opportunity to work on it and translate it into the more recognisable feelings of guilt and self-reproach that will eventually, inevitably, disturb the fully awakened conscience. Dixon fends these off for as long as possible, but physical repose offers little respite: 'Dixon heeled over sideways and came to rest with his hot face on the pillow … This, of course, would give him time to collect his thoughts, and that, of course, was just what he didn't want to do with his thoughts; the longer he could keep them apart from one another, especially the ones about Margaret, the better.'[34] It would be far easier,

---

32   See David Amigoni, Paul Barlow and Colin Trodd (eds), *Victorian Literature and the Idea of the Grotesque* (Farnham: Ashgate, 1999).

33   See Jean Paul Sartre, *Nausea*, trans. Robert Baldick ([1938] London: Penguin, 2000).

34   Amis, *Lucky Jim*, pp. 63–64.

indeed something of a comfort, to focus on the body alone. But regret lurks with embarrassment and, combined with weary resignation at the sheer scale of the possible consequences for his career and personal relationships, is expressed through a helpless grimace, imponderables and inarticulacy recalling Birnam and McKisco:

> He pushed his tongue down in front of his lower teeth, screwed up his nose as tightly as he could, and made gibbering motions with his mouth. How long would it be before he could persuade [Margaret] first to open, then to empty, her locker of reproaches, as preliminary to the huge struggle of getting her to listen to his apologies?[35]

The hangover also serves Amis in another way by enabling him to divert the romantic plot in Dixon's favour. Famously any immediate opportunity for the kind of extensive self-reproach and meditation upon human weakness that we have seen in McKisco and Amory – and which one feels might be just around the corner – is denied to Dixon by his realisation that he is surrounded by the aftermath of a small conflagration from a cigarette that he failed to extinguish before passing out the night before. A crisis usually has the effect of sharpening calcified wits but, twinned with Dixon's cognitive impairment, this results not in clarity but in further chaos as the unintentional arsonist attempts to conceal the singed bed sheets and charred rug by hacking at them with a razor blade and hiding a damaged bedside table in a lumber room.

The resultant farce disgorges Dixon's larger sense of misery and denial, attributed to his unhappiness with his vocation and desire to avoid a romantic relationship with Margaret. Margaret is the voice of reason: 'You couldn't have gone to Mrs Welch and explained, of course'?[36] But if Dixon internalises her chastisement to any degree (he briefly declares that he hates himself), this is offset by the pity and perspective of the clear-headed Christine Callaghan, girlfriend of Bertrand, whom Dixon has also insulted the previous night. Christine good-naturedly assists Dixon in rearranging his room and remaking the bed to disguise the scorched linen. Her general sense of the ridiculousness of Dixon's plight sets her in sympathetic contrast to Margaret, which enables Amis to introduce the first stirrings of the romance between them that will eventually blossom.

35   Amis, *Lucky Jim*, p. 64.
36   Amis, *Lucky Jim*, p. 75.

Christine's complicity in the crime symbolically aligns her for the first time with Dixon against Bertrand's pomposity, Welch's pedantry and Margaret's self-pity. Nevertheless, it is Dixon's deep sense of breakage that takes centre stage, proving instrumental in forcing him to confront his personal malaise and break Margaret's unhealthy stranglehold. In reading Dixon's hangover, it becomes apparent that the body both exacerbates the severity of what we might call moral consequences, but Dixon deflects onto assignable symptoms (albeit temporarily) the less easily addressed, but often more deeply troubling, psychosocial issues. In the confusion of mind on his initial waking, the two occur almost simultaneously.

The way in which assignable symptoms relate to environment can also be identified in the case of Fallow. We pick him up as he arrives at work at the offices of *The City Light* newspaper, where he catches his reflection in a mirror:

> He had the beginnings of a belly and was getting too fleshy in the hips and thighs. But this would be no problem now that he was finished with drinking. Never again. He would begin an exercise regimen tonight. Or tomorrow, in any case; he felt too bilious to think about tonight. It wouldn't be this pathetic American business of jogging, either. It would be something clean, crisp, brisk, strenuous ... English. He thought of medicine balls and exercise ladders and leather horses and Indian clubs and pulley weights and parallel bars and stout ropes with leather bindings on the end, and then he realized that these were the apparatus of the gymnasium at Cross Keys, the school he had attended prior to the University of Kent. Dear God ... twenty years ago. But he was still only thirty-six, and he was six-foot-two, and he had a perfectly sound physique, fundamentally.[37]

This might seem like a fairly generic response to a hangover, but it shows Fallow's identity is a product of his time. His self-image is noticeably disrupted or, more accurately, corrupted as the values upon which that image depend – notions of English sophistication, deriving from his schooling, which are pitted against the more vulgar Americanisms we saw represented by Streptolon and Metalon – are invoked as a counterbalance to the damage done by drink. Not only does the body suffer, but also a larger sense of cultural identity. If the body discloses this – through the seedy appearance and thickening waist in this case – it represents a

---

37   Wolfe, *Bonfire*, p. 177.

failure to meet acceptable standards of behaviour. It induces feelings of shame, emphasised by the threat of exposure or being 'seen'. Fallow's feelings may not be visible to others, but his own gaze is loaded with the cultural judgements he has internalised.

Fallow is reflected in a mirror that is also held up to systems of thought and belief of the sort that Durkheim and Foucault suggest shape individuals. The beer belly is not always viewed so negatively, as we find in the case of Shakespeare's heavy-drinking lothario, Sir John Falstaff, who, in *The Merry Wives of Windsor* (1600), is particularly proud of his 'portly belly' (I, iii, 59), which he associates with virility, or in any number of examples from the middle ages or early modern period (witness the beer drinkers in William Hogarth's *Beer Street* [1751] [Fig. 3.1] for instance), when a prominent gut was often associated with power and good health.[38] Of course Falstaff is defined by hubris, and we might add that when Verdi recasts him in his comic opera *Falstaff* (1893) it is noticeable that he evaluates more openly physical signs of excessive drinking in relation to ageing in such a way that his hangover aria, following his submersion in the Thames – 'Ehi! Taverniere! Mondro ladro' (Act III) – shows that just as the body suffers so too does his self-image on which it depends: 'If my magnificent belly hadn't kept me afloat I'd surely have drowned. A horrible death. Bloated with water. Wicked world! There's no decency left … May heaven help me. I'm getting too fat. I'm losing my hair.'[39] Familiar signs of excess pursued into later life appear unacceptable without the lubrication of drink as Verdi explores the social and cultural judgements passed upon the association of ageing with pleasure and excess. (Falstaff's spirits are noticeably revived, however, by another glass of wine.)

The difference between the behaviour of Fallow and the Falstaff of *Merry Wives* derives primarily from their self-fashioning, although we are also led to believe that they differ in their levels of tolerance. Hangover tolerance is a subject that has occupied science and may initially appear less pertinent to a study of literature. The notion of personal severity is, however, worth pausing over in concluding this chapter, because although it is likely to depend on a number of physical things – for instance, an ordinarily low or high pain threshold, metabolic rate, general health of the immune system, age and gender – some issues

38 William Shakespeare, *The Merry Wives of Windsor*, ed. Giorgio Melchiori (Walton-on-Thames: Arden, 2000); see Georges Vigarello, *The Metamorphoses of Fat: A History of Obesity* (New York: Columbia University Press, 2013), pp. ix–x.

39 Giuseppe Verdi, *Falstaff*, dir. Franco Zeffirelli (Hamburg: Deutsche Grammophon, 2009).

relate to culture and upbringing, such as high or low levels of moral sensitivity or shame-proneness.

Evidently not everyone suffers to the same degree and recent scientific research has debated whether a minority of people may be immune to the physical symptoms of hangovers.[40] On the other hand, a genetic predisposition to suffer intolerably from the physical after-effects of alcohol is one explanation given for the variance in symptoms in twins.[41] A recent study of hangover tolerance, led by the aptly named Sherry Span and Mitchell Earleywine, indicates that the desire to offset the symptoms of hangovers nearly always influences the negative decisions made by individuals with a high familial risk of becoming alcohol dependent (in other words one or both parents are known to be alcoholics). They propose two possible responses to the hangover: first, the 'Traditional-Punishment' model in which 'individuals who experience the punishing effects of hangover will reduce their drinking' accordingly and seek some form of reparation; second, the 'Withdrawal-Relief' model, or the 'hair of the dog', which 'might lead individuals to drink alcohol again in order to alleviate withdrawal symptoms'.[42]

We should be wary of bifurcating the hangover, but these categories are more profitable for a literary and cultural enquiry than the kind of body/mind or body/spirit split that I rejected in my introduction and I will regularly employ them in this book. The frequency of their occurrence makes them useful markers for orientating some of the broader continuities and contrasts I draw in the following chronological chapters. They invite focus on personal responsibility – the hangover is, in most cases, self-inflicted – that cannot be wholly explained in terms of physiology. We have already seen the first model in operation: Fallow constructs a punitive, Traditional-Punishment response to restore his self-esteem. The Withdrawal-Relief recovery method is, however, his next port of call when, under provocation from an annoying colleague, he resorts to quaffing from a bottle of vodka concealed in his coat. Withdrawal-Relief is also the amusing climax of Amis's 11-step plan to remedy the physical hangover in *On Drink*: 'About 12:30pm, firmly take a hair (or better, in Cyril Connolly's phrase, a tuft) of the dog that bit

---

40   See research presented at the ECNP conference in 2015 by Joris Verster. <https://www.sciencedaily.com/releases/2015/08/150829123815.htm.> Accessed 4/10/2018.

41   See: S. H. Wu, 'Heritability of Usual Alcohol Intoxication and Hangover in Male Twins: The NAS-NRC Twin Registry', *Alcoholism, Clinical and Experimental Research*, 38.8 (August 2014), pp. 2307–13; W. S. Slutske, 'Genetic Influences on Alcohol-related Hangover', *Addiction*, 109.12 (December 2014), pp. 2027–34.

42   S. A. Span and M. Earleywine, 'Familial Risk for Alcoholism and Hangover Symptoms', *Addictive Behavior*, 24.1 (Jan–Feb 1999), pp. 121–25.

you. The dog, by the way, is of no particular breed; there is no obligation to go for the same drink as the one you were mainly punishing the night before.'[43] The study of literature allows me to develop the ramifications of choosing one model over another, to understand the subjective responses that lead to the decisions taken during a hangover, in ways that Span and Earleywine's quantitative data analysis does not. As this chapter has demonstrated, such terms become meaningful when they are fleshed out and contextualised and one of the best ways to do that is through the fine-grained study of hangover literature that I have begun in this chapter.

We now have a flavour of the way in which study of the literary representation of hangovers can illuminate our critical reflections on things like the interrelation of the drinker's body and mind – things that cannot be tabulated – and the manner in which cultural values are expressed through reactions to drinking. Issues such as susceptibility to shame or guilt, habits of acceptance and denial and the ability to tolerate the after-effects of alcohol, to accept or resist moral appraisal, need to be viewed in terms of socio-cultural contexts as well as physiology. Moreover, the very notion that there is a 'traditional' response to a hangover indicates that these contexts do not emerge out of thin air. We can chart their development, beginning in this case with literature of the early modern period in England.

43   Amis, 'The Hangover', p. 83.

Chapter 2

'The Nausea of Sin':
The Early Modern Hangover

Introduction

Literary and cultural accounts of the consumption of alcohol, drinking cultures and its associated discourses in seventeenth-century England have too often accommodated hangovers without really acknowledging that they are there. Despite the growing body of fine work on drinking that has appeared over the last decade or so – including Adam Smyth's *A Pleasing Sinne* (2004), studies of alehouses and fellowship by Bernard Capp (2012) and Mark Hailwood (2014) and Phil Withington and Angela McShane's *Cultures of Intoxication* (2014)[1] – the physiological state, but also the political, religious and social ramifications, of hangovers in early modern literature and culture are usually lost in our accounts of inebriation and intoxication.

Historically there may be good reasons why hangovers are often ignored by scholars of early modern drinking cultures. In perhaps the most conspicuous and pervasive form of drinking literature at the opening of the seventeenth century – the verse often called Anacreontic, in reference to the Greek poet Anacreon, practised notably by Ben Jonson and his acolytes, the 'Tribe of Ben', which celebrated sophistication and moderation – hangovers evidently have little place. The hangover's elision in the Anacreontea and its offshoots has, I believe, set a tone in much

---

1   See: Adam Smyth (ed.), *A Pleasing Sinne: Drink and Conviviality in Seventeenth-Century England* (Cambridge: D. S. Brewer, 2004); Mark Hailwood, *Alehouses and Good Fellowship in Early Modern England* (Woodbridge: The Boydell Press, 2014); Phil Withington and Angela McShane (eds), *Cultures of Intoxication, Past and Present*, 222.9 (2014). See also Phil Withington, 'Food and Drink', in *The Ashgate Companion to Popular Culture in Early Modern England*, ed. Andrew Hadfield, Matthew Dimmock and Abigail Shinn (Farnham: Ashgate, 2014), pp. 149–62. Also relevant is Amanda Flather's discussion of social space in *Gender and Space in Early Modern England* (Woodbridge: The Boydell Press, 2007), pp. 98–108.

recent criticism, which has led it to focus almost exclusively on social aspects of drinking and tavern culture: fellowship, conviviality and their political significations.

In the early modern period hangovers are, however, often hiding in plain sight; we just need to know where to look for them to open up a surprisingly rich topic of study. The hangover's grammar of rise and fall, which often makes it a useful metaphor for articulating generational decline – the 'Saturday Night and Sunday Morning' or 'lost generation' topos that I introduced in Chapter 1 – no doubt plays a part here. In this chapter I will demonstrate that in the early modern period, images of hangovers cluster around the many political and social upheavals of the century, registering regularly, for example, in Puritan tracts and sermons of the early Stuart period, in Royalist drinking culture during the interregnum, in the writing of conventiclers following the Restoration of the monarchy and in Tory and Whig factions in the 1680s and 1690s. In each of these historical moments, hangovers provide a shared vocabulary with which social, political and, particularly, religious commentators were able to address spiritual shortcomings and the perceived erosion of moral values.

However, more than just marking change, hangover literature contributes significantly to our store of knowledge of early modern attitudes to alcohol. Specifically, the period advances, largely due to the emergence of particularly stern manifestations of Protestantism, our understanding of some of the components of what Span and Earleywine call a Traditional-Punishment response to a hangover.[2] Regularly invoked as a sign of sinfulness by religious enthusiasts, I argue that the assignable symptoms of a hangover – those symptoms discussed in the previous chapter that are generally perceived to belong to the body – were used to draw attention to its metaphysical concomitants. The vocabulary of nausea is my central motif, and I will show that it belongs to both the body and the soul in religious writing where it is interpreted as a product of guilt and shame. The early modern period plays a key role in establishing the link between the hangover and remorse or the guilty conscience, by connecting the somatic and ontological aftershocks of alcohol consumption in ways that become commonplace in later periods. At the same time, and in response to moral censure, the literature of the period demonstrates ways in which the Withdrawal-Relief method of combatting the hangover became associated with resisting moral judgement in bawdy song and drama.

If the dominant motif of drinking throughout the period is indeed sociability – particularly male sociability – then it is perhaps unsurprising

2   See Chapter 1, p. 30.

that the hangover, marking the after-effects of alcohol consumption, plays a part in the writing of those who wanted to censure and control excessive public drinking. Early modern hangovers are represented more frequently than we have perhaps been led to believe and demonstrate the moral values that drinking is perceived to upset, although I will begin by elaborating upon the reasons why I think the hangover has not previously been addressed in any extensive way in accounts of seventeenth-century drinking.

Anacreontea

The seventeenth century opens with the English parliament trying to come to terms with the popularity of taverns and alehouses (four bills to control drunkenness were passed between 1604 and 1625)[3] and concludes with a country waking up to a newly acquired taste for gin, which was heavily promoted by an anti-French administration and a Dutch monarch. A considerable amount of alcohol was consumed in the intervening years, despite increasingly vocal religious objections to the nation's drinking habits, and yet the period's hangovers have so far received little, if any, attention.

One of the key reasons why the hangover frequently escapes the notice of the literary critic interested in the 'textual constructions of drunkenness', as Smyth puts it, has to do with genre or mode. The most famous and celebrated manifestations of seventeenth-century excess – the 'Anacreontic-Horatian symposiastic tradition' indebted to the Greek Anacreon and the Roman poets Horace and Lucretius, popularised in England by Abraham Cowley's 1656 collection of verse on the theme – are designed precisely to deny the hangover its form and function.[4] Anacreontic verse has been a popular topic for literary critics interested in the customs of tavern culture in recent times. It is a particularly performative literature: in many examples the verse is not just written in praise of drinking but designed to be read or recited while drinking and so has proved useful in historical reconstruction.[5] The ideal of Ben Jonson

---

3   See James Nicholls, *The Politics of Alcohol: A History of the Drink Question in England* (Manchester: Manchester University Press, 2009), pp. 13–17.

4   Adam Smyth, '"It were far better to be a *Toad*, or a *Serpant*, then a Drunkart": Writing about Drunkenness', in Smyth (ed.), *A Pleasing Sinne*, p. 193 (pp. 193–210).

5   See David Fairer, 'Lyric and Elegy', in David Hopkins and Charles Martindale (eds), *The Oxford History of Classical Reception in English Literature*, 4 vols (Oxford: Oxford University Press, 2012), III, pp. 533–36 (pp. 519–46). In relation to historical reconstruction of performances of Anacreontic verse in the later Romantic period,

– 'the first major writer to make wine's association with "wit" central to his poetic vocation'[6] – and the 'Tribe of Ben' was, as Stella Achilleos has argued, elite and temperate sociability that eschewed overindulgence and the more vulgar public house.[7] We find such conviviality celebrated in famous lyrics like 'An Epistle Answering to One That Asked be Sealed of the Tribe of Ben', which excludes the negative effects of 'fevery heats, or colds' (67) and 'Oily expansions' (68) associated with the hangover. Jonson's speaker is unshaken by alcohol, comfortably able to 'dwell as in my center ... / Still looking to, and ever loving, heaven' (60–61).[8] A type of handbook for such refinement is found in Richard Brathwaite's *Laws of Drinking* (1617) where he sees the Anacreontic symposium as an event arising out of *'pure affection*, as mutual courtesies are shewne among friends for no other cause than merely for friendship'.[9]

Moderate drinking ought not to lead to a hangover. When Jonson composes the short lyric 'Inviting a Friend to Supper' some time between 1605 and 1610, he cajoles his partner to the convivial occasion firstly through his catalogue of food and drink, but secondly by guaranteeing a clear conscience the next day:

> Nor shall our cups make any guilty men:
>   But, at our parting, we will be, as when
> We innocently met. No simple word
>   That shall be uttered at our mirthfull board
> Shall make us sad next morning, or affright
>   The liberty, that we'll enjoy to-night. (37–42)[10]

Jonson has a specific political purpose, which is to ensure his addressee that his table shall be free from spies and other government informants, permitting them to speak without censure on a range of topics while

---

      see Ian Newman, *The Romantic Tavern: Literature and Conviviality in the Age of Revolution* (Cambridge: Cambridge University Press, 2019), pp. 149–75.

6   Joshua Scodel, *Excess and the Mean in Early Modern English Literature* (Princeton, NJ and Oxford: Princeton University Press, 2002), p. 201.

7   Stella Achilleos, 'The Anacreontea and a Tradition of Refined Male Sociability', in Smyth (ed.), *A Pleasing Sinne*, pp. 21–35.

8   *The Cambridge Edition of the Works of Ben Jonson*, ed. David Bevington, Martin Butler and Ian Donaldson, 7 vols (Cambridge: Cambridge University Press, 2012), VII.

9   Richard Brathwaite, *Laws of Drinking* (1617), Boddeleian Douce D. 34, p. 3, cited in Michelle O'Callaghan, 'Tavern Societies, the Inns of Court, and the Culture of Conviviality in Early Seventeenth-Century London', in Smyth (ed.), *A Pleasing Sinne*, p. 44 (pp. 37–54).

10   Bevington, Butler and Donaldson (eds), *Works of Ben Jonson*, V.

they enjoy the 'rich Canary wine' (29), but the sentiment can be taken as emblematic of a drinking culture allegedly untroubled by hangovers. Symposiastic pleasure thus envisaged ought, according to Robert Herrick's 'Hymn to Bacchus', to 'let us be / From cares and troubles free' (25–26) and his caveat 'So long as thou dost heat us' (9) registers weakly in the context of this type of song.[11] Jonson's invitation to drink may be more moderately constructed than those of Herrick – who, in 'On Himself', famously wrote the lines 'This day Ile drown all sorrow; / Who knowes to live tomorrow?' (5–6) – and some of the later Cavaliers and libertines, as Joshua Scodel has argued, but both writers aspire to present versions of a drinking culture free from the hangover. They promote 'a mirth that knows no tomorrow'.[12]

That last description belongs to Leah S. Marcus and pertains to her analysis of another, later, iteration of Anacreontic verse, which is the Royalist drinking song of the Civil War period, specifically Richard Lovelace's 'The Grasse-hopper. To my Noble Friend, Mr. CHARLES COTTON'. If the hangover is not usually part of the Anacreontic algorithm, Marcus's reading of 'The Grasse-hopper' provides us with another, slightly different, reason for its almost complete neglect in recent accounts of early modern drinking: that is its failure to declare, and so make available for analysis, its features within the era's discourses of excess.

'The Grasse-hopper' is an allegory of the Royalist defeat to Cromwell, probably composed prior to the execution of Charles I, but first published in 1649 in the *Lucasta* volume. It develops the common associations of the grasshopper with revelry in the classical Anacreontea where it is the 'Epicuraean animal' (32) that Cowley hymns in his 1656 poem.[13] Unlike some of the outright hedonism seen in the Cavalier verse of Cowley, William Habington and Thomas Randolph, however, Lovelace blends the typical signifiers of drunken pleasure with a more subtle vocabulary that demonstrates ambivalence towards Caroline excess, tinged with melancholy and remorse. Scodel argues that the lyric promotes 'heavy carousing' as an appropriate response to the 'wintry times' of the commonwealth',[14] but rather than knowing no tomorrow, Lovelace

---

11 L. C. Martin (ed.), *The Poetical Works of Robert Herrick* (Oxford: Clarendon Press, 1956). All references to Herrick's poetry are to this edition.

12 Leah S. Marcus, *The Politics of Mirth: Jonson, Herrick, Milton, Marvell, and the Defense of Old Holiday Pastimes* (Chicago, IL and London: University of Chicago Press, 1986), p. 230.

13 L. C. Martin (ed.), *Abraham Cowley: Poetry and Prose* (Oxford: Oxford University Press, 1949).

14 Scodel, *Excess and the Mean*, p. 228.

carefully accommodates within his opening sequence a morning scene, which seems to radiate complicated feelings of discontentment and disturbed bodily imagery throughout the first three stanzas:

> Oh thou that swing'st upon the waving haire
>   Of some well-filled Oaten Beard,
> Drunke ev'ry night with a Delicious teare
>   Dropt thee from Heav'n, where now th'art reard.
>
> The Joyes of Earth and Ayre are thine intire,
>   That with thy feet and wings dost hop and flye;
> And when thy Poppy workes thou dost retire
>   To thy Carv'd Acron-bed [*sic*] to lye.
>
> Up with the Day, the Sun thou welcomest then,
>   Sports in the guilt-plats of his Beames,
> And all these merry dayes mak'st merry men,
>   Thy selfe, and Melancholy streames. (1–12)[15]

The unsettled feelings owe much to the hangover's infiltration of diction and imagery that actually works against the grain of Anacreontic celebration. Despite Lovelace's emphasis on weightlessness – the 'waving haire' on which the grasshopper swings, for example – and the heavenly origin attributed to alcohol, there is something distinctly corporeal in the proximity of 'haire', 'well-filled' and 'Oaten Beard' that carries more than a suggestion of the drinker's hangover consciousness. 'Delicious teare' is an oxymoron, which incorporates melancholy, and so minimises its difference, within the pleasurable state of intoxication. The second stanza introduces the poppy that suggests the narcotic effects of a sleeping draught, an image that partakes both of the feeling of euphoria but also of a need to forget.

As Lovelace turns to consider the following morning at stanza three, there appear, in typical Anacreontic fashion, to be no incommodious effects following the grasshopper's night of revelry. Yet, even in the Anacreontea, there are hints that the hangover may only be kept in abeyance. As Marcus points out, the last line is 'notoriously cryptic': although it is probable that Lovelace intends it to read that the morning sun 'operates as a general panacea' for 'Melancholy streames', readers often feel that the final clause is disconcertingly removed from the

---

15   C. H. Wilkinson (ed.), *The Poems of Richard Lovelace* (Oxford: Clarendon Press, repr. 1963).

apparent modifier 'mak'st merry'.[16] Melancholy seems to have its place in the grasshopper's dawn despite the overwhelming insistence on mirth. Negative implications are reinforced in stanza four where Lovelace bemoans the 'Sickle' (13) and 'Sharpe frosty fingers' (15) of winter. Conventional images celebrating excess are then fully overturned in the second half of the poem where Lovelace turns his back on the grasshopper – an emblem of Charles's hedonism – to embrace the voice of experience and the 'sober gravity' of the final Stoic sentiment: 'he / That wants himselfe, is poore indeed' (39–40).

The poem's rueful conclusion is more than enough to suggest that 'The Grasse-hopper' is an example of a hangover used to mark time that also tells us much about how it feels to suffer one. It presents an allegory of the Royalist hangover – the aftermath of the good times of the 1630s – but the opening of the poem is particularly instructive. Earl Miner noted that the poem's overall trajectory is 'enacted within the general downward movement of imagery in each stanza'.[17] True, there is a downward movement in stanzas one to three, but it is undoubtedly blurred in the upward trajectory to such a degree that it becomes difficult to say where pleasure ends and feelings of melancholy, remorse and perhaps even self-disgust, begin. The hangover fails to wholly signify, but is nevertheless there, ghosting the central and familiar Anacreontic conceits. Its presence hints that if moderation was an aspiration of Anacreontic drinking it was not always a reality.

Old Red Eyes is Back

I have proposed that the links perpetuated between drinking and sociability in Anacreontic verse – despite being under strain in some of its manifestations – have set the tone for much recent writing about alcohol in early modern literature. If, however, Anacreontic poetry attempts, in its purest form, to fend off consequences for pleasurable actions or to assimilate them into the experience of intoxication, then it is important to note that this is only one strand, albeit perhaps the most prominent, of early modern writing about drunkenness. Elsewhere hangovers do stand out more distinctively, indicating that the bodily sensations we associate with them were being used to explore the hangover's so-called metaphysical superstructure.

16   Marcus, *Politics of Mirth*, p. 230.
17   Earl Miner, *The Cavalier Mode from Jonson to Cotton* (Princeton, NJ: Princeton University Press, 1971), p. 287.

One example is the moral tract. Moderation, of the sort commended by Jonson, is only theoretically a prophylactic against the hangover, but less conviviality and decorum, and a lot more intemperate behaviour of the sort that we would expect to lead to a hangover, is indicated by a document such as Thomas Heywood's *Philocothonista, or, the Drunkard, Opened, Dissected, and Anatomized* (1635). Unsurprisingly, hangovers are a much more visible component of Heywood's reflection upon drunkenness as his title derives from the Greek Philocothonista who 'drank immoderately, and above his strength'.[18] He presents his reader with a series of tawdry contemporary drunken scenes, a short history of 'great quaffers' from antiquity (including most famously the account of the death of Alexander the Great after downing 'at one draught' more than two gallons of wine),[19] a survey of national drinking habits, and a bestiary of drunken 'types' (a genre popularised by Thomas Nashe in *Pierce Penniless* [1592]). Heywood's technique is to exploit the pangs of conscience, to draw out shame and guilt and prompt remorse in his reader through a mixture of grotesquery and moralising in which hangovers feature prominently. Presenting to his (supposedly) 'Sober' reader the actions undertaken in the heat of drink, he reveals that 'Wine will make the wise man sing foolishly, the temperate man laugh outrageously; The stayd man dance ridiculously, the silent man utter secrets openly.'[20] Drunkenness is a toxic assault on good judgement that is followed by humiliation. In the verse Preface, 'The Author of the Booke', decries '*Froggs*, not content / To live in water, (their sole nutriment) / But ever croaking (to find something new) / After the evening and the morning's dew' (13–16). Heywood depicts hangovers that are typically periods of laziness and anti-social behaviour. Inebriates who 'looke not on the Sun' (20) and keep regular hours, preferring instead to 'lay their heads, / When th'early Cock calls other from their beds' (21–22) are a source of condemnation and ridicule.[21]

In 'The Reader: To the Author', John Ford plays the role of respondent, labelling those 'Guilty of wilfull Shipwracke' (9) who ignore the cautionary tales contained in *Philocothonista*.[22] The drunkard catalogued as *Ebrietas Asinina* – the Drunken Ass – is cautioned against indiscretion in 'boasting what either they have, or might have done, when their more

---

18   Thomas Heywood, *Philocothonista, or, The Drunkard, Opened, Dissected, and Anatomized* (London: Robert Raworth, 1635), p. 10.
19   Heywood, *Philocothonista*, p. 11.
20   Heywood, *Philocothonista*, p. 8.
21   Heywood, *Philocothonista*, p. i.
22   Heywood, *Philocothonista*, p. iii.

sober consciences can Justifie against their toxed Insolence'. *Cave Ebreus*!
The potential antagonist of the Ass is *Ebrietas Vulpina* – the Drunken
Fox – who, as Jonson feared in 'Inviting a Friend to Supper', urges
the Royalist custom of drinking healths 'for no other purpose than to
intrap [men] in their speeches, and bring them into trouble, or to catch
some advantage at their words'. Heywood deploys the period's proverbial
commonplace: 'the Vine bringeth forth three *Grapes*; The first of Pleasure,
the second of drunkennesse, the third of Repentance'.[23]

If, however, Heywood aims to discourage drinking by amplifying
its deleterious after-effects then one of the problems of *Philocothonista*
is his evident relish for his subject matter. Adam Smyth has argued
that *Philocothonista* is 'written with a verve that suggests a dangerous
familiarity with the drunkenness being condemned'.[24] This seems to be
particularly true of the series of 'domesticke examples' of hangovers in
Chapter XVIII: 'Divers stories of such whom immoderate drinking hath
made ridiculous'. Heywood is at his most entertaining in recounting the
tale of the 'sharke' at a gaming club who 'would save his purse ... and
yet would devoure more Wine than any Two in the Company' whilst
the rest are occupied with their cards. In order to get revenge, once he
nods off, the company put out the tavern lights: he wakes in confusion,
hearing the gamesters continuing to play and believing he has gone blind.
The group play upon his conscience suggesting a 'judgement was fallen
upon him for some great sinne he had committed'.[25]

Likewise, in the story of another company of drunkards, one
particularly befuddled man rises in the morning 'with the purpose to
pisse in the Chimney'. On standing in the hearth he appears to undergo
some form of temporary amnesia and, unable to see with his head in
the 'Mantle-tree', believes he has fallen down a well:

> [He] first walked from one end of the Chimney to the other, then
> backe againe and felt about with his hands, but could find no way
> out, at which he began to blesse himselfe and wonder where he was,
> and in his devotion casting up his eyes he perceived a light above
> (for it was then day) by which he presently apprehended, that he
> was fallen into a well; but seeing by the distance betwixt him and
> it, it was so deepe that there was no possibility for him to get out
> without helpe, hee began to be in despaire.[26]

23 Heywood, *Philocothonista*, pp. 3, 5, 7.
24 Smyth, 'Writing about Drunkenness', p. 195.
25 Heywood, *Philocothonista*, p. 73.
26 Heywood, *Philocothonista*, p. 77.

Having cried out for help, the rest of the company eventually rescue him from his disorientation. The episode is narrated in such a way, with the arrival of daybreak, the symbolic depths of the well and the resultant 'despaire', that it is elevated from simple comic vignette to an allegory of sinfulness.

The hungover penitents that feature in *Philocothonista* act as a counter-weight to the temptations of public conviviality, which are demonstrated to entail deception, betrayal and subsequent embarrassment and humiliation, rather than Jonson's cordiality and good conscience. It is always the case that the short-term effects of a hangover are difficult to separate from long-term issues when the focus is on chronic, rather than occasional, drinking, and Heywood maximises this indistinctness in portraying more sinister consequences. Somatic effects range in severity from those that suggest hangover symptoms such as 'trembling of the Joynts' and 'stammering of the tongue' to threats to the inveterate drunkard of a 'diseased life'. Heywood uses scripture and Christian philosophy to buttress his arguments against immoderation, variously citing Proverbs 23:20 ('Keepe not company with drunkards'), Proverbs 31:4 ('It is not for Kings to drinke Wine'), Ephesians 5:17 ('And be not drunke with Wine, wherein is excesse, but bee satisfied with spirit'), and proclamations of Augustine and Boethius against the sins of intemperance.[27]

In the tract's final section Heywood becomes more introspective, turning to the mode of Protestant self-interrogation, paraphrasing at length the Proverbs of Solomon, in order to denigrate the man (because this is, like Jonson's, a world from which women are largely excluded) who can rise in the morning with a clear head and unburdened conscience following a night of overindulgence; the man who can remark: 'They have stricken me ... but I was not sicke; they have beaten me, but I knew not, when I awoke, therefore I will seeke it yet still' (Proverbs, 23:35). He counters with 'Saint *Luke* 21.3, 4. *Take heede to your selves, least at any time your hearts be oppressed with surfets and drunkennesse.*'[28] Suitably, *Philocothonista* finishes by posing the series of questions attributed to Solomon: 'To whom is woe? To whom is sorrow: To whom strife: To whom is mourning?; To whom wounds without cause? And to whom is the rednesse of the eyes?' (Proverbs, 23:29). The answer in each case is, of course, the man who suffers from a hangover. Tellingly the damage done by drunkenness is firstly to the soul: in this biblical context the body is used as a vehicle to make legible the more abstract metaphysics of guilt and sin. Heywood's accounts of hangovers are a direct product of the religious climate in England. In the

27   Heywood, *Philocothonista*, pp. 85, 88.
28   Heywood, *Philocothonista*, p. 89.

sermon literature of the period, as we will now see, we are reminded of the role that socio-cultural factors play in increasing our awareness of the interconnection of body and mind during a hangover.

Qualms of Conscience: Sermons and Tracts

Philocothonista is a good example of the end to which most writing on hangovers in the tracts of the first half of the seventeenth century tends: an invocation to biblical authorities on the theme of temperance or an appeal to the conscience of a remorseful drinker who, according to Richard Allestree in *The Practice of Christian Graces* (1658), 'ruines his reason, yea his soul'.[29] In post-Reformation Europe, the rise of Protestantism, particularly the conventicles of the Puritan non-conformists in England, meant that drinking, which had previously played a major role in religious life on holy days and feast days, began to be associated more regularly with sinful behaviour. According to Rod Phillips, while wine – along with beer – was consumed regularly in the Protestant countries of northern Europe, as it was in the Catholic south, 'Protestants were more rigorous towards alcohol consumption' than Catholics and tried to suppress excessive drinking. John Calvin attempted to make taverns less hospitable places for socialising and Martin Bucer opposed all public drinking establishments. Measures to close alehouses were likewise proposed by Puritan reformers across England.[30]

Allestree's intended readership was manifestly not moderate drinkers such as those idealised in the Anacreontea, but, as with Heywood, those who drank to excess. As the alehouse historian Peter Clark notes, 'One of the main concerns of sermons and pamphlets, in the Elizabethan and early Stuart period, was with what was seen as an advancing tide of heavy drinking and drunkenness.'[31] Similarly, as Bernard Capp has argued, attempts to regulate the production and consumption of alcohol, particularly amongst the plebeian classes, played a prominent part in the later 'culture wars' of the interregnum during which Allestree was preaching and poets like Lovelace were writing.[32] Charlotte McBride

29   Richard Allestree, *The Practice of Christian Graces, or, The Whole Duty of Man* (London: D. Maxwell for T. Garthwait, 1658), p. 179.

30   See Rod Phillips, *Alcohol: A History* (Chapel Hill: University of North Carolina Press, 2014), pp. 87–89.

31   Peter Clark, *The English Alehouse: A Social History* (London: Longman, 1983), p. 108.

32   Bernard Capp, *England's Culture Wars: Puritan Reformation and its Enemies in the Interregnum, 1649–1660* (Oxford: Oxford University Press, 2012), pp. 152–62. See also, Keith Wrightson, 'Alehouses, Order and Reformation in Rural England,

has argued that early Puritan pamphleteers developed 'a rhetoric that introduces drunkenness into the political debate, increasingly framing it as a characteristic vice of the court and the Protestant ruling classes'.[33] This does not mean that there were no sermons written against the abuse of alcohol by supporters of the crown – Allestree, Regius Professor for Divinity at Oxford, was a Royalist – but that the general shift in England towards a stricter Protestantism meant a newly austere attitude towards drinking developed, first articulated in the sermons and tracts composed by Puritan divines prior to the Civil War such as Thomas Young's *Englands Bane: or, the Description of Drunkennesse* (1617), William Prynne's *Healthes: Sicknesse* (1628) and *A Monster Late Found out and Discovered* (1628) by Richard Rawlidge, but extending throughout the period of the commonwealth and beyond.

Given the new stress placed upon the burden of shame and sinfulness in relation to heavy drinking, it is unsurprising to find that the rhetoric to which McBride alerts us in tracts and sermons of the period incorporates frequent references to its after-effects. The turbulent religious situation in England explains why the hangover gained a rhetorical life in this period through formulations of the features of a Traditional-Punishment response, of which we have already seen something in *Philocothonista*.

In the early Puritan tracts, the hangover is invoked as a markedly gritty, sometimes grotesque, phase in a sinner's existence, focalised through the body, which sets a tone for many subsequent sermons in the century. Like Heywood, Young draws out the bestiality of the drunkard who, in varying states of debauchery, 'fights or quarrels ... dances, capers, and leapes about', before he eventually 'vomits, spews and wallows in the mire'.[34] Composed during the interregnum when he was acting as intermediary between the future Charles II in Brussels and Royalists in England, Allestree's *The Practice of Christian Graces* is typical of the type of rhetoric McBride describes. Paramount is the association of a drunkard's spiritual condition with hellish punishments enacted on the flesh. In the chapter concerning temperance Allestree rails:

> If all this be not enough to affright thee out of this drunken fit, thou must still wallow in thy vomit, continue in this sottish, senseless

1590–1660', in Eileen Yeo and Stephen Yeo (eds), *Popular Culture and Class Conflict, 1590–1914: Explorations in the History of Labour and Leisure* (Brighton: Harvester, 1981), pp. 1–27.

33   Charlotte McBride, 'A Natural Drink for an English Man: National Stereotyping in Early Modern Culture', in Smyth (ed.), *A Pleasing Sinne*, p. 185 (pp. 181–92).

34   Thomas Young, *Englands Bane: or, the Description of Drunkennesse* (London: William Jones, 1617), pp. 40–41.

condition, till the flames of Hell rowse thee, & then thou wilt by sad experience find, what now thou wilt not believe, that *the end of these things,* as the Apostle sayeth, *Rom. 6. 21. is Death.* God in his infinite mercy timely awake the hearts of all that are in this sin, that by a timely forsaking it, they may *flye from that wrath to come.*[35]

Familiar effects associated with the hungover body, including vomit and sottishness – a word indicating an addled mind that the *OED* finds applied to drunkenness and its after-effects from about 1648 – lead rhetorically into a discussion of guilt and shame or 'sad experience'. For Allestree the after-effects of drinking occasion a crucial opportunity for repentance and reaffirmation of faith. Softening his tone, and changing focus from the punishment of the body to the rewards of the soul, he aims to be more suasive: quoting 1 Peter 5:7, he asks his reader to relinquish his cares to Christ rather than the bottle: 'Christianity will direct thee to one, on whom thou must *safely cast all thy cares, for he careth for thee.*' That comfort is nearly always accompanied by more strident warnings, however, that stress the ephemeral delights of intoxication and the inevitability of the subsequent hangover: 'whilst thou art in the height of the drunken fit, keepe thee from the sense of thy cares, yet when it is over, they will return again with greater violence, and if thou have any conscience, bring a *new care* with them, even that which ariseth from the guilt of so foul a sin'.[36] That warning is the antithesis of the Anacreontic-Horatian tradition of Herrick and Jonson: far from provide alleviation from the cares of life, drunkenness only serves to intensify them, adding extra burdens of physical distress and shame. This hangover is not a matter of a few hours spent feeling foolish but a kind of purgatory: transient, though potentially foreshadowing permanent damnation.

Allestree's deployment of the hangover as a deterrent from sin is notable for what I have called 'hangover consciousness' – the process through which the mind translates physical sensations into emotions and, potentially, moral judgement. He is typical of the period in attending to sickness and purgations within what is primarily a spiritual context. Headaches and fevers, tremors and agitation abound, but the conscience is most often reached, semantically at least, via the stomach. An explanation for this can be found in the etymology of some of the hangover vernacular of the period. Medical documents, such as Humphrey Brooke's *Ugieine, or A Conservatory of Health* (1650), for

---

35 Allestree, *Christian Graces*, p. 196.
36 Allestree, *Christian Graces*, p. 181.

example, are notable for the way in which they take assignable hangover symptoms as evidence of sinfulness. Brooke warns against the long- and short-term effects of hard drinking in a hybrid religio-medical discourse (not dissimilar to Heywood's) advising moderation:

> That Delight is best, which is most lasting, such is the Temperate mans, His all the year long continues; Whilst the other, for his Deliciousness to day, is fain to lie by it to morrow: nay, is distracted amidst his Pleasure, by the foreknowledge of what will follow: And how can that be termed delight, which is intermixt with an expectation of Sorrow. There will bee Qualms and Surfets, a necessity of frequent Purgations, Vomitings, Bleeding, making Issues; And then the former Surfets are called to mind, and repented of; then we condemn our selves for preferring a sickly and momentary Pleasure before a sound and lasting.[37]

Brooke's intermixture of delight and sorrow leading to repentance typifies an orthodox Traditional-Punishment response to a hangover. He deliberately occludes distinctions between pleasure and remorse by including the 'foreknowledge' of misery within his account of overindulgence. Enforced bodily evacuations range from purgation and vomiting to bloodletting to ease circulation. The unpleasant sounding 'Surfets' and 'Issues', speak more generally of repletion followed by unspecific, and no doubt unwelcome, discharges: Jonson's 'Oylie Expansions' come to mind. All the bodily effects of 'Qualms ... Purgations, Vomitings' prepare the way for repentance wherein the conscience baulks at a pleasure that has become 'sickly' rather than, as it earlier appeared, delicious. It is tricky to say where health, to invoke Brooke's title, transitions from being a physical condition to a spiritual one rendered through somatic vehicles (the same mode is indicated by Prynne's title, *Healthes: Sicknesse*).

The word 'qualm' is a particular favourite of Allestree and Brooke. In association with vomiting and purgation, qualms belong firstly to the language of the stomach and digestion. The *OED*'s primary definition, 'To have a qualm; to swoon; to feel sick' is first recorded in Thomas Cooper's *Thesaurus linguae Romanae & Brittanicae* (1565). Related to this is the slightly earlier meaning of 'A sudden fit, impulse, or pang of sickening fear, misgiving, despair', first used by William Tyndale in an account of Jonah and the whale. Emerging from both is our more familiar modern usage of 'qualm' – 'A scruple of conscience; a pang of guilt; a doubt, esp.

---

37   Humphrey Brooke, *Ugieine, or A Conservatory of Health* (London: R. W. for G. Whittington, 1650), p. 97.

as to the rightness of one's actions' (*OED*) – which is initially recorded in 1617, roughly at the beginning of the period of the sermons under consideration. It can be no coincidence that the hangover becomes so closely associated with a guilty conscience at this time.

That a qualm was a type of nausea particularly experienced during the morning or on first waking, as distinct from more general stomach ache, is suggested by the common attribution of qualms to women in accounts of morning sickness. This is the tenor of the use of the expression in the fake pregnancy plot in John Dryden's bawdy comedy *The Wild Gallant* (1669), wherein Lady Constance attempts to trick Lord Nonsuch into believing his unmarried daughter is pregnant:

> *Isa.* ... I think she's grown fat o' th' sudden
> *Non.* O Devil, Devil! What a fright I am in!
> *Isa.* She has qualms every morning: ravins mightily for green-fruit; and swoons at the sight of hot meat.
> *Non.* She's with Childe! I am undone: I am undone! (IV, ii, 65–69)[38]

In another fake pregnancy plot in *The Abdicated Prince* (1690), the queen is told to counterfeit a 'small fit of *Hawking* and *Reaching*' (IV, ii) on waking.[39] But, in hangovers of the early modern period, qualms stand at a juncture between body and the conscience, increasing our awareness of their interconnection. Hence, John Adams warns that after a debauch a 'Qualm of mind will always follow'. They also feature in Allestree's *The Gentleman's Calling* (1660), where we find a drunkard's 'mornings qualm is revenging on him'.[40]

Hangover qualms reappear amongst the non-conformists and conventiclers of the 1670s and 1680s, including Bunyan and Isaac Barrow. The latter deploys the figure of the qualm of conscience in the posthumous collection *Sermons Preached Upon Several Occasions* (1679): '[The pleasures of Christ] are Pleasures indeed, in comparison whereto all other pleasures are no more then brutish sensualitys, sordid impuritys, superficial touches, transient flashes of delight; such as should be insipid and unsavoury to a rational appetite; such as are tinctured with sourness and bitterness, have painfull remorses

---

38 John Harrington Smith and Dougald MacMillan (eds), *The Works of John Dryden*, 12 vols (Berkeley and Los Angeles: University of California Press, 1962), VIII.

39 Anon. *The Abdicated Prince, or, the Adventures of Four Years* (London: John Carterson, 1690).

40 John Adams, *A Sermon Preached at White-hall on Sunday, the 17th of February ...* (London: printed by Benj. Motte, 1695), p. 14; Richard Allestree, *The Gentleman's Calling* (London: printed for T. Garthwait, 1660).

or qualms consequent'.[41] Barrow attributes another series of noxious feelings to the state of sin, consequent on 'brutish' and 'sordid' actions along with the 'transient flashes of delight' evocative of the Anacreontea. He blurs physical sensations and negative affect, but the body is a vehicle to express sin: 'rational' appetite is disturbed and the primary feeling of disgust – as is often the case with grotesquery – centres upon the mouth. Appetite fails – a product of nausea – but due to the absence of reason (again a cipher for moral rectitude).

For his part, Bunyan gives his most extensive condemnation of what he perceived to be a tide of heavy drinking and immorality sweeping the nation in the conduct book, *The Life and Death of Mr. Badman* (1680), which he composed following the first part of *The Pilgrim's Progress* (1678). Mr Wiseman tells the tale of Badman's wickedness, much of which involves his drunken consorting with prostitutes and abuse of his wife. Badman courts impoverishment, illness and early death, stealing and embezzling to fund his habit. The only check comes when he breaks his leg whilst reeling home from the alehouse, but he quickly forgets his attempts at amendment: 'his conscience was choked before his leg was healed'.[42] The pattern of pleasure followed by bodily and spiritual discomfort is more dramatic in some of Bunyan's sermons, such as *The Barren Fig Tree* (1673) where we even find a dramatic vignette of the sinner on his sickbed relayed through hangover symptoms:

> … Death come with *Grim* looks into the Chamber, ye and Hell follows with him to the Bed-side and both stare this Professor in the face yea, begin to lay Hands upon him; or smiting him with pains in his Body, with Head-ach, Heart-ach, Back-ach, Shortness of Breath, Fainting Qualms, Trembling of Joints, Stopping at the Chief and almost all the *Symptomes* of a Man past all recovery. Now while *Death* is tormenting the Body, *Hell* is doing with the Mind and Conscience.[43]

It was not unusual for the conventicler to describe the hangover as a type of hell in this manner, just as many Puritans figured hell as a hangover, as in Richard Carpenter's *The Downfall of Anti-Christ* (1644),

41   Isaac Barrow, *Sermons Preached Upon Several Occasions* (London: printed for Brabazon Aylmer, Cornhill, 1679), pp. 55–56.

42   John Bunyan, *Grace Abounding & The Life and Death of Mr. Badman* (London: J. M. Dent & Sons Ltd., repr. 1953), p. 269.

43   John Bunyan, *The Barren Fig Tree, or, the Doom and Downfall of the Fruitless Professor* (London: printed for J. Robinson, St Paul's Church-yard, 1688), p. 90.

where the deceased drunkard 'being layd, and his mouth stopt with dirt, hee ceases to reele; till at last, hee shall reele, body and soule, into hell: where, notwithstanding all his former plenty, & variety of drinks, hee shall never be so gracious, as to obtaine a small drop of water, to coole his tongue'.[44] Hell is an eternity of such dehydration.

The figure of the qualms of conscience could also be used to intercede in specific political and religious debates. In a sermon preached at Whitehall – the site of court preaching – in January 1660 (eventually published in 1669), Allestree develops a detailed argument advocating temperance. Its contents are significant coming on the eve of the Restoration of the Stuart monarchy. The argument that, 'it prevails with us to indulge our selves' and that 'to do otherwise were to evacuate Gods purpose in the making; Did he give us good things not to enjoy them?',[45] is the one that had long been attributed to Catholics, as in Spenser's May eclogue in *The Shephearde's Calendar* (1579).[46] Allestree revisits the debate, equipped with the discourse of the early modern hangover, to fashion a new riposte to those who were arguing, including perhaps Charles II (identifying with Catholicism although fortifying the position of the Church of England), that 'it prevails with us to indulge our selves the full use of lawful pleasures, and for this the Flesh will urge, it is the end of their Creation'.[47] Allestree argues that the flesh instead leads to sin when it is 'sauc'd with pleasures' and, recalling the drunkard's use of the Withdrawal-Relief recovery method, temporarily offers to 'take off all cares', but also 'thoughts of any joys hereafter'.[48]

As with Bunyan and Carpenter, Allestree brings the hangover into conjunction with death: 'his Soul hath dying qualms, caused as much by the Nausea of sin as by the fear of Hell'. He further contrasts the spiritual banquet of Christ with the deleterious effects of overindulgence in worldly pleasure:

---

44   Richard Carpenter, *The Downfall of Anti-Christ* (London: John Stafford, 1644), p. 22.

45   Richard Allestree, *Eighteen Sermons Whereof Fifteen Preached the King, the Rest Upon Publick Occasions* (London: printed by Tho. Roycroft for James Allestry, St Paul's Church-yard, 1669), p. 6.

46   Spenser's debate between the Protestant Piers and Catholic Palinode is weighted decidedly in favour of the former who 'Sike worldly sovenance he must foresay' (*Maye*, 82) to avoid 'Heaping up wauves of welth and woe' (*Maye*, 93). William A. Oran *et al* (eds), *The Yale Edition of the Shorter Poems of Edmund Spenser* (New Haven, CT & London: Yale University Press, 1989), pp. 90–91.

47   Allestree, *Eighteen Sermons*, p. 6.

48   Allestree, *Eighteen Sermons*, p. 6.

The Artificial pleasures of the Palate whether in meats or drinks, forc'd tasts, that do at once satisfie and provoke the Appetite, will rellish ill when I begin to swallow down my spittle; but sure I am, I am invited to the *Supper of the Lamb, to drink new Wine with Christ in my Father's Kingdom;* The *fatted Calf* is dressing for my Entertainment, and shall I choose to be a while a Glutton with the Swine, rather than the eternal Guest of my Father's Table and Bosom? and refuse these for a few sick Excesses which would end in qualms, and gall, and vomits, if there were no guilt to rejolt too, and which will kindle a perpetual Feaver?

Allestree again indicates the interfused physical, emotional and spiritual dimensions of the hangover in the seventeenth-century sermon whereby – prompted by a surfeit of food and drink – the sinner ends swallowing down the saliva that accompanies nauseous feelings of the stomach. Guilt may even 'kindle' the 'perpetual Feaver' – simultaneously physical and spiritual – of the confirmed sinner. Although the Anacreontea claims to know no tomorrow, in the January sermon Allestree uses the spectre of physical sickness and pounding head to force his reader to face it squarely: 'another [drunkard], as if [he] had learnt to fulfill our Saviours command, and *take no care for the morrow,* will not think of the next mornings pains and Headach'.[49]

Nausea, vomiting, headache, fevers, indeterminate and unwelcome bodily 'issues', unexpected joint pain, trembling, dizziness and balance problems: for the authors of the tracts and sermons of the seventeenth century, the hangover, whether it was literal or used as a metaphor for other types of sin, was undoubtedly one of the key occasions for, or instigators of, repentance. Assignable symptoms were not held to be exclusive to the body, but were rather a sign of moral and spiritual sickness. This explains why penitents were often imaged through physical ailments associated with heavy drinking of the extensive kind that Penning, McKinney and Verster reproduce in their scale of Alcohol Hangover Symptoms (Fig. 1.2). As I have been arguing, those physical symptoms are culturally determined by the association of feelings of guilt and melancholy with a divine judgement on debauchery and vice particular to the religious attitudes of the day. The hangover regulated alcohol use as much as any law. In the Protestant sermon, the sensations we associate with hangovers are interpreted as physical signs of a bad conscience, which force a reappraisal of the conduct of the dutiful Christian.

49   Allestree, *Eighteen Sermons*, pp. 79, 87–88, 8.

Sociable Stuarts or Crop-sick Cavaliers?

In *The Beauty of Holiness* (1653), Thomas Hall claims that melancholy is shunned by hungover inebriates despite being a 'Preparative to grace'. Melancholy can lead in one of two ways – which tally with the Traditional-Punishment and Withdrawal-Relief responses to the hangover – to Christ or to further dalliance with the bottle. In the latter case the conscience is drowned in liquor: 'they runne to drunken companions, gaming, idlenesse, &c. yea for fear of melancholy runne almost mad, and bring themselves into a thousand sorrows'. Hall advises that it is better to dwell upon those melancholy feelings, as they will ultimately lead to God, rather than to attempt to overcome them through resorting to Withdrawal-Relief: 'of two evils we should chuse the least; and if it cannot be avoided, better undergo ten thousand melancholies, then the least sin'.[50]

At the heart of *The Beauty of Holiness* is a division. On one side stands conviviality and clubbability, on the other the alternative 'holy company', which the former encourages the good Christian to forsake. The two are mutually exclusive in seventeenth-century, Protestant England. According to Allestree, the companionship, or 'mutual kindness', sought out by the social drinker helps to weaken his resolve: 'Let others joy in Friends that Wine does get them; such as have no qualification to endear them, but this, that they will not refuse to sin and to be sick with their Companions.'[51] A critical attitude to masculine arenas of conviviality and indulgence was staple territory within tracts and sermons throughout the seventeenth century, but, following the Restoration, it became a significant focus of condemnation within secular literature too.

Here the status of male social gatherings in the period needs to be explained. Prior to and during the Civil War sociability was considered one of the hallmarks of Cavalier excess: the consumption of wine, particularly claret, canary and sack being linked to wit and good humour as in the earlier flourishing of Anacreontic verse, epitomised by Shakespeare's Sir John Falstaff who, in *2 Henry IV* (1600), extols at length the virtues of 'a good sheris sack' (IV, i, 44–45).[52] During the interregnum, drinking in company took on a greater political significance as it came to symbolise

---

50   Thomas Hall, *The Beauty of Holiness* (London: printed by Evan Tyler for John Browne, St Paul's Church-yard, 1653), p. 123.

51   The Fourth sermon preached at Whitehall, October 12 1662, in Richard Allestree, *Forty Sermons Whereof Twenty One Are Now First Published* (Oxford and London: printed for R. Scott, G. Wells, T. Sawbridge, R. Bentley, 1684), p. 52.

52   William Shakespeare, *2 Henry IV*, ed. Giorgio Melchiori (Cambridge: Cambridge University Press, 2007), p. 134.

loyalty to the exiled Charles and compensation for the Stuart defeat to Cromwell. Parliament's ban on drinking healths and toasts meant that the custom came to be seen as an act of defiance against the commonwealth. As Alexander Brome put it: 'They Vote that we shall / Drink no healths at all / Nor to King nor to Common-wealth, / So that now we must venture to drink 'um by stealth' (I, 8–11).[53] Following the Restoration, the refusal to partake in toasts to the king was viewed as an act of treachery, which prompted works of protest such as Charles Morton's *The Great Evil of Health-Drinking* (1684). Even the choice of alcoholic drink could be seen as a political act: in Royalist propaganda, Parliamentarians were associated with beer drinking, which was reputed to dull the senses, and Cromwell was ridiculed for his family's alleged ties to the brewing trade.[54]

The political division between libertines associated with the court of Charles II and sober Parliamentarians who hankered after the 'good old cause' of the commonwealth gradually gave way to the party politics of Tories and Whigs in the 1680s. Nevertheless, the politicisation of drinking cultures and sociability continued in what were largely recognisable forms. In the late 1670s, the accusations of debauchery were aimed at the Tory faction, as they had earlier been at the Cavaliers, while, according to Angela McShane Jones, Whigs were characterised as 'miserable, miserly and bad company', as the Parliamentarians had been before them.[55] Quakers were sometimes seen as hypocrites who preached against drinking but imbibed on the sly. McShane Jones argues that 'there was a connection between sobriety and sedition': anti-social behaviour, or the refusal to drink, was politicised and deemed by some to be a threat to the stability of the country.[56]

Conspicuous drunken behaviour was also an increasing problem in urban centres. As McShane Jones writes: 'In all English towns a large proportion of cases brought before magistrates related to riotous drunkenness, tippling, unlawful entertainment, or the selling of ale without a licence.'[57] John Spurr notes a growing reformist agenda during the 1670s, partly prompted by debates about how to accommodate

---

53   Alexander Brome, 'Song XXV: The Prisoners', in *Songs and Other Poems* (London: printed for Henry Brome, 1664). A similar example of stealthy toasting occurred later when Jacobites would silently raise a glass of wine above one of water signalling the Pretender, James Stuart, or 'The King Over the Water'.

54   See Nicholls, *The Politics of Alcohol*, p. 25.

55   Angela McShane Jones, 'Roaring Royalists and Ranting Brewers: The Politicisation of Drink and Drunkenness in Political Broadside Ballads', in Smyth (ed.), *A Pleasing Sinne*, p. 78 (pp. 69–78).

56   McShane Jones, 'Politicisation of Drink', p. 78.

57   McShane Jones, 'Politicisation of Drink', p. 77.

religious dissenters within the Church of England, but more overtly by 'the urgent need for action against the wits, atheists, Hobbists, libertines, and other sinners of this profane generation'.[58] He could have added drunkards to this list, amongst the most notable being the prominent aristocrats of the Carolean court, where 'violence, drunken and mindless, was rife'.[59] These included the Duke of Monmouth, Lord Buckingham, Sir Charles Sedley and John Wilmot, Earl of Rochester. Rochester was not only a famous libertine but also implicated in the murder of several men and notorious for his violent debauches. On one occasion, he smashed the king's sundial in the privy garden and, on another, was involved in a scandalous brawl with locals at Epsom in which there was a fatality. These courtiers may well have been a 'swaggering minority' but their behaviour was celebrated and copied by numerous other would-be roués.[60]

Many of these social and political issues can be seen in the literature concerning the consumption of alcohol and drinking culture of the Restoration. The popular Broadside ballads of the culture wars could take either side to task for their attitude to drink. Fellowship and good company are at times straightforwardly endorsed, as in *The Young Gallant's Tutor* (c. 1674–79) and the popular *The Wine Cooper's Delight* (1681), or denigrated as in the ballads that depict the reformation of libertines, including *The Prodigal Son Converted* (1665). Set against the background of this new social encoding of alcohol, the cultural signif-icance and function of the hangover within literature begins to develop in new directions too. Indeed, we might argue that the politicisation of drink entailed a corresponding politicisation of the hangover. Its currency within satirical attacks on drinking culture, usually penned by writers with Whig sympathies, is, for example, quite different from the way that hangovers were represented within the new, usually comic, literature celebrating mirth and merriment written by defenders of the crown. In the latter case, verse and drama written by, or representing the behaviour of, drunken aristocrats during the Restoration, is not afraid to entertain a hangover. If anything, the opposite is true.

For the Royalist it appears that the hangover is not excluded from the ideological claims about drunkenness with which religious non-conformists were berated. This is the tenor of some of the drinking songs celebrating the return of the king, such as the Cavalier Henry Bold's 'Song LVI. A Round' from his *Poems lyrique, macaronique, heroique.* (1664):

---

58 John Spurr, *England in the 1670s: The Masquerading Age* (Oxford: Blackwell, 2000), p. 70.
59 Spurr, *Masquerading Age*, p. 70.
60 Spurr, *Masquerading Age*, p. 70.

I

A Pox on those *Od-mates*!
And half witted *Clode-pates*!
That ne're knew the *price*, of a *Pottle!*
Nor ever took *part*,
Of a tedious *Quart*,
But tamper their *Chaps*,
On the dow-back't *Sops*.
Of pittyful *Aristotle*!

Chorus. Blaze up to the *King*, say I,
Fill the *Cup*,
Tope it *up*,
Let it pass, 'tis the *vote* of the *Commons*,
To *Sing, Drink* and *Fight*,
In the world's despight.
That the Crown may be *Charles* his, or no *mans*.

II

A fig for *Jandunus!*
Here's *Sack* that can tune us,
In our *mirth*, to a *note* above *Ela*.
While the *Round-head Rogues*,
Like *Birds* (call'd *Hogs*)
In damnable qualms,
Howle out *Wisdomes psalms*
To a *Presbyterian Selah*
Chorus. Blaze up, &c.[61]

Bold's song is a good example of the association usually made between the king's supporters and mirth and the Parliamentarians and seriousness, but it is also noticeable that the latter are excluded from the conviviality due to their 'damnable qualms'. The implication is that, unlike the singer and his Cavalier companions, Puritans are unable to hold their drink and are plagued by guilt. Later in the century it became a popular notion that toping Whigs consumed beer only in half-pint measures, as they so feared both the physical and spiritual after-effects of heavy drinking.

---

61   Henry Bold, *Poems lyrique, macaronique, heroique, &c.* (London: printed for Henry Brome, 1664), pp. 90–91.

For the libertine or rake, in contrast, the hangover is treated in more playful and positive fashion, a necessary concomitant of sociability and sign of good breeding, gallantry and manliness. Rochester, evidently no stranger to hangovers, records one in 'Tunbridge Wells' (1675; 1697) where he recounts rising at five in the morning to take the town's spa waters, but mostly to observe the 'fools, buffoons, and praters / Cuckolds, whores, citizens, their wives' (4–5).[62] Having roused himself with Withdrawal-Relief – 'My squeamish stomach I with wine had bribed' (6) – he juxtaposes the nausea of his stomach with that inspired in him by the unnatural behaviour of his fellow men. Emblematic of the alternative moral outlook of the libertine is the notorious lyric beginning 'I Rise at Eleven' (1680), attributed to Rochester, but more frequently supposed to be a satire on a rake's 'average' day.[63] The speaker, apparently detached from morality, makes an ostentatious eschewal of the effects of heavy drinking, defying any physical and emotional repercussions:

> I Rise at Eleven, I Dine about Two,
> I get drunk before Seven, and the next thing I do;
> I send for my Whore, when for fear of a Clap
> I Spend in her hand, and I Spew in her Lap:
> There we quarrel, and scold, till I fall asleep,
> When the Bitch, growing bold, to my Pocket does creep;
> Then slyly she leaves me, and to revenge th' affront,
> At once she bereaves me of Money and Cunt.
> If by chance then I wake, hot-headed, and drunk
> What a coyle do I make for the loss of my Punk?
> I storm, and I roar, and I fall in a rage,
> And missing my Whore, I bugger my Page:
> Then crop-sick, all Morning, I rail at my Men,
> And in Bed I lye Yawning, till Eleven again. (1–14)

The heroic couplets provide the perfect balance to parade the circularity of the debauchee's life. The concluding couplet sends the reader back to the first line, meaning that the initial shock value of the vivid description

62 *The Works of John Wilmot, Earl of Rochester*, ed. Harold Love (Oxford: Oxford University Press, 1999). All references to Rochester's poetry are to this edition unless stated.

63 Paddy Lyons attributes the poem to Rochester in his Everyman edition (*Complete Poems and Plays* [London: Everyman, 1993]), but he is alone amongst modern editors. Harold Love, in the most authoritative modern edition of Rochester's works (*The Works of John Wilmot, Earl of Rochester* [Oxford: Oxford University Press, 1999]), prints it but classes it as 'about' Rochester.

of the hangover is made doubly powerful by the disclosure of its routine nature. Emotional disengagement from his subject matter – 'in Bed I lye Yawning' – is indicated by the speaker's nonchalant tone that contrasts the earlier 'storm', 'roar' and 'rage'. The crop-sickness mentioned is, as in the case of qualms, a feeling of illness often used in representations of the hangover (which continues well into the eighteenth century) and is part of its vernacular. The 'crop' (also known as the craw) refers in this case to the gullet of a bird, usually a fowl, which helps soften grain prior to digestion. In *Enquiries into Human Nature* (1680), Walter Charleton gives a clue as to the origin of the expression as used in 'I Rise at Eleven': 'Fowls for the most part, chiefly the Grainivorous, feed their young with half-digested chyle, or corn macerated, puking it from the crop into their mouth, as is commonly observ'd in Doves and Rooks; which they could not so commodiously have done, if the crop had not been seated so near the mouth.'[64] That definition helps explain the word's appearance in the lexicon of the hangover: crop-sickness applies to a particular type of nausea that is seated 'near the mouth'. Johnson's *Dictionary* (1755) defines crop-sickness as being 'sick with excess and debauchery'. Interestingly, in *A New Dictionary of the Canting Crew* (1699), 'Crop-sick, queasy Stomackt' is given as the definition for 'Qualmish', confirming a link between the two words.[65]

Whether Rochester was the real author or the satirical object of 'I Rise at Eleven', it is evident that the poem flaunts the libertine's drunken behaviour to shock the reader. Absence of shame is a product of political affiliation: showing disdain for the ordinary physical effects of a hangover was as much a rejection of Puritanism as was the drinking of toasts and the Withdrawal-Relief recovery method became associated with resisting moral judgement. The pattern is illustrated and developed more extensively by Thomas D'Urfey's play *Trick for Trick, or, The Debauch'd Hypocrite*, first acted at the Theatre Royal by 'his Majestie's servants' in 1678, wherein sources of shame are many, but remorse barely registers. D'Urfey's plot is thin and at times lacks plausibility: Monsieur Thomas, the play's anti-hero, pretends to be a reformed character with a 'sober look' (I, i) following his return from France in order to win the virtuous Celinda, but he continues to drink and whore in secret 'defaming Ladies, debauching their Women, beating Constables, breaking Glass

---

64 Walter Charleton, *Enquiries into Human Nature* (London: printed for M. White by Robert Boulter, 1680), p. 36.

65 Samuel Johnson, *A Dictionary of the English Language...*, 2 vols (London: W. Strahan, 1755), I, n.p.; B. E., *A New Dictionary of the Canting Crew...* (London: printed for W. Hawes, P. Gilbourne and W. Davis, 1699), n.p.

Windows' (I, i), *à la* Rochester.[66] His father, the aptly named Sir Wilding Frolick, is an unreconstructed libertine who bemoans his son's apparent reformation and contemplates disinheriting him.[67] As with Aphra Behn's *The Rover* (1677), the play is most shocking for a foiled rape plot: in the final act Celinda's father is made to watch helplessly as Monsieur Thomas assaults his daughter, while Sir Wilding cheers encouragement.[68] The drama concludes not with a moral assessment of these scenes but with a reunion of the rakes who had earlier fallen out suggesting that the values of the play derive from the kind of masculine bonding that is built on shared experience of vice.

Lacking any moral outcome to the behaviour of the aristocratic males, the values of the play are underlined by the protagonists' dismissive attitude to the hangover. When Franck, another libertine, falls ill of the 'Mulligrubs', a melancholy feeling induced by his crop-sick stomach, Monsieur Thomas prescribes Withdrawal-Relief in the form of 'Old Sack', which 'refines the Spirit, revives the Person, removes the Disease, Restores the blood' (III, i). Sir Wilding exhibits a dismissive attitude to the hangover, which he claims as a necessary sign of 'Man and Mettle', chiding his upright daughter Dorothy, 'thou can'st snore, and sleep, and Chatter bawdy in thy Dreams, – and the next morning wake and go to breakfast, and nothing else – but [Monsieur Thomas's] life shou'd be otherwise' (III, ii). If Dorothy's conscience is clear, however, Sir Wilding's 'otherwise' should not be taken as the attribution of guilt or shame to his son whose ability to overcome the hangover, affirmed by imbibing 'something' else, preserves the dubious gallantry of D'Urfey and 'His Majestie's servants'. D'Urfey demonstrates that the young Cavalier feels bad in body only; his conscience, in this libertine environment, is undisturbed, reminding us that the hangover is a response to the values of a socio-cultural context as much as a physical reaction to alcohol.

Other Restoration sex comedies entertain the hangover in similar ways, although they do not always appear to sanction the kind of position that we might ascribe to writers like Rochester and D'Urfey. Two examples are worth noting. The first is found in Act IV of Reuben Bourne's *The Contented Cuckold; or, the Woman's Advocate* (1692). In a conversation between two rakish aspirants the morning after a night's

---

66 Thomas D'Urfey, *Trick for Trick, or, The Debauch'd Hypocrite* (London: printed for Langley Curtis, 1678). I provide only Act and scene references as the edition does not contain line numbers.

67 The reasons why Sir Wilding could not be informed of the duplicity, which he would heartily endorse, are never explained.

68 See Anne Greenfield, 'Introduction', in Anne Greenfield (ed.), *Interpreting Sexual Violence, 1660–1800* (Oxford: Routledge, repr. 2016), p. 1 (pp. 1–13).

excess, the hangover functions as a key site in renegotiating the type of gallant masculinity earlier associated unproblematically with the Carolean courtiers and poets:

> SPARKISH: 'Tis the Wine I drank last Night lies in my Head. I wonder how you rub through with it so well as you do; I am as Squeamish as a new married Woman, that's breeding her first Child; when she is in one of her breeding fits, she resolves never to have any more Children; and I in one of my sick qualms, never to drink any more Wine: But you see how quickly we break our Resolutions; the first kind proffer, and the first good Company, make us run the hazard of a disorder, tho we have experienced the sad effects before.

> FRIENDLY: Bear up man, ne're give way, and part good Company for the Head-ach, or disaffected Stomach; 'tis so Childish, I am ashamed to hear thee name it: One Bottle sets thee right again, and makes thee as sound as a Rock; there's no Medicine I know like it, 'tis beyond all the Pills in the World. (IV)[69]

It is clear from the rallying speech of Friendly that the hangover is, as the pulpit has already shown, the enemy of carousing. Friendly embodies the pressure of male bonding, labelling Sparkish unmanly, although he has already aligned himself with feminine signifiers, repeating the link between the qualms of the hangover and morning sickness that we saw previously. Although the voice of Friendly is the more assertive of the two, and ultimately wins out, the misgivings of Sparkish are entertained for long enough to demonstrate the weakening of masculine resolve in the face of the combined physical and emotional effects of a hangover. Acknowledgement of the weakness of the aristocratic drunkard's will, and his failure to carry through the resolutions made when hungover, evince a dissenting voice within the dominant bawdy of the play.

The second example can be found in Aphra Behn's *The Debauchee; or, the Credulous Cuckold* (1677). If the remorse entertained by a libertine like Sparkish might be explained by the altered political landscape at the time Bourne's farce was written – following the end of the Stuart dynasty rakes were characteristically presented as less extreme figures on the stage – Behn's comedy boldly uses the hangover to make similar

---

69   Reuben Bourne, *The Contented Cuckold, or, The Woman's Advocate* (London: printed by Randall Taylor, 1692), p. 37.

criticisms during the reign of Charles II. Significantly in this case, the aristocratic drunk is not the subject but the object of discussion, as his behaviour is observed and pondered upon by Simon, butler to Sir Oliver Thrivewell. Behn uses this lower-class figure as a mouthpiece for caution in a prose soliloquy on the morning after a drunken night:

> 'Tis a meer folly to go to bed now, 'tis time to rise. – Well, *Simon*, well, thou art bound to give God thanks, thou wert not born a Gentleman, – some comfort that. – Mercy upon us, what lives they lead! never rise till three of the clock after noon, (or very rarely) and then they are damnable dry, and crop-sick, – but not at all hungry, so they lose both breakfast and dinner, (two great blessings;) instead of Prayers, the first words they speak, as soon as awake, are – Damn me, how cursed drunk was I last night! Hay, *Jack* – some small Beer, you Vermin, – (very fine) – well – at last he gets himself dress'd, calls for his Coach (and not a word of dinner) rouls to Play-house, to that that has the bawdiest Play (for that settles his stomach,) tells as many as he meets (that he knows) how he was claw'd away last night, but forswears drinking again, for at least a day or two; then spys me a Vizard, over the benches he stalks, and there thunders a deal of leud bawdy, till he has won her heart quite; away they go, sup and get drunk in spight of vows of sobriety, and then to some convenient Mansion of pleasure, where they spew and snore away the remaining part o'th' night, and then comes repentance, and never till then have they any grace before their eyes.[70]

Simon's ironic honorific to his master's dedication to the life of the gentleman is not just wittier but more revealing than the flawed chumminess depicted by Bourne. The servant half-heartedly rejoices in not having to prepare breakfast and dinner. Instead of rising to prayers, Sir Oliver wakes with a curse. The remedy for his dryness and sickness is small beer followed by a trip to the theatre where he brags about his excesses before attempting to ensnare a bawd. A quick recovery from a hangover is a crucial feature of the mythology of the amoral libertine: an affirmation of his commitment to a life of pleasure despite the pressure of moral censure. Noticeably, cultural defiance is almost always underpinned by some version of the Withdrawal-Relief

---

70 Aphra Behn, *The Debauchee; or, the Credulous Cuckold* (London: printed for John Amery, 1677), p. 30.

recovery method.[71] What Behn captures most brilliantly is, however, the restorative power bequeathed here to the bawdy play. To overcome his hangover, Sir Oliver attends the very kind of play in which he features and in which his values are (ostensibly) celebrated. It 'settles his stomach'. Art reinforces, and becomes an alibi for, life, while the emphasis on repentance is undermined, as in 'I Rise at Eleven', by the insistence on the routine nature of the hangover. Behn holds up to moral censure the prevailing socio-cultural values that allow a figure like Sir Oliver to thrive well even when crop-sick.

Anti-Symposiasts

The textual evidence of the period indicates that for those writers who spoke on behalf of the crown, or later the embryonic Tory party, hangovers were less about a guilty conscience than a sign of a return to good times. They were a necessary part of good living – almost an inversion of the hangover's 'Saturday Night and Sunday Morning' topos that Lovelace adopts – to be embraced and overcome as a mark of gallantry and belief in an ideology that derived ultimately from the Stuart monarchs. It shows that the drinkers respond to their environment

71 Small beer was by far the most common hangover remedy from the early modern period up until the nineteenth century. It was usually produced in a second stage – the 'second runnings' – following the initial brewing of ale and contained 1 per cent or less alcohol. Its weakness meant that it was not considered an alcoholic beverage and so did not qualify as the 'hair of the dog' in the same way as sack or brandy. The difference in popular perception is underlined by the fact that small beer was generally linked to feelings of penitence and alcoholic remedies to defiance. Nevertheless, the refreshing qualities of small beer mean that it often served a similar function to the 'hair of the dog'. Its consumption was also a precursor to stronger alcoholic remedies, which is why I consider it as a 'version' of Withdrawal-Relief in this context. The poet-laureate of small beer was undoubtedly 'Rambling' Ned Ward who wrote 'A Poem in Praise of Small Beer' in 1705. He hymns small beer for its capacity to repair and refresh the body: 'drouthy', 'Scorching and raving in a Fever' (23), Ward's 'soothing Dose' (11) of small beer relieves the 'flaming Heart' (11), 'cools [his] inside by a Belch or Fart' (12), a 'hissing Draught as down it goes' (21) (Edward Ward, *A Satyr Against Wine. With a Poem in Praise of Small Beer* [London: B. Brag, 1705]). When it came to consuming stronger alcohol as a remedy, Ward wrote in his more typical rambunctious fashion, as in *The Rambling Fuddle-Caps: or, A Tavern Struggle for a Kiss* (1706), evoking the Carolean rake: 'In order to quench our immod'rate Droughts, / That burnt in our Stomachs, and scorch'd up our Mouths, / We leap'd out of Bed with a strong *Appetitus*, / To swallow a Hair of the Dog that had bit us' (23–26) (Edward Ward, *The Rambling Fuddle-Caps* [London: B. Bragge, 1706]).

as much as to the physical sensations of a hangover, which, in this case, do not carry the stigma that we have seen elsewhere.

On the opposite side of the political divide, Whigs used the hangover in a quite different way, as we will now see, that strengthened the pejorative cultural associations found in the sermon but added to them a series of other factors linked to the heavy drinker's failure to abide by acceptable norms of civic and familial responsibility. The hangover, more so than drunkenness, is represented as a period during which cultural values were witnessed and contested, and the social obligations of individuals restated.

The final decades of the seventeenth century see the brief flowering of a genre of poetry that we might dub 'Anti-Symposiastic', because of the way it explodes, usually in a mock-heroic vein, the conceits on which the Anacreontic poets with which I began this chapter, and later the more debauched libertines, established their literary and cultural credentials. The setting of these poems, by hitherto neglected writers such as John Dennis, Sir Charles Darby and Richard Ames, is ordinarily the tavern. Unlike the public house, this was largely an establishment for gentry, where wine, not beer, was sold. It was not uncommon for topers to drink to a stupor and depart the tavern at dawn and Anti-Symposiastic verse reflects this type of drinking culture. What this means for the student of the hangover is that the blood alcohol level of these sots has almost certainly not returned to zero. Nevertheless, it is apparent that hangovers are deployed in this kind of poetry as a moral curb to persuade heavy drinkers to abstain from sociability.

Typically, the speaker is invited to join, or manages to infiltrate, a private group of drinkers, from which perspective he is able to comment on, and even participate in, the drunken evening as it unfolds while maintaining a critical distance from his subject matter. The specific political affiliation and social status of the drinkers tends to be varied – often suggesting an alignment with the anti-Catholic and anti-French sentiments of the Whigs – but the occasions are always delivered in the mode, and through the motifs, of Royalist drinking culture. One joke of Darby's in *Bacchanalia: Or a Description of a Drunken Club* (1680), even suggests that – *in vino veritas* – otherwise sensible Whigs will eventually reveal Tory sensibilities when in their cups: 'The Censor's gone, / ... Words now, like Thieves in *Interregnums*, break / Their prisons' (VI).[72]

Bacchanalia introduces the reader to a series of drunken 'types' – the would-be soldier, the amateur politician and the religious casuist – who

---

72 Charles Darby, *Bacchanalia, or, A Description of a Drunken Club* (London: printed for Robert Boulter, 1680). There are no line numbers, so I give section numbers.

pontificate on their subject of choice, becoming increasingly boastful and vain as the poem proceeds. Darby devalues the posturing, revealed by their garrulousness, by turning the tropes and classical allusions of drinking songs back upon themselves. This mock-heroic mode is best evidenced by the stanzas concerning the battle at the table, where each drink is a blow 'level'd ... against the Soul's chief Seat, the Head', or in the biblical 'deluge of Reason', where Reason is a maiden unprotected by the rising tide of drunkenness:[73]

> I saw
> Dame Reason trembling stand upon
> The top of her Conarion,
> Dreading a deluge from the Floods below.
> As Mortals in Deucalion's Flood, on cliff
> Of Caucasus, or Tenariff,
> On Aiery Alps, or Apennine,
> Prolong'd that Fate, which they could not decline. (V)

Amongst a variety of contemporary topics up for discussion is the popish plot, in which Titus Oates fomented anti-Catholic feelings by fabricating a conspiracy to assassinate Charles II. As in any tavern of 1680, the drunkards in *Bacchanalia* speculate on the recent murder of Sir Edmund Berry Godfrey – found on Primrose Hill impaled on his sword but also strangled – concluding that this is evidence of Catholic intrigue.

The end-point of these scenes of over-indulgence arrives in the final three stanzas of the poem in Darby's return to the conceit of the deluge, this time in the form of what can best be described as a carnival of vomit:

> So slept they sound; but whilst they slept,
> Nature, which all this while, had kept
> Her last reserve of strength,
> In Stomachs mouth, where *Helmont* saith,
> The Soul its chiefest Mansion hath,
> Began at length
> To kick, and frisk, and stoutly strove
> To throw the Liquid Rider off.
> For now Her Case, like Mariners, was grown,
> In leaky Ship, She must or pump, or drown.
> Or whether that the Wine, which, till this time,

---

73   For discussion of the loss of rationalism in *Bacchanalia* see Smyth, 'Writing About Drunkenness', pp. 194–98.

Was wont to dwell in Cellar's cooler Clime,
Now put in Stomachs boiling-Pot,
Found its new Habitation too hot?
What e're it was, the Floods gusht out
From ev'ry spout,
With such a force; they made a fulsome fray.
One, who athwart his Neighbour lay,
Did right in his Pocket disembogue;
For which the other would have call'd him Rogue,
But that his forestall'd mouth (brawls to present)
Replenisht with the same Element. (XIX)

The collective expurgation of the club members is delivered in comic terms, but a descent into scatology sees the speaker reach his own stomach's limit:

The surly Element,
With Orall Channels not content,
Reverberates; and downwards finds a Vent
Which my Nice Muse to tell forbears,
And begs, for what is past, the pardon of your Ears. (XIX)

As the drawer presents a huge bill for the wine that none of the company can dispute because ''twas all beyond Man's Memory', Darby's speaker steps into the midst of the group, embodying the form and function of the hangover in a sententious epilogue. The ingredients that instil shame and embarrassment are various and include 'ruin'd Health', the loss of time ('Think of those Hours consum'd in sordid Vice') and a 'Bankrupt Reputation' ('Epilogue'). Financial impoverishment, the damaging effects to the family and other wider social responsibilities are more prominent here than previously witnessed:

Think of that abused Wealth,
Due to your Families, or the Poor;
Think how you swallow, in each Drunken Health,
The Widows Tears, and starved Orphans Goar. ('Epilogue')

Darby asks the hungover group to finally consider the fate of their 'guilty Souls', but it is particularly the domestic charges that resonate in the epilogue, as they were to in literature of the later eighteenth century. Significantly, the voices of the company are given no right of reply, but are advised to 'think on't soberly' ('Epilogue').

Darby requests the shame-faced inebriates think not only of the effects of heavy drinking to themselves but also of the effects on others; this hangover functions outside a religious context as a form of personal and social conscience. John Dennis's burlesque of the drinking club, *The Triumvirate: or, The Battle* (1692), follows suit, but in this case the rebuke comes not from another male within the group but from the drinker's wife (his argumentative friend takes the final part of the three) who intrudes on the evening's entertainment, 'and took her Vagrant, / *Ipso Facto*, in Guilt that's flagrant'.[74] An ideological and physical battle follows as Ned encourages his friend with arguments that come close to those we saw Friendly use in *The Contented Cuckold*:

> Old Bob, quoth he, Old Bob so doughty,
> Wilt thou be Cow'd by such a Dowdy?
> Take Crab-tree here Old Boy, and Bast her,
> Until she owns her Lord and Master.[75]

Undermining wine's association with wit, on this occasion it is the wife who has the best lines:

> Vile Sot said she to Ned, but such
> A Title honors thee too much;
> For Sot supposes something Human,
> Thou art a Bear, not born of Woman;
>
> ...
>
> For Men a Nights n'er see thee Sup,
> But what they've eat themselves comes up,
> Whilst thou devouring meat, dost cram it
> More nauseously than they theirs Vomit:
> Why should Beasts love Debauches, fit
> Only for Men, and Men of Wit?[76]

Ned is excluded from the elite traditions of the symposiasts by the breaking of the spell that had forged together, and upheld the actions

---

74   John Dennis, *The Triumvirate: or, The Battle*, in *Poems in Burlesque* (London: printed for the Booksellers of London and Westminster, 1692), p. 4. The text gives no line numbers, so I provide page references in the notes.

75   Dennis, *The Triumvirate*, p. 5.

76   Dennis, *The Triumvirate*, p. 6.

of, male drinkers and writers earlier in the century. The drinking party in *The Triumvirate* are abashed not only by the unwelcome spectre of domesticity and responsibility, but by the emptying out of Anacreontic conceits as the speaker witnesses a fight between the three, reflecting that if once the 'Bottle in Fellowship Men unit[ed]', it has now become an instrument 'made for Fighting'. Unlike the unifying symbol of the entrenched Cavaliers during the Protectorate, Dennis's wine leads to an unchivalrous battle; his 'Civil War' is one in which 'Friend fell foul on every Friend' and his speaker hurriedly leaves in the final lines of the poem as dawn is breaking 'and firmly Swore / Never to mix with Monsters more'.[77] Here, the hangover is not just about the fact of drinking, but, sending us right back to the start of this chapter, has actually become the main weapon in countering the representational strategies through which the patterns of early modern drinking culture validated itself.

Undoubtedly the most dominant voice to intercede in the alcohol question of the 1690s was Richard Ames, whose *Fatal Friendship; or, The Drunkard's Misery* (1692), published the year before his death, directly addresses, as its title suggests, the damage that the myth of conviviality and fellowship did to young men. Addressed 'To All Gentlemen, and Others; More particularly, To the Sworn Friends of the BOTTLE', Ames's speaker asks 'urge me no more my Friend' to drink in company.[78] This is the voice of experience (Ames had earlier gained fame with *The Search after Claret* [1691] in which he described his vain attempts to find a tavern serving claret following the increased taxation levied on the French wine by the Whigs).[79]

Ames firstly wonders about the hangovers of social drinkers in his prose preface:

> 'Tis a very strange thing, that a Man should *do* that *over-night*, which he must *ask Pardon* of his Constitution for *next Morning*. How *Penitent*, and *Crop-sick*, have I seen a *Spark*, after a Debauch? His *Body* Feaverish, his *Head* out of order; then *Small-Beer*, and *Coffee*, are his Beloved Liquors, and he abhors *Wine* for some time, equal with a *Mussel-man*; till nature throws it off, and then the *Bottle*

---

77 Dennis, *The Triumvirate*, p. 8.

78 Richard Ames, *Fatal Friendship, or, The Drunkard's Misery being a Satyr against Hard Drinking* (London: printed for Randal Taylor, 1693). There are no line numbers so I give section numbers.

79 For a recent discussion of Ames's earlier works on drink see Charles Ludington, *The Politics of Wine in Britain: A New Cultural History* (Basingstoke: Palgrave Macmillan, 2013), pp. 37–43.

must be ply'd pretty warmly, to redeem the time lost in *Sobriety*.
('The Epistle Dedicatory')

Echoing the words of Behn's butler in *The Debauchee*, the expression of
remorse is almost immediately overturned, and the weak will of the
libertine held up for censure. As with Darby and Dennis, Ames's primary
technique is to undermine the established patterns of drinking culture
and their dominant tropes, but Ames stands out for his greater variety
of targets. The twin bases of fellowship and wit are drained of their
colour like liquor from glasses. Health drinking quickly descends into
suspicion, violence and recrimination:

> To each Man's Health the Glass goes briskly round,
> And nought but Mirth and Jollity is found;
> But when one Bottle ushers in another,
> And this Half Flask brings in his younger Brother:
> A Scene quite different appears,
> For now with Wine inflam'd each petty Jar,
> Will 'mongst these Friends create a Civil War. (VII)

Friendship founded on drinking is depicted throughout the poem as
delusive and shameful. The enemy to sociability is discovered, most
damningly, not without but within the very customs that aim to preserve
it. The same is true for wit. Rather than promote good conversation,
Ames's speaker instead witnesses tedious jokes that fail to mask a general
feeling of awkwardness and purposelessness. Quite unlike the 'Tribe
of Ben', to whose spirit the drinkers aspire, Ames finds that 'Learned
Talking is Kickt out of Doors' (XX) by the consumption of wine, which
is reduced to the status of beer and ale through its association with
dullness.

Ames's speaker takes an oath against heavy drinking – 'Some
Irksom things one would for Friendship do, / Yet a Man's Health must
be regarded too' (II) – but feels nostalgia for lost sociability and risks
being labelled '*Squeamish Fool*, and *sober Sot*' (IV) (he wittily sets a
sober 'Health' against those toasts of the Royalists). So he is located
away from the tavern in pastoral 'Groves and Fields' where, rather than
feel crop-sick, he will 'crop the sweets, the lovely Garden yields' (III),
recalling occasions of previous excess from a safe distance. Unlike the
tavern company, the speaker associates his life with 'Health and Liberty',
but periodically finding himself in company, he recalls the temptation
to drink again – 'Now I've a doubtful Task to chuse, / Either to Drink,
or else refuse' (V) – and the expectations of the homosocial collective.

Opposed to fellowship, the hangover is a restraint against any misgivings experienced about the termination of sociability. Rhetorically, Ames suggests at times the early modern sermon, as when he argues that drunkenness is the parent of other sins, including murder. The return to sobriety is an accompanying part of social justice: 'oft a sad Repentance is his Lot, / And the Lewd Frolicks of a Drunken Sot, / End with a Halter, and a Psalm, / If drunk you kill, you must be hang'd when Calm' (VI). Ames turns to consider the drunkard's regrets:

Homeward 'tis time, that now he reels,
Insensible yet, but who can tell's
The Pangs his serious Thoughts next Morning feels,
When he considers what th' effects may be
Of his last Nights Vain, Sinful Jolity. (IX)

Other physical consequences are scrutinised in turn, including the gout, premature ageing, weight gain, weight loss and sexual impairment: 'Not able to perform what he once did.' Economic consequences also make a reappearance: 'The Body is the smallest Sufferer: / Too often the Estate the Damage feels, / And a House totters whilst its Master reels' (XV). Those unable to afford to maintain the lifestyle are abandoned by their friends and 'he who once esteem's no *Wines* too dear, / Now wets his throat with Penitent small beer' (XV). Eventually, feeling 'quite weary of the nauseous Town' (XVII), Ames forsakes it.

The role of the hangover in early modern writing about drunkenness is wider ranging than has ever really been acknowledged. Partly, as I have argued, this is due to the fact that modern critical interest in the topic, with its emphases on issues such as celebration and conviviality, means that the hangover is almost by necessity forgotten or overlooked. Even in discussions of censorship and reform, the hangover has previously made little impact because critics are so often drawn to the patterns of drinking culture, rather than to the personal and social aftermath. And yet this chapter has demonstrated that hangovers, whether directly addressed, as in sermons, tracts and the drinking satires penned by Anti-Symposiasts, or through the way in which they infiltrate representational modes that otherwise pay homage to the delights of drinking like the Anacreontea, reveal the cultural beliefs and social practices that surround alcohol consumption. Literature of the early modern period, partly because it often demonstrates stark political and religious divisions, enables us to better understand the guilt characteristic of a Traditional-Punishment response and the reasons why a Withdrawal-Relief response might indicate defiance. Chiefly, the hangover provides a different route into understanding the religious climate and the political symbolism of the period to those found in more general accounts of drinking customs. For any writer wanting to intercede in debates about the status of alcohol in the seventeenth century, the hangover was a useful weapon. To be crop-sick or to suffer qualms meant something more than just feeling physically ill or emotionally unsettled. To suffer a hangover in the early modern period was no straightforward business: in fact, it could very well define you in political, religious and cultural terms.

Chapter 3

'Baneful to Public and to Private Good': Hours of Illness and Idleness in the Long Eighteenth Century

Introduction

If drunkenness often induces temporary feelings of liberty from prevailing cultural norms, then the hangover usually leads to reappraisal of the standards of social conduct required of an individual, even if that does not necessarily result in penitence. In the previous chapter, I established that in the culture wars of the seventeenth century the hangover was largely identified as a period of remorse for sins committed when drunk. In the long eighteenth century in Britain, a period covering the later Stuart and Georgian age, hangovers carry a similar stigma, but they typically throw more light on the relationship between the individual drinker and the state. James Nicholls has rightly argued that at this time public debates about alcohol were 'shot through with anxieties over class, the economy, national identity and the protection of moral norms',[1] but it is my contention that hangover literature gives us a particularly strong sense of what those cultural anxieties consisted of. A study of hangovers furthers our understanding of the ways in which the moral questions that surrounded alcohol consumption in the eighteenth century became focused on economics, issues of nation building and the centrality of the family, rather than the fate of the drunkard's soul. To introduce this chapter, I will consider two examples of texts wherein hangovers disclose the social and commercial costs of heavy drinking.

In 1747 the Reverend Robert Colvill, a minister from Fife, and sometime poet, published his second volume of verse titled *Britain: A Poem*. A work of uneven quality, it alternates barbed observations on the habits of the idle and degenerate upper classes with Colvill's vision of

---

1   James Nicholls, *The Politics of Alcohol: A History of the Drink Question in England* (Manchester: Manchester University Press, 2009), p. 34.

a more democratic – and sober – Albion (III, 'The Argument').[2] Colvill
reflects the mood of many social commentators of the period when he
associates good habits, manners and gentlemanliness with the health of
the nation and sees the hangover as evidence of a 'shameful progress
in luxury' and moral deterioration. Written at the time of the War of
the Austrian Succession (1740–48), Colvill's poem juxtaposes a British
and Austrian morning:

> View the confed'rate realm, what temp'rance reigns
> And frugal plenty joyous thro' the land:
> Grateful they take the bounteous gift of heaven,
> And strong for toil with rising morn awake,
> The gallant champions of defended faith;
> Whilst Britain's sons, wore out by vicious joy,
> Their task o'er night, in deepest slumbers ly,
> Sunk on the couch of indolence and shame. (III, 57–64)

'Sinful nights' of 'revel and debauch' (III, 20) and the subsequent
hangovers fatigue 'Britain's sons' who are unfit to defend the realm.
Luxury and status – 'Sunk on the couch' – only serve to amplify the
degree of 'indolence and shame'. Colvill proceeds to use the somatic
and emotional features normally associated with hangovers to elaborate
on his primary targets: a government at odds with itself, armed forces
hamstrung by indecision ('the chance of war / Breathes panic thro'
your armies and your fleets' [III, 72–73]) and a body politic drained of
its vigour and direction ('This is the noxious malady, which hangs / So
deadly now on thy infeebl'd arm' [III, 65–66]). Embodied in the image
of the arm sapped of its strength, Britain's hungover gentry are not
only morally condemnable, but emasculated, fit only to lounge away the
morning amidst soft furnishings. These are 'shameful days ..., / Which
our industrious fathers never knew' (III, 53–54); the moralist presents
the past as a time marked, in contrast to the present age, by hard work
and diligence. His century's 'lengthened banquet' has a 'luxurious cost'
(III, 50) and the hangover is the price of collective overindulgence: an
enemy of regular hours, good habits, commitment and endeavour that
are the hallmarks of a morally upstanding nation.

The second example is concerned with the opposite end of the social
spectrum. In 1751 the author and magistrate Henry Fielding published
An Enquiry into the Causes of the Late Increase of Robbers, making a direct

---

2   Robert Colvill, *Britain, a Poem in Three Books* (Edinburgh: Wal. Ruddiman, Jr. &
     Co., 1747).

Fig. 3.1   William Hogarth, *Gin Lane* and *Beer Street* (1751). Images
courtesy of The Metropolitan Museum of Art.

link between the rise in consumption of spirituous liquors, particularly
gin, amongst the poor and an increase in criminal activity. This was
the same year that William Hogarth produced his famous engravings
Gin Lane and *Beer Street* (Fig. 3.1), which attempted to capture the
catastrophic social impact of the uncontrolled production of cheap
gin on the nation. For the conservative Fielding, the discussion of
gin was an opportunity to examine a number of arguments for the
benefits of increased legislation – contributing to the decisive Gin Act
of 1751 – including legal provision for the poor and a more efficient
penal system. Fielding's image of the nation is more classical than
Colvill's, but it partakes of the same logic: 'By the *Constitution* [of
this country] is … meant something which results from the Order
and Disposition of the whole … many of the Greeks imagined the
Soul to result from the … Composition of the Parts of the Body;
when these were properly tempered together'.[3] When disordered by
the consequences of heavy drinking, the body, like the body politic,
fails to function healthily and morally. Relative economic prosperity
has led many poorer members of society to covet the luxuries, and
adopt the bad habits, of the upper classes, which upsets the political

3   Henry Fielding, *An Enquiry into the Causes of the Late Increase of Robbers and Related
Writings*, ed. Malvin R. Zirker (Oxford: Clarendon Press, 1988), p. 66.

homeostasis: 'In free Countries ... it is a branch of Liberty claimed by the people to be as wicked and as Profligate as their Superiors.'[4] 'Not being able by the Fruits of honest Labour to support the State which they affect', Fielding proceeds, '[the poor] disdain the Wages to which their Industry would intitle them.'[5] In Hogarth's *Gin Lane*, men and women are likewise unfit to work and only the owner of the pawnshop and the undertaker do any trade; according to Daniel Defoe, in his pamphlet opposing Humphry Mackworth's workhouse scheme, *Giving Alms No Charity* (1704), once the Englishman has his wages he is inclined only to 'be idle, or perhaps drunk'.[6] The former was most likely consequent on the latter.

As Sarah Jordan has demonstrated, idleness was an increasing source of moral unease at both ends of the social scale, and for both sexes, in Georgian Britain. Idleness and indolence had long been the privilege of the landed gentry, but 'the knowledge and moral authority of the leisured gentleman was no longer a given' in the context of a democratising Britain.[7] The nation's desire to appear industrious meant closer inspection of the cultural authority and value of the hereditary rich and never did they appear more indolent than while hungover. Likewise, the plebeian and emergent middle class were defined by their capacity or failure to work.[8] British industry was often contrasted with the perceived laziness of other nations – 'the free Countries' invoked by Fielding – but the incursion of French habits was a less potent danger to enterprise than the after-effects of heavy drinking. Fielding's poor – allegedly mimicking the sort of well-heeled inebriate depicted by Colvill – no longer form a 'working' class, but a set of idlers, alternately drunk and hungover, likely to drag their families into extreme poverty or crime.

Issues that dominate public debates surrounding the consumption of alcohol in the eighteenth century focalise my discussion of the hangover in this chapter. These are anxieties that orbit around the damage done by drink to social and domestic well-being, the moral responsibility attendant on affluence, the economic and personal benefits arising from a healthy work force and a perceived crisis in the character of

4   Fielding, *Enquiry*, p. 77.
5   Fielding, *Enquiry*, p. 77.
6   Daniel Defoe, *Giving Alms No Charity*, in *The Shortest Way with Dissenters and Other Pamphlets* (Oxford: Blackwell, 1927), p. 186 (pp. 153–88).
7   Sarah Jordan, *The Anxieties of Idleness: Idleness in Eighteenth-Century British Literature and Culture* (Lewisburg: Bucknell University Press, 2003), p. 14.
8   Jordan argues that both upper and lower classes were defamed for idleness by the growing middle class (*Anxieties of Idleness*, p. 19).

both the labouring and professional man, and the leisured man and woman. In this book's introduction, I mentioned that the effect of the hangover on work is often publicly debated, most recently in 2014, when the Institute of Alcohol Studies reported on the extent to which workforce productivity in Britain was disrupted by hangovers, with 77 per cent of respondents indicating that the hangover was the main cause of absence through sickness.[9] According to John Crofton and Richard Stephens, estimating the societal cost of drinking is 'prone to inaccuracy' precisely because those costs related to the hangover, such as 'lateness, accident risk, poorly performed work and disputes', are hard to measure accurately.[10] The hangover literature I examine in this chapter does not aim for the statistical precision of data collection, but it places the hangover at the centre of debates about fitness to work and fitness to govern.

In the first half of the chapter I summarise the politics of the gin craze and then analyse the representation of hangovers in the period leading up to the second Gin Act of 1736. The physical symptoms of the hangovers of spirit drinkers are here represented as more severe than those experienced by drinkers of beer and wine. Hangovers also feature extensively in representations of the landed gentry and young professionals (usually bachelors) in comic drama, satirical verse, life writing and domestic fiction. These texts are full of hungover idlers, sweating and cursing and fretting away their mornings, evidently incapable of work. In the second half of the chapter, I range more widely back and forth across the period's literature to explore how the hangover disrupted the home for both men and women. The domestic space is significant for analysing hangovers in the period because, as Amanda Vickery has argued, 'the home was crucial to traditional political theory, since the household was taken to be a microcosm of the state'.[11] Or, as Colvill puts it, the hangover was dually 'baneful to public and to private good' (III, 56). In what follows, I will attempt to show how hangovers disclosed social anxieties about civic duty, the real level of industriousness of the British workforce and the moral status of the unoccupied man and woman of means in the long eighteenth century.

9   Institute of Alcohol Studies, *Alcohol in the Workplace Factsheet* (March 2014), p. 4.
10   Richard Stephens *et al*, 'A Review of the Literature of Cognitive Effects of Alcohol Hangover', *Alcohol and Alcoholism*, 43.2 (2008), p. 163 (pp. 163–70). See also John Crofton, 'Editorial: Extent and Costs of Alcohol Problems in Employment: A Review of British Data', *Alcohol and Alcoholism*, 22.4 (1987), pp. 321–25.
11   Amanda Vickery, *Behind Closed Doors: At Home in Georgian England* (New Haven, CT & London: Yale University Press, 2009), p. 7.

The Gin Craze

Ladies Delight. Cuckold's Comfort. Mother's Ruin. Colic Water. Madame Geneva, and so on and so forth. The many colloquial expressions for gin in the eighteenth century are testimony to its cultural pervasiveness and inevitably representation of the hangover at this time was intertwined with the gin craze in numerous ways. Before explaining these, we need to consider the reasons why gin had such an impact on public consciousness and the body politic.

Writing about drunkenness in the first half of the eighteenth century is dominated by parliament's attempts to police spirits. The word 'gin' was a shortened version of 'geneva', which derived from the French for 'juniper', the berry with which the alcohol was flavoured. Its explosion in popularity at the beginning of the eighteenth century is partly explained by the legislation through which William III gave support to new technologies in distillation. His political and economic motivation was to establish gin as an alternative to French claret and brandy, importation of which was banned from 1689 to 1695 and during the War of the Spanish Succession (1701–14). Gin quickly became a symbol of Britain's ideological hostility towards Catholic France and of its support of Dutch interests in Europe. In a nation that increasingly defined itself through its trade relations, an indigenous distilling industry was a sign of economic strength. Even so, political sponsorship of gin was partly opportunistic: a response to a series of good harvests in the 1690s that led to a surplus of corn – it is commonly agreed that the distillation of gin aided the financial interests of the landed gentry – and capitalisation on advancements made in farming and distillation.[12]

Whichever way it is presented, the extent of the gin phenomenon from the 1720s onward is startling. Although exact figures are contested, most commentators are in agreement that *per capita* consumption of gin rose dramatically throughout the first half of the eighteenth century spiking in the early 1740s. Roy Porter calculates that in London at this period, men, women and children consumed roughly two pints of gin a week and it was speculated that every eighth house sold spirits.[13] James R. McIntosh estimates that, prior to 1690, British consumption

12   See Patrick Dillon, *Gin: The Much-Lamented Death of Madame Geneva* (Boston, MA: Justin, Charles & Co., 2003), p. 82.

13   Roy Porter, *London: A Social History* (Harmondsworth: Penguin, 2000), p. 219. The degree of uncertainty surrounding precise calculations of gin production, retail and consumption is indicated by the variability of this particular figure. H. A. Monckton sets it at one in six houses (*A History of the English Public House* [London: Bodley Head, 1969], p. 64), while M. Dorothy George estimated that

of gin was little more than half a million gallons, whereas by 1750 it had risen to 11 million gallons.[14] According to Rod Phillips, the 'man, woman, and child' calculation is usually an unreliable abstraction in discussions of *per capita* consumption, but it is more applicable to the gin craze than to other alcohol because, as Hogarth captures starkly in *Gin Lane*, 'much of the anxiety rested on the belief that gin was being abused not only by men, but also by women and children'.[15] Gin was sold at dram shops, rather than in taverns or public houses, but also in a wide variety of other premises including barbers shops, workhouses and brothels. The novelty – and danger – of gin in the early eighteenth century is underlined by the absence of the kind of well-established legal regulations that controlled brewing: unlike other forms of alcohol, up until 1729, gin could be sold without any form of licence. Nicholls observes that gin presented 'a kind of legislative tabula rasa, being unencumbered by either centuries of tradition or the muddle of laws which covered the licensing of both wine and beer'.[16] Effectively anyone who wanted could sell gin at the beginning of the eighteenth century.

The first attempt to legislate the production of gin came with the Gin Act of 1729, which introduced a £20 excise licence on retailers and a duty tax of two shillings per gallon of spirits. The effect of the 1729 Act was not to diminish a nation's thirst, however, but to increase the amount of adulterated gin on the market as producers attempted to evade restrictions. Early ineffectual legislation led directly to a more severe stance on gin by Robert Walpole's administration and a second Act was passed in 1736, which aimed to make gin prohibitively expensive to the working class (now perceived to be the largest consumers and the group most at risk from the pernicious consequences of gin). Hiking the licence fee to £50 for retailers wanting to sell gin in quantities of less than two gallons led to riots on the streets of London and the Act was repealed in 1743.

New stricter legislation was partly a response to the agitation of influential prohibitionists such as Thomas Wilson and Sir Joseph Jekyll, but on the other side of the argument there were many prepared to speak on behalf of gin and the distillers. In 1726 Daniel Defoe,

in the area of St Giles one in four houses sold gin (*London Life in the Eighteenth Century* [Harmondsworth: Penguin, 1925], p. 54).

14   James R. McIntosh, 'Gin Craze', in Jack S. Blocker, Jr., Ian R. Tyrrell and David M. Fahey (eds), *Alcohol and Temperance in Modern History: An International Encyclopedia* (Santa Barbara, CA, Denver, TX and Oxford: ABC Clio, 2003), pp. 265–67.

15   Rod Phillips, 'Gin', in Blocker, Tyrrell and Fahey (eds), *Alcohol and Temperance in Modern History*, p. 264 (pp. 263–65).

16   Nicholls, *Politics of Alcohol*, p. 39.

for example, addressed *A Brief Case of the Distillers and the Distilling Trade* to parliament, arguing that the economic benefits of distillation were indisputable: 'As the consumption increases, the publick revenue increases of course, without the Addition of new Taxes, with this undeniable Advantage to *England* ... The Quantity of Lands to be cultivated, will encrease: The Advantage to the Farmer, the Employment of Cattle, and Men, will increase.'[17] Increased productivity meant more jobs. Defoe also countered the 'health-of-the-nation' objection by arguing that the spirit distilled from corn was wholesome. Ale and beer had long been thought to provide sustenance that was not qualitatively different from bread and meat, as demonstrated by Hogarth's stout and healthy beer drinkers in *Beer Street*. Defoe now maintained that the same was true, if not more so, for gin: 'the Spirit only is the nutritive Part of all our Food, whether Meat or Drink'. The spirit was superior in fact to food for being separated from 'the gross and humid Parts'.[18] In any case, the problems of excessive drinking were not, according to Defoe, the responsibility of the distillers but of consumers. The economic argument was not one that he would maintain. Only two years later, gin had become a more toxic subject for its perceived contribution to crime and poverty and in *Augusta Triumphans* (1728) Defoe called for similar state intervention to that advocated by the likes of Wilson and Jekyll.[19]

Part of the variance in responses to gin is because, as Nicholls explains, the stakes were so high: the gin phenomenon went to the very heart of capitalism, raising 'fundamental questions about the role of the modern state'.[20] Fielding, for one, was concerned with the question of 'How far is it the business of the Politician to interfere in the Case of Luxury?'[21] At all levels of public debate the moral argument needed balancing against the commercial one and politicians sought a way of mediating 'wild Notions of Liberty that are inconsistent with all Government, and those pernicious Schemes of Government, which are destructive of true Liberty'.[22]

---

17   Daniel Defoe, *A Brief Case of the Distillers and the Distilling Trade* (London: printed for T. Warner, 1726), p. 10.
18   Defoe, *Distillers*, pp. 10–11.
19   See Daniel Defoe, *Augusta Triumphans: Or, the Way to Make London the Most Flourishing City in the Universe* (London: J. Roberts, 1728).
20   Nicholls, *Politics of Alcohol*, p. 39.
21   Fielding, *Enquiry*, p. 71.
22   Fielding, *Enquiry*, p. 73.

Caput Mortuum

In *The Politics of Alcohol*, Nicholls titles his chapter on the gin craze, 'A new kind of drunkenness'. But in order to understand 'how the 1736 Gin Act came about' and 'how [the] message of economic collapse', which I outlined above, 'gained currency', we would be better served by focusing on a new kind of hangover.[23] For those who campaigned against the distillers, the aftermath of drinking could be just as grisly as the kind of intoxication Hogarth depicted in *Gin Lane*, and one of the commonest observations about the gin epidemic was that the aftershocks of consumption were more detrimental to both individual and public good than those experienced by other drinkers.

A representative example of the way in which the hangover was used to intervene in the economies of the gin question is *The Trial of the Spirits* ... (1736), which will be my primary focus here. The essay was addressed to Walpole and Jekyll and published during the period leading up to the Gin Act of September of that year. As a consequence, it is often considered to be one of the most influential pieces of parliamentary lobbying on the gin question. Attributed to the pseudonymous 'Philanthropos', Jonathan White argues that it was probably authored by a clergyman.[24] That the technology of distillation was still only partly understood is apparent from the way that Philanthropos distinguishes between spirits and other forms of alcohol such as beer and wine, using the pseudo-medical language of the humours. The product of distillation is described as a 'Composition of acid Phlegm and Earth' and, as so often at this period, gin is portrayed as an inflammatory liquid, particularly detrimental to drinkers disposed to be fiery and aggressive. 'Chymists', Philanthropos continues, term the 'Spirit' of fermented liquids a 'Residuum' and '*Caput Mortuum*', or worthless remains, 'the bare Tast of [which]', unlike beer, 'will give the Patient a Vomit'.[25] The *Caput Mortuum* – literally the 'dead head' redolent of a hangover – is an indigestible by-product – 'the *Liquor* being rarefied and evaporated, the *Caput Mortuum* remains in their

---

23 Nicholls, *Politics of Alcohol*, p. 38.

24 Jonathan White, 'The "Slow But Sure Poyson": The Representation of Gin and Its Drinkers, 1736–1751', *Journal of British Studies*, 42.1 (2003), p. 43 (pp. 35–64). A note to the Goldsmiths' Library copy conjectures that the author was Adam Holden, but this is probably a mistake made because Holden wrote a defence of the *Trial* titled *A Vindication of a Pamphlet Lately Published, Entitled 'The Trial of the Spirits'* (London, 1736).

25 'Philanthropos', *The Trial of the Spirits: Or, Some Considerations Upon the Pernicious Consequences of the Gin Trade to Great Britain* (London: printed for T. Cooper, 1736), p. 7.

Stomachs' – leading directly to many physical hangover symptoms and, in extreme cases, to the conditions indicative of alcoholic withdrawal: 'Hence a Train of *universal Disorders*, such as Indolence, Depravation of Appetite, Weaknesses, Nervous Convulsions, Epilepsies, Apoplexies, Death.'[26]

Philanthropos's discussion of the physical effects of excessive spirit drinking is a preface to the real subject of his essay, which is the impact of a collective *Caput Mortuum* on the nation's economic prosperity. He argues for the prohibition of gin on proto-Benthamite grounds, with individual happiness subservient to the larger social good, predicting that the habitual spirit drinker is likely to be so incapacitated or immobilised by hangovers, rendered 'so *stupid* and *enervated*, that instead of being a *useful Member* of the Community, he is actually become a *scandalous Burthen* upon it'. Sketching consequences for drinking in broad social and economic terms, Philanthropos, echoing the sentiments of Colvill, targets the masculine spheres of the military and the workplace: 'Hence then, Sirs, you will easily perceive, that the Nation must in a little Time be destitute of both *Labourers* and *Soldiers*. The *One* will not be able to carry a Musket, no more than the *Other* a Burthen, and what then must become of Society, especially this Fertile, Trading Island?'[27] In *The Trial of the Spirits*, the *residuum* of gin is firstly an emasculating weakness: physical aftershocks of drinking deprive the body of its energy. Philanthropos animadverts on the common belief that gin, associated in the public consciousness with the Netherlands and often called 'Hollands', provided soldiers with 'Dutch' courage. Indirectly his prose also gestures towards impaired sexual performance or sterility: gin is a threat to the 'Fertile' island nation.

What for Defoe helped men fight and labour lustily while inebriated – he perpetuates the myth of Dutch courage in *A Brief Case of the Distillers* – has quite the opposite effect for Philanthropos when it came to the morning after.[28] Invoking medical authorities he argues that recognisable physical

---

26   'Philanthropos', *Trial*, p. 7. In alchemy, the *caput mortuum* was a useless substance left over during a chemical experiment.

27   'Philanthropos', *Trial*, p. 7.

28   In *A Brief Case of the Distillers*, Defoe had invoked the popular myth that the armed services thrived on spirits. In one example it is the navy: '[T]he Captains of the *Hollanders* Men of War ... usually set a Hogshead of Brandy abroach ... and bid the Men *drink lustick*, then they might *fight lustick*: and our poor Seamen felt the Force of the Brandy' – in another the army: 'It was strange to observe, how [gin] prevail'd in the Army; how the Soldiers were surprised at the Goodness of it; the Spirit, the Vigor it put into them' (p. 18). The same belief prevailed in America and it was not until 1862, largely as a result of the agitation of temperance reformers, that the navy's rum ration was revoked.

hangover symptoms – which here include the stated indolence along with *'Depravation* of *Appetite, Vomitings, Relaxation* of the *Coats* of the *Stomach'*[29] – so debilitated the system of the average drinker that it rendered him unable to work and so contribute to the nation's productivity. If it was the case, as Nicholls argues, that some observers believed the gin industry encouraged subsidiary trades – including 'toolmakers, corn-reapers, maltsters, carriage-drivers and so forth'[30] – Philanthropos countered with the argument that many men would be unfit to carry out such work during the days following a drinking bout. Scale was everything for those campaigning against the distillers. Examples of the greater severity of hangovers in spirit drinkers were useful proof of gin's extensive grip on the workforce. Spirit drinkers put additional pressure on poor relief and the state by producing needy women and children: 'the *Parish Work-Houses* are fill'd with their poor, starv'd Families, *Trade* and *Country* depriv'd of their *Manufacturers* and *Labours'*.[31]

Amongst their list of alcohol hangover symptoms, Penning, McKinney and Verster note the deleterious effect on appetite (Fig. 1.2). Philanthropos raises the economic stakes of the nation's hangover when he enlarges on the nausea, vomiting, tainted palate, indigestion and heartburn (redolent of the 'acid Phlegm' of the liquor itself), which was typically ascribed to the hangovers of spirit drinkers. Countering the belief that the distillation of gin served the landed interest, he maintained that spirit drinking negatively affected the trade of farmers, bakers and butchers through its debilitating effects on the nation's constitution. First, 'the Consumption of *Wheat* must be greatly lessened', he argues, 'from a total Inappetite of these poor Wretches'.[32] The economic benefits deriving from the use of surplus corn in distillation were, as a consequence, negated by the corresponding fall in the production and consumption of bread. Moreover, if the worker's debilitated stomach could not take the wholesome, *'light* and *inoffensive'* sustenance of bread, what would it make of heavier food such as meat?

> For if the Stomach, through its Depravity, occasion'd by the Reception of those Liquors, rejects so *light* and *inoffensive* a Food as *Bread*, that can offend or oppress no Stomach in any *tolerable* Condition, either by its Weight, Smell or Tast, and which would give light and natural Nourishment: How must it not Nauseate *Butchers*

---

29   'Philanthropos', *Trial*, p. 10.
30   Nicholls, *Politics of Alcohol*, p. 39.
31   'Philanthropos', *Trial*, p. 12.
32   'Philanthropos', *Trial*, p. 10.

Meat, offensive to the Smell of every sick person, heavy to Digest, and so substantial Nourishment?[33]

Food frequently turns the hungover stomach and Philanthropos depicts spirit drinkers courting illness by rejecting nourishment. The message was the opposite of that found in Hogarth's *Beer Street*, where the hearty appetite of ale drinkers is signalled by the labourer brandishing a haunch of meat. The personal suffering of the gin drinker, indicated by the emaciated figures in *Gin Lane* and by *The Trial of the Spirits*, was an index of a greater social malaise that had consequences for the nation's economic constitution.

Philanthropos argues for state intervention in the distilling industry by linking the physical and economic *residua* of gin. As with other commentators, this meant grandstanding the most overt somatic symptoms associated with hangovers – headache, nausea, vomiting, tremors and hot and cold flushes – to demonstrate that the morning after might be a prelude to the chronic and extensive health issues that would disorder the body politic. 'Is there no *other* Way of preserving our *Constitution*, but by letting it fall into a *deep Consumption*?' he laments.[34] Naturally, Philanthropos is concerned with the state of inebriation – with the social impact of drunken behaviour – and this ought at times to be distinguished from the hangover. Yet, *The Trial of the Spirits* underlines what is perhaps the most important point about the moral panic that surrounded the gin phenomenon, which is, as Ernest Abel has argued, that public debates about gin were not really about drunkenness *per se* but about class and whether or not labourers were fit to work.[35] These issues were predominantly framed by the aftermath of drinking: 'Gin drinking among the "inferior class" in the second quarter of the 18th century', Abel argues, 'was attacked as an unprecedented problem not because drunkenness was more commonplace, or because of benevolent concern that it was impairing the health of the poor as individuals, but because of its perceived dangers to the Nation's welfare and economy.'[36] Significantly, his research demonstrates that 'when the London Grand Jury met at the Old Bailey in 1735 to present to the Lord Mayor "such publick Nusances as disturb and annoy the Inhabitants of the City"', its main complaint was not, as we might expect, drunken and disorderly

---

33   'Philanthropos', *Trial*, p. 12.
34   'Philanthropos', *Trial*, p. 27.
35   Ernest L. Abel, 'The Gin Epidemic: Much Ado About What?', *Alcohol and Alcoholism*, 36 (2001), pp. 401–405.
36   Abel, 'Much Ado', p. 402.

behaviour, but that 'gin was robbing the "lower kind of people" of their will and power "to labor for an honest livelihood, which is a principal Reason of the great Increase of the Poor"'.[37] Hence, Philanthropos argues that gin fuels male aggression and violence, but the subsequent social consequences are more devastating: 'During [a drinking bout] the *Hero* swells … but the *Fury* at length being over, the *hero* subsides in proportion, and sinks into a miserable *Invalid*, his whole Strength and Courage being intirely demolish'd.'[38] If the hangover was understood to be a state of physical incapacity or bodily enervation, the greater severity and duration of hangovers amongst gin drinkers appeared to threaten the fabric of working life in London and beyond. Fiery gin was literally leaving the workforce burned out, 'parch'd or crisp'd', as Philanthropos puts it.[39]

Philanthropos was one of the commentators to most effectively direct parliamentary legislation against the gin distillers but he was not alone in drawing attention to the social *Caput Mortuum*. *A Dissertation Upon Drunkenness* (1727) focuses on spirit drinking (though beer and wine are not exempt from attack), adding to the catalogue of physical ailments linked to gin in *The Trial of the Spirits* the language of remorse and penitence commonly associated with a Traditional-Punishment hangover response. The anonymous author predicts that if the gin epidemic 'does not soon abate, that in the next Age all our Arts, Sciences, Trade, and Manufactures will be entirely lost, and the whole Kingdom become nothing but a Brewery or Distillery, and the Inhabitants all drunkards'.[40] Alcohol was altering the foundations of daily life and distorting the economic conditions on which the ability to trade were based by destroying the health that was the 'Gift of God'. The author of the *Dissertation* bemoans the temptations that the city offers to young beaus and country squires, but his social concerns are revealed by his principal focus on the tradesmen who frequent alehouses and dram shops, 'the Rendezvous of *Joiners*, *Shoe-makers*, and *Taylors*'. Heavy drinking has led 'many honest fellows' to lose 'the best of Places'. For these individuals, the hangover is an economic one comprising 'a well-stretched Score', or the arrears with alehouse keepers, 'impending over their Heads, threatening heavy Judgments'. Dram shops are temptation for the servants of the nobility and gentry, unable to pay their tab, causing 'them to wrong their Masters in greater Matters'.[41]

37   Abel, 'Much Ado', p. 402.
38   'Philanthropos', *Trial*, p. 6.
39   'Philanthropos', *Trial*, p. 10.
40   Anon., *A Dissertation Upon Drunkenness. Shewing to What an Intolerable Pitch that Vice is Arriv'd at in the Kingdom* (London: printed for T. Warner, 1727), p. 2.
41   Anon., *Dissertation*, pp. 17, 5, 9–10.

The *Dissertation* touches on many of the issues that we see raised in *The Trial of the Spirits*, but again the negative effects of hangovers on the industry of the labouring class feature most prominently: '*Geneva*, never fails to produce an invincible Aversion to Work and Labour.' The *Dissertation*'s rhetoric surrounding laziness is particularly melodramatic: '[Gin] charms the Unactive, the Desperate and the Crafty of either Sex, and makes the starving Sot behold his Rags and Nakedness with stupid Indolence, or banter both in senseless laughter and more insipid Jests.' Nothing is 'more destructive, either in Regard to the Health, or the Vigilance and Industry of the Poor'. It warns that spirit drinking 'has broke and destroyed the strongest Constitutions' and the physical after-effects of gin drinking that the inebriate can expect will ultimately extend beyond indolence, 'Loss of Appetites' and 'Fevers', to 'Black and Yellow Jaundice, Convulsions, Stone and Gravel, Dropsies, &c.' In the long term the drunkard 'lays in Fuel for a distempered old Age', but only if he does not die young. Once again these physical effects are never considered in isolation but in the utilitarian light of their consequences on trade and 'publick Welfare'. Notably, the hangover provides the moral arbiter on the drink question with a maxim drawn from the language of commerce: the drunkard 'to please an unruly Appetite, *purchases* tormenting Guilt and endless Woe' [emphasis added].[42]

For the author of the *Dissertation*, hangovers are a natural corrective to individual drinking, but they reflect the larger social and economic problems contingent on drunkenness. The difficulty in reforming the endemic drinker emerges when the physical, moral and economic deterrents of the hangover cease to function. 'If', the anti-gin campaigner writes, 'Shame and Fear, if Love and Knowledge are powerful Restraints to keep us from offending, how necessarily must the intemperate Man, who has lost his Guards and Security, fall into the manner of Sin.'[43] He goes so far as to claim that the spirit drinker is beyond help because he lacks a conscience, or the ability to experience the remorse that identifies a Traditional-Punishment response: 'In truth I must suspect the Drunkard feels none of this Remorse, and is so far from repenting of his evil Course of Life, that he would run over again the same Excess of Riot, if he had the Power and Opportunity.'[44] What the absence of 'Power' suggests, on the other hand, is that the physical weakness, and perhaps even the loss of money or 'Opportunity', of the hungover drinker is, more than any moralising, the most effective deterrent against the immediate prospect of another drinking binge. In the textual responses to the gin craze, the hangover, at a personal and national level, was firstly a matter of economics. Drinkers purchasing gin were also 'purchasing' guilt for their idleness, but the semantics of the hangover suggested that society as a whole was picking up the tab.

Sullen Matrimonial Creatures

In 1755 a housewife named Susan Bacon commissioned a noted artist to paint a portrait of her husband as a marriage gift. What the husband thought of his depiction is not recorded, but the painting – in oils by the aforementioned William Hogarth – survives and is on display in Norwich Castle Museum titled *Francis Matthew Schutz in His Bed* (Fig. 3.2). The bed is a four-poster, and the rich red curtains and drapery

Fig. 3.2   William Hogarth, *Francis Matthew Schutz in His Bed* (1755?). Image courtesy of Norfolk Museums Service (Norwich Castle Museum & Art Gallery).

and ornate furnishings indicate wealth, refinement and good taste. Far from resting at his ease in such sumptuous chambers, however, Francis Matthew Schutz is depicted half tumbling from his crumpled sheets, vomiting into a chamber pot, his expression vacant with what looks like a hot towel wrapped around his head. He is evidently suffering from a severe hangover.

A lyre adorns the wall and next to the bed is an inscription from an Ode of Horace: '*Vixi puellis nuper idoneus, &c*', translating as 'Not long ago I kept in shape for the girls'. As Ronald Paulson observes, the implication is that he has either given up carousing – as with Horace's speaker he has 'hung up his lyre and his lechery' – or, what is more likely, is unable to fulfil his marital duties. Paulson calls the picture 'a pious temperance exordium', designed by Bacon to present her dissolute husband with a stark warning about the state of his health, his morals and his marriage once the euphoria of drunkenness has worn off.[45] It is a much more vivid version of Colvill's idle fop on his couch, but is drawn from the same field of censure.

The painting is certainly an amusing depiction of a hangover, but the incongruous setting means it retains some of its shock value. It should be set in the context of wider considerations about the way that hangovers were revealing tensions in Georgian households of quite different social standing up and down the land. The new importance of the domestic household to national prosperity is well known, encapsulated in the 'family–state analogy', delineated by Michael McKeon, whereby the health of the latter was seen to depend on the regulation of the former.[46] If moralists wanted to tackle middle-class drinking then they needed to turn their attention from the public house or dram shop to the home and the surest way to do this was to follow the example of Susan Bacon and focus on the drinker's hangover. Schutz was newly married and the painting has something of what McKeon describes as an 'emergent discourse' against libertinism, whereby 'the reformative powers of a female-dominated interior space' were conflated 'with the authority of public government'.[47] As Amanda Vickery puts it, a feeling arose that 'male extravagance', and the subsequent idleness, could be 'tempered and domesticated by female refinement'.[48] The hangover's contribution

45   Ronald Paulson, *Hogarth: Art and Politics, 1750–1764* (Cambridge: The Lutterworth Press, 1993), p. 269.

46   Michael McKeon, *The Secret History of Domesticity: Public, Private, and the Division of Knowledge* (Baltimore, MD: Johns Hopkins University Press, 2005), p. 120.

47   McKeon, *Secret History*, p. 186.

48   Vickery, *Behind Closed Doors*, p. 19.

to the contest between male and female priorities in the home, which has hitherto been a neglected subject, was becoming more significant for writers who began to note that it was in the private sphere that they could be used to explore, and provide a commentary on, gender norms, the state of marriage and, hence, the nation.

Prior to the eighteenth century the history of the domestic hangover is a fairly short one. In Chapter 2 we saw a couple of brief examples, but the tendency was to interpret hangovers as a commentary on sinfulness. Perhaps the most notable document to anticipate the way that hangovers would be used to show marital tensions in the late Stuart and Georgian periods is John Taylor's 'Skimmington's lecture to her husband which is the errant scold' from his *Divers Crabtree Lectures* (1639). The wife's role in upbraiding her spouse is a humorous one that would become a stereotype:

> What not a word this morning, are you all alike, drunke and sober, cannot you speake, or have you lost your tongue, you may be ashamed, had you any grace in you at all, to bee such a common drunkard, a pisse-pot, a beast, nay worse then a beast, for they can tell when they have sufficient, but thou canst not tell; every day foxed & at night brought home by a watchman; and the next morning you are then a little crop-sick, and then to cure your squeezy stomacke, you get a haire with the same dog, you know what I meane you drunken sot, a cup of the same wine burnt or muld that you dranke raw over night, this you call Physicke and say it is good and wholsome once a month, and this is your course of life, from one weeks end to the other. As I am a sinner I am ashamed of thee thou art such a noted Taverne hunter.[49]

The skimmington was, as McKeon notes, 'a ritual enactment of the disordered household' and a 'skimmington ride', later made famous by Thomas Hardy in *The Mayor of Casterbridge* (1886), was a grotesque pageant or ritual intended to humiliate erring women.[50] The fear of shame associated with the household is represented by the wife as nagging termagant. Pestered husbands characteristically adopt a Withdrawal-Relief recovery method, or the 'hair of the dog', to mitigate physical symptoms of sickness or 'squeezy' stomach. Here, shame is mainly a result of loss of

49 John Taylor, *Divers Crabtree Lectures Expressing the Severall Languages that Shrews Read to Their Husbands, Either at Morning, Noone, or Night* (London: I. Okes for John Sweeting, 1639), pp. 132–34.
50 McKeon, *Secret History*, p. 243.

status: on the one hand in class terms – he is a 'common' drunkard – on the other, more fundamentally, he is depicted as abhuman. This scene is an antemeridian form of 'curtain lecture', whereby women privately reprimanded their spouse in bed for shameful misdemeanours usually including drunkenness, gambling and other forms of carousing. Shame is located within the home although in this case the wife is a comic antagonist whose reproofs are undermined by the humorous mode.

McKeon tells us that the domesticated skimmington became more popular in the eighteenth century and the 'regime of sexual difference' whereby the wife 'internalized authority that had previously been gendered male' was notable.[51] Edmund Harrold, a wig-maker from Manchester, whose surviving diaries (1712–15) provide a valuable record of a professional man, and heavy drinker, from the period epitomise the kind of position in which the hungover husband found himself. Harrold evidently went on regular benders or what he called 'rambles', but he documents his return home regularly and vividly including the curtain lectures, both whilst in his cups and hungover: 'Came home and went to bed, but my wife scolding and upbraided me with drunkenness, houghting and coughing and would not be easie.' His work is interrupted 'with wife['s] clamours about my last dr[u]nken bout'. Likewise, on visiting a friend about securing a housekeeper he 'had a lecture for my debauches ye month past, and instead of caunsel [I had] discouragement in my condition'. Harrold's wife had good reason to complain about her husband's behaviour as he would regularly disappear for days on end or return inebriated in the early hours of morning: 'Yn we fell on ramble on Shud[e] Hill, and yn I home in ye morn. I found him in bed, yn we drank and I b[ought] [Alex] Cockras hair [for] 12s, yn I cam[e] to dinner, and yn I rambl'd TWs mothrs Jolvers[?]. Yn to Aunt Barrows with John Davie, so home to bed.' The next day Harrold records 'Very ill, lay long, Could not work, eat little.' Later in the day 'cured gravel kidneys with purg[e] and vomit and fasting'.[52]

Harrold's somatic symptoms are long and severe, including his regular feelings of nausea, vomiting and headache. A heavy night at the *Bull's Head* and *Royal Oak* 'set [him] on shitting'. He is also frequently dehydrated, 'burn'd up with thirst and heat' during a hangover.[53] Kidney stones reveal more serious health problems, but, in-keeping with the century's denunciation of idleness, Harrold's shame is particularly

51   McKeon, *Secret History*, p. 243.
52   *The Diary of Edmund Harrold, Wigmaker of Manchester 1712–15*, ed. Craig Horner (Aldershot: Ashgate, 2008), pp. 43, 23, 57, 91.
53   *Harrold Diary*, pp. 43, 29, 90.

associated with poor work-life balance and his hangovers remind him of his commercial and domestic responsibilities as a husband. He regularly aims to reform for the sake of his wife and laments loss of employment due to his illnesses. Following what appears to be the most monumental drinking binge – his diary is blank for a period of 14 days – he records 'Promis'd a restauration of self to w[i]f[e]', and the subsequent two days, 'Mist church, but meditated at home', and 'Ive promised w[i]f[e] sobriety for greatness'.[54] One of the most amusing series of entries following a binge is rendered in the following simple form:

January
16 This day ill till noon. Made a sad week, ram[bling] and ill
17 18 19 20 21 22 23 24 25 Worse of all, EV, WG, A Thyer, GG, JK, T[homas] G[enkinson], W[illiam] C[ook], J[ohn] C[hadwick, AC, JC.
26 Ill.
27 Worse.
28 Mended.
29 As so.
30 Under penance.[55]

The names are evidently Harrold's drinking companions during the course of a week. Throughout his hangovers Harrold has an admirable sense of stoicism about his inability to temper his behaviour, but entries such as these say much about his unpopularity at home and work as do his more extended reflections on impropriety during which he read sermons and prayed to God for a stronger will.[56]

In comic verse and drama of the early eighteenth century, Anya Taylor tells us that a high level of tolerance for alcohol was still a 'criterion of manliness', as it had been for the Cavaliers and libertines of the Stuart court discussed in Chapter 2. But the eighteenth century also saw unreconstructed versions of masculinity contested more frequently by a female perspective on the hangovers of men, leading to what amounted to 'a war between club and home ... riot and domesticity, male group solidarity and isolated female discontent'.[57] That domestic

---

54   *Harrold Diary*, p. 103.
55   *Harrold Diary*, p. 115.
56   See, for example, the entries on the subject of Norris on p. 44 and Tillotson on p. 95.
57   Anya Taylor, *Bacchus in Romantic England: Writers and Drink, 1780–1830* (Houndmills: Macmillan, 1999), p. 191.

tension is captured in Robert Gould's *Sylvia's Revenge, or, A Satyr Against Man* (1709) in which a wife voices her misery within the private sphere. Her husband's hangovers are typified by bad temper and violent mood swings:

> A Drunken *Husband* may pretend good Nature:
> But here's a *Sullen, Matrimoniall Creature*:
> Will, and will not, will ask, and will deny;
> Is peevish, Cross, and cannot tell for why.
> Not one kind Look he will to Spouse afford,
> Not one kind Smile, perhaps not one good Word.
> All the obliging Arts that she can use,
> To reconcile this angry peevish Spouse,
> Avail no more.[58]

The wife can tell for why. This hungover, peevish husband's mood is impaired not just by his bodily symptoms but by his inability to perform the role of *paterfamilias*, unfit to attend to his domestic responsibilities. This is a hangover about the gendering of power. If the man exerts himself whilst drunk, during his hangover he sacrifices authority to the voice of his wife. Audio-sensitivity on such occasions – one of the hangover's notable somatic symptoms – is always implied by the voice of a nagging partner: 'the wife has no weapon but her tongue'.[59] Domestic negligence is emphasised by the wife's pun on the head of a household: 'You have told us *Man* must be our *Head*', yet 'what's the Head, when the Sense is gon?'[60] The hungover husband jeopardises the hierarchical constitution of the household, symbol of national order, expressed through his inability to justify his actions when being scolded, while the wife is reduced to the role of 'nurse'. A husband's failures at home were an index of his inability to uphold civic responsibilities.

The lines are echoed in the poem *A Modest Defence of Chastity* (1726), where the responsibility to '*carry on Trade*' and keep order in the home – note the customary accusation of idleness – devolves to the wife who is reduced to nothing more than 'a better sort of servant', whose

---

58   Robert Gould, *Love Given Over: Or, a Satire Against the Pride, Lust, and Inconstancy, &c. of Woman with Sylvia's Revenge, or a Satyr Against Man, in Answer to the Satyr Against Woman* (London: H. Hills, 1709), p. 23. There are no line numbers for this poem so I give page numbers in the notes.

59   McKeon, *Secret History*, p. 23.

60   Gould, *Sylvia's Revenge*, p. 23.

main function is to nurse the male wastrel with 'Hot-Suppings when Crop-Sick'.[61] These women alternately antagonise and pacify men, but are not just idle bystanders and provide a moral perspective on male drinking habits. Defoe's Roxana alternately pities and condemns her first husband for his 'way of living', which entails 'ten Hours of the Day, half-asleep on a Bench at the Tavern-Door where he quarter'd'.[62] In Thomas Chaloner's *The Nauseous and Insipid Sot: Or, The Woman's Answer* (1732), hungover men are 'Cropsick and mad at what past over Night, / They'll quarrel with all that appears in their Sight' (7–8). They 'seek their own Ruin each Day of their Lives, / And falsely accuse their industrious Wives' (43–44).[63] While the women work, their husbands are hungover, unproductive layabouts.

It is important to note that ill and idle wives were not exempt from similar judgements and, for some observers, the parties and balls of the London season were, as the doctor who attends Fielding's Amelia reminds Captain Booth, 'very improper to be frequented by a chaste and sober Christian Matron', particularly a young mother.[64] Defoe's Colonel Jack laments his wife's sottish habits, the impact on her looks a guide to her character: 'her fine Face, bloated and blotch'd, had not so much as the Ruins of the most beautiful Person alive'. After being 'twice exposed in the most scandalous manner, with a Captain of a Ship', he notes that 'instead of her being asham'd, and repenting of it, when she came to her self, it hardened her in the Crime, and she grew as void of Modesty at last as of Sobriety'.[65] Her hangover hosts none of the repentance characteristic of a Traditional-Punishment reaction to a hangover that Jack associates with the good breeding and domestic habits she forsakes, although her transgressions are noticeably sexual, anticipating the hangovers of the 'ladettes' we find in literature of the late twentieth century.

---

61   Anon., *A Modest Defence of Chastity* (London: A. Bettesworth, 1726), p. 7. For a discussion of women's resentment about male conviviality and drinking culture that includes some evidence from the later eighteenth century, see Anna Clark, *The Struggle for the Breeches: Gender and the Making of the British Working Class* (Berkeley, Los Angeles, London: University of California Press, 1995), pp. 79–83.

62   Daniel Defoe, *Roxana*, ed. David Blewitt ([1724] Harmondsworth: Penguin, 1987), p. 133.

63   Thomas Chaloner, *The Merriest Poet in Christendom: Or, Chaloner's Miscellany, Being a Salve for Every Sore* (London: George Lee, 1732).

64   Henry Fielding, *Amelia*, ed. Martin C. Battestin ([1751] Oxford: Clarendon Press, 1983), p. 423.

65   Daniel Defoe, *Colonel Jack*, ed. Gabriel Cervantes and Geoffrey Sill ([1722] Ontario: Broadview, 2015), pp. 278–79.

Later in the period, the setting for Jane Austen's *Persuasion* (1818) is provincial rather than urban, but laziness consequent on overindulgence carries the same stigma away from the metropolis as evidenced by the temperamental Mary Musgrove, sister of heroine Anne Elliot. Mary has touches of a hypochondriac disposition, quite unlike the dependable and pragmatic Anne: 'While well, and happy, and properly attended to, she had great good humour and excellent spirits; but any indisposition sunk her completely. She had no resources for solitude; and, inheriting a considerable share of the Elliot self-importance, was very prone to add to every other distress that of fancying herself neglected and ill-used.'[66] This is never truer than following an evening of sociability where her house is an emblem of domestic disarray. Summoning Anne to Uppercross from Kellynch, Mary is discovered 'lying on the faded sofa of the pretty little drawing-room, the once elegant furniture of which had been gradually growing shabby under the influence of four summers and two children'. Charles Musgrove is absent at a shooting party while the children run amok. Mary, unable to 'bear their noise', bemoans they 'do me more harm than good'.[67] Languishing under the weight of an illness of obscure etiology manifested largely in heightened audio-sensitivity, Mary is different to the industrious Anne, who is otherwise busy with the arrangements for her father's move from Kellynch Hall. Mary's maudlin reveries on the subject of the Miss Musgroves suggest a mild persecution complex: 'I never want them, I assure you. They talk and laugh a great deal too much for me. Oh! Anne, I am so very unwell! It was quite unkind of you not to come on Thursday.' But the mystery of Mary's excessive melancholy has its source in the previous evening's festivities:

> ... 'but you have never asked me one word about our dinner at the Pooles yesterday.'
> 'Did you go, then?' I have made no inquiries, because I concluded you must have been obliged to give up the party.'
> 'Oh, yes! I went. I was very well yesterday; nothing at all the matter with me till this morning.'[68]

Anne, who provides a 'cure' in the form of reassurance, but also an opportunity for gossip that noticeably speeds Mary's recovery, indulges her sister's selfishness, and hangover.

---

66   Jane Austen, *Persuasion* (London: Penguin, 1994), p. 35.
67   Austen, *Persuasion*, p. 35.
68   Austen, *Persuasion*, pp. 36–37.

The ballroom was not necessarily a drinking environment – Fielding's *Amelia* only consumes lemonade – although the dinner party invariably was, and Austen was not unfamiliar with the consequences of overindulgence. In a letter to her sister Cassandra of November 1800, for example, she confesses: 'I believe I drank too much wine last night at Hurstbourne; I know not how else to account for the shaking of my hand to-day.'[69] But Mary Musgrove's behaviour whilst hungover is specifically a moral commentary on her selfish temperament and domestic negligence. The absent husband is spared Anne's cynical eye in this case, although more often than not tensions arise in the provinces, as in the city, from the clash between the values of the domestic realm and those of the masculine public sphere that we have witnessed. As Vickery notes, not all husbands were 'fully house-broken', and 'the man who forsook the parlour for his old drinking cronies was a stock rogue of female complaint'.[70] The squirearchy were particularly notorious for heavy drinking amidst their other country pursuits of game shooting, horse riding and coursing, satirised in figures such as John Vanbrugh's Sir Polydorus Hogstye of 'Beast-Hall in Swine-County', Squire Western in Fielding's *Tom Jones* (1749) who swears by his 'morning-draught' of ale and Sir Tunbelly Clumsey, regularly discovered drunk in the day in Sheridan's *A Trip to Scarborough* (1777).

The prototype is Squire Sullen in George Farquhar's *The Beaux' Stratagem* (1706). According to Steven Earnshaw the depiction of domestic drunkenness 'begins to take on a more pointed, less codified, aspect' in the eighteenth century and the wife's voice is heard more urgently in Mrs Sullen's account of Squire Sullen's incorrigible behaviour than it was in Taylor's skimmington:[71]

> O Sister, Sister, if ever you marry, beware of a sullen, silent, Sot … He came home this Morning at his usual Hour of Four, waken'd me out of a sweet Dream of something else, by tumbling over the Tea-table, which he broke all to pieces; after his Man and he had rowl'd about the Room, like sick Passengers in a Storm, he comes flounce into Bed, dead as a Salmon into a Fishmonger's basket, his

69 Deirdre Le Faye (ed.), *Jane Austen's Letters*, 4th edn. (Oxford: Oxford University Press, 2011), p. 62.

70 Vickery, *Behind Closed Doors*, p. 80.

71 Steven Earnshaw, *The Pub in Literature: England's Altered States* (Manchester and New York: Manchester University Press, 2000), p. 136.

Feet cold as Ice, his Breath hot as a Furnace, and his Hands and
his Face as greasy as his Flanel Night-cap. (II, i, 73–89)[72]

It is important that the audience initially views the drunken sot through
the jaundiced eyes of his other half. The caricature drunk is enriched
by Farquhar's use of images of nausea, sweat and nocturnal stumbling.
Mrs Sullen's feelings of physical revulsion are magnified by the image
of her husband as a dead fish. The hangover seeps, both literally and
figuratively, into the matrimonial bed. Mrs Sullen continues to recount
her interrupted sleep: 'my whole Night's Comfort is the tuneable
Serenade of that wakeful Nightingale, his nose. – O the Pleasure of
counting the melancholy Clock by a snoring Husband!' (II, ii, 93–96).
The Sullens' marriage bed ironically stages 'Serenade' and 'Pleasure' of
a non-romantic sort, reminiscent of the lament of the wife in *Sylvia's
Revenge* who tells a similar tale of the 'too too happy Bride, / that has a
Husband snoring by her side; / Belching out *Fumes* of undigested wine'.[73]

Mrs Sullen's voice is not that of an isolated woman, however, as this
is not a curtain lecture, but a lament to her sister-in-law, Dorinda, in the
more genteel surroundings of Lady Bountiful's House where she comes to
realise the fallacy of her confidence that her husband, 'being a well-bred
man ... will beg my pardon' (II, i, 98). Squire Sullen's hangovers only
exacerbate his general irritability and entrench him in his beastliness.
Initially announcing that 'My Head akes consumedly' (II, ii, 99), he
refuses to apologise the following morning (on the instigation of his sister)
and re-establish domestic accord through the symbolic act of taking tea
('It may do your head good' [II, i, 90]), instead renewing commitment to
male drinking culture by calling his servant, Scrub, for 'a Dram ... the
Venison-Pasty, and a Tankard of strong Beer' (II, ii, 112–14). The wife
gives vent to her frustrations; the husband remains silent and sullen,
Withdrawal-Relief offering the quickest route to recovery. Unable to
appeal to his better self – he does not have one – Mrs Sullen resorts to
the threat of sexual insecurity, common in Restoration and sentimental
comedy. As Sullen calls for Scrub to shave his head, Mrs Sullen quips
on the theme of cuckoldry – 'Have a care of coming near his Temples,
Scrub, for fear you meet something there that may turn the Edge of your
Razor' (II, ii, 133–35) – which presents her with the idea of the hoax
affair with a French Count designed to make Sullen jealous. The Squire's
level of domestic negligence is fully disclosed, however, when he responds

72   George Farquhar, *The Beaux' Stratagem*, in David Womersley (ed.), *Restoration Drama:
      An Anthology* (Oxford: Blackwell, 2000), p. 743.
73   Gould, *Sylvia's Revenge*, p. 23.

by requesting that, if his wife must pursue extramarital relations, she do it discreetly and try to avoid the French.

Squire Sullen is a man not fully housebroken and his hangovers are the site of tension between incompatible domestic and homosocial codes. They indicate that, as Jordan comments, the 'moral authority' of the landed gentry was thrown into doubt by their hours of idleness. We see Squire Sullen hungover more often than we see him drunk and, even though this initially highlights Mrs Sullen's helplessness, it is, ironically, a hangover that enables her to eventually escape the legal ties of marriage and seek a divorce. Her brother, Sir Charles Freeman, gets Squire Sullen to make a drunken promise to an annulment and, despite failing to remember this the next morning, the Squire suffers so badly from another headache that he has no choice but to comply and release his wife on the proviso that he retains her dowry. This is denied him, but only because Archer – one of the Beaux of the play's title – acquires enough money to buy off Sullen and take Mrs Sullen's hand.[74]

The Sullens emblematise the collision of two worlds when she remarks 'I can't drink ale with him' and he responds, 'Nor can I drink tea with her' (V, iv, 268–69). Tea was by no means the exclusive province of women: it was the diurnal drink of choice for rambunctious men too, as we see in the case of Captain Mirvan in Frances Burney's *Evelina* (1778).[75] Nevertheless, Farquhar uses the contrast to communicate his point that the hangover throws doubt on the belief that male excess could ever really be 'tempered or domesticated by female refinement'. It underlines the threat that excessive drinking posed to the home and the nation, which was reflected in the gentry's apparent disdain of moral standards.

In this context it is usually the case that female craftiness was no match for male sullenness and indifference. There are, however, a couple of entertaining examples in the poetry of Anne Finch, Countess of Winchilsea wherein female speakers go the extra mile in an attempt to reform dissolute men, recalling the intervention of Susan Bacon. Anya Taylor notes that Finch was one of very few women to enter the masculine sphere of drunken conviviality in the eighteenth century.[76] In 'The Prevalence of Custom' (1713) the setting is again domestic and the

74   The plot is resolved, partly because the embattled Squire is too enfeebled by a hangover to protest otherwise, although the sexual politics of marriage remain intact. Mrs Sullen is an unequal partner, whoever her husband may be; the male and female spheres will remain separate and the Squire is manifestly unrepentant.

75   Frances Burney, *Evelina*, ed. Susan Kubica Howard (Toronto: Broadview, 2000).

76   Taylor, *Bacchus*, p. 204.

agents are husband and wife. Rather than take the approach of Mrs Sullen and directly request an apology, here the wife devises an outlandish 'Stratagem to prove' (3) her husband by taking advantage of his hangover, dressing as a devil and pretending to transport him to a crypt:

> Finding him overcome with Tipple,
> And weak, as Infant at the Nipple,
> She to a Vault transports the Lumber,
> And *there expects* his breaking Slumber.
> A Table she with Meat provided,
> And rob'd in Black, stood just beside it;
> Seen only, by one glim'ring Taper,
> That blewly burnt thro' misty Vapor.
> At length he wakes, his Wine digested,
> And of her Phantomship requested,
> To learn the Name of that close Dwelling,
> And what offends his Sight and Smelling;
> And of what Land she was the Creature,
> With outspread Hair, and ghastly Feature? (5–18)[77]

The sequence recalls the improbable 'domesticke' examples of Thomas Heywood's *Philocothonista* that we saw in Chapter 2, but here physical suffering is part of an infernal parody of the well-ordered home of the eighteenth century rather than the pub or club, with the hungover husband nauseated by the sight and smell of food. The 'devil' proceeds to tell her bemused spouse that she will discover his appetites by offering him his favourite food before depriving him of it for eternity. Those scare tactics prove to be ineffective, however, as the male drinker argues that since he is already dead he might as well attempt to eat what is on offer and a Traditional-Punishment scenario yields to one of Withdrawal-Relief: 'Thou Guardian of these lower Regions' (35), continues the husband, 'Who of our Victuals thus art Thinking, / If thou hast Care too of our Drinking, / A *Bumper* fetch' (39–41). In exasperation, the wife breaks character at the poem's conclusion:

> Quoth she, a *Halter*,
> Since nothing less thy Tone can alter,
> Or break this Habit thou'st been getting,
> To keep thy Throat in constant wetting. (41–44)

---

77   Anne Finch, Countess of Winchilsea, *Miscellany Poems, on Several Occasions* (London: W. Taylor, 1713).

Taylor rightly argues that the humorous outcome of 'The Prevalence of Custom' demonstrates the poem should be read as less than serious and that Finch 'acknowledges the difficulty of managing a drunken husband but plays the game coquettishly'.[78] In the second example, 'A Song for my Br. Les: Finch. Upon a Punch Bowl' (1713?), Finch's female speaker braves the male sanctuary of the tavern and is more successful in her manipulation. Beginning with the ordinary premises of a drinking song, she invites her brother to join her in a bowl of punch. Co-opting the stereotypical braggadocio about tolerance she orders a giant bowl of rack punch: 'The half Globe 'tis in figure; / And would it were bigger' (7–8).[79] The tone of the first half of the poem shifts, however, on the introduction of the classical motif of Alexander the Great's murder of Clytus in a drunken quarrel:

> 'Twas a World, like to this,
> The hott Graecian did misse,
> Of whom History's keep such a pother,
> To the bottom he sunk,
> And when one he had drunk
> Grew maudlin, and wept for another. (13–18)

Finch skilfully contests her brother's wish to certify his masculinity through downing the contents of the enormous bowl, with a cautionary tale about the ruptures in homosociality. Her allusion is well chosen: the argument of the two soldiers arose from Alexander's bragging about his military achievements and Clytus's jealousy. Finch's brother is similarly imagined at the end of the poem repenting in melancholy and weeping for other worlds to conquer. In this case the hangover, it is implied, has done its remedial work.

Single and Stewing in Bed till Noon

Unlike Francis Matthew Schutz or Squire Sullen it appears that the target of Finch's Song is an unmarried man: it is the sister on this occasion, rather than wife, who enters the male drinking environment in order to shame her brother. Drinking clubs and coffee shops were 'the first space of masculine performance' for single Georgian men, as Vickery

---

78 Taylor, *Bacchus*, p. 206.
79 Katharine M. Rogers (ed.), *Selected Poems of Anne Finch, Countess of Winchilsea* (New York: Ungar, 1987).

remarks, and bachelorhood was seen as a 'natural phase' in which 'exuberance and some licence' was expected before men embarked on the sober duties of marriage.[80] Finch's confrontation with the bachelor drinker suggests, however, that the matter was more complicated than that. As Katherine Snyder notes, it was in the mid-eighteenth century that bachelor became a term for 'an unmarried man of marriageable age', but that simultaneously greater focus on the unmarried state 'moved the definitional context of bachelorhood into a world and a set of relations – the private sphere, the family, marriage – from which bachelors themselves were nominally excluded'. At the same time, as we have already seen, 'middle-class masculinity itself was coming to be equated with the emerging concept of occupation' and idleness considered a violation of civic duty, 'especially with respect to an ideal of male productivity'.[81] It is therefore unsurprising to find that, far from being exempt from castigation for his drinking habits, the bachelor was regularly reminded of his own need to reflect on an indeterminate social status, future professional and domestic duties and interpersonal relationships. The same was true for young unmarried women who likewise belonged to the set of domestic relations that Snyder describes. The bachelor at the tavern, coffee house or club, and the debutante or socialite frequenting the assemblies, ballrooms and dinner parties during the season were equally upbraided for the hours of illness and idleness after a late night.

The hangover demonstrates that the 'emergent discourse' against libertinism, identified by McKeon, often framed the Traditional-Punishment response in the eighteenth century and was in full effect in relation to the single, as well as the married, life. Hence in *The Task* (1785), William Cowper begs to be saved 'from the gaiety of those / Whose head-aches nail them to a noon-day bed' (499–500). His hungover bachelor suffers physically and emotionally: the hangover 'fills the bones with pain, / The mouth with blasphemy, the heart with woe' (504–505).[82] The indisposed gentleman is a city-dweller and abiding happiness is located in the country. It was a common lament of the period that urban vice would corrupt rural wholesomeness in naïve young men and women – despite the debauchery associated with landed squires – and in Thomas Baker's *Tunbridge-Walks* (1703) a country father

80   Vickery, *Behind Closed Doors*, p. 77.
81   Katherine V. Snyder, *Bachelors, Manhood and the Novel, 1850–1925* (Cambridge: Cambridge University Press, 2004), pp. 20–21.
82   William Cowper, *The Task and Other Selected Poems*, ed. James Sambrook (London and New York: Routledge, 2013).

fears his daughter will receive 'a Town Education' in London, where 'instead of rising early to inspect your families, you stew in bed till Noon' as a result of too many late nights.[83] For Lady Sophia Burrell, 'the vulgar country' was likewise threatened by the fashion of turning 'night to day'. Midday was the apex of shame, with rakes and socialites unwilling to 'quit their bed till noon, / Loath to be seen unfashionably soon'. They invoke a debauched version of the carpe diem spirit of the Anacreontea: 'Let mirth and pleasure laugh at care and sorrow – / We'll live TO-DAY, and think not of TO-MORROW.'[84]

A town education is perceived as a particular threat to the behaviour and moral compass of the titular character of Burney's *Evelina*. Raised in an isolated rural hamlet, Evelina takes the opportunity to travel to London with the Mirvans and encounters the eligible Lord Orville at Ranelagh where she is overwhelmed by the glamour of the company and 'brilliancy of the lights'. We are not told whether Evelina drank, but the experience leaves her worn out and the following day her feelings of regret are analogous to a hangover. These concern fears of social exclusion, worries about ineptness, and a general sense of foolishness for her behaviour at the assembly, but she is also vexed at giving way to a sore head that means she misses an opportunity to meet Lord Orville the following day:

> This morning was destined for seeing sights, auctions, curious shops, and so forth; but my head ached, and I was not in a humour to be amused, and so I made them go without me, though very unwillingly.
>
> They are all kindness. And now I am sorry I did not accompany them, for I know not what to do with myself. I had resolved not to go to the play to-night; but I believe I shall. In short, I hardly care whether I do or not.
>
> I thought I had done wrong! Mrs. Mirvan and Maria have been half the town over, and so entertained! – while I, like a fool, staid at home to do nothing. And, at the auction in Pall-mall, who should they meet but Lord Orville. He sat next to Mrs. Mirvan, and they talked a great deal together; but she gave me no account of the conversation.

---

83 Thomas Baker, *Tunbridge Walks: or, The Yeoman of Kent* (Dublin: printed for William Smith, repr. 1758), p. 28. There are no line numbers given for this poem.

84 Sophia Burrell, *Poems. Dedicated to the Right Honourable the Earl of Mansfield* (London: J. Cooper, Bow Street, Covent Garden, 1793), p. 301. There are no line numbers given for this poem.

> I may never have such another opportunity of seeing London;
> I am quite sorry that I was not of the party; but I deserve this
> mortification, for having indulged my ill-humour.[85]

Symptoms include the stated headache and ill humour along with a
general sense of lassitude and indecision – 'I know not what to do with
myself' – but Evelina is a conscientious paragon and full of self-reproach.
Burney uses the epistolary mode to construct an intense Traditional-
Punishment response of the sort that becomes more common as the
novel develops as a genre through the nineteenth century, anticipating
examples we will see in Charles Dickens's *David Copperfield* (1850) and
Thomas Hardy's *Jude the Obscure* (1895). Evelina is a young woman
killed with kindness as the sympathy of the Mirvans – which cannot
be extrapolated from the suspicion of social judgement – only serves to
amplify her sense of shame at self-inflicted injuries and her regret spikes
when she discovers the missed opportunity to socialise with Orville.
The class-consciousness that rises during her hangover is a primary
feature of Evelina's self-rebuke and is a painful reminder of her social
position that means she 'may never have such another opportunity of
seeing London'. She resolves never to attend such assemblies again. The
morning after the night at Ranelagh Evelina is disabused of any emergent
self-regard and her memories are filled with characteristic examples of
social awkwardness – 'He bowed to me; I courtesied, and I am sure I
coloured'[86] – now internalised in a form of self-flagellation.

Inhabiting a precarious social position, Evelina cannot afford to
lounge away the morning in the fashion of a socialite like Alexander
Pope's Belinda in *The Rape of the Lock* (1712). Her lack of occupation is a
reminder of insecure means that heighten moral jeopardy, rather than
an indication of the dangers of entitlement without responsibility. It
was one thing to be rich and idle, another to suffer a hangover without
the resources necessary to keep up appearances. George Hilton, of
Beetham, Westmorland, whose journal covers the period from 1700 to
1723, would no doubt have agreed. Born a gentleman in 1673, Hilton
was impoverished by legal disputes and a dissolute temperament. As
a Catholic in the early eighteenth century he was unable to train for
the law, the Church or take a degree at Oxford and filled his days
with horseracing, shooting, backgammon and regular heavy drinking
bouts. Although his journal suggests that he may have been married,
he lived the life of an idle, largely unemployed bachelor, estranged from

---

85   Burney, *Evelina*, p. 131.
86   Burney, *Evelina*, p. 131.

his wife as a consequence of his debauchery. Anne Hillman notes that 'The constraints and frustrations of his position, both financial and social, shaped his lifestyle', but these were given particular piquancy during his many hangovers.[87]

Hilton marked his diary with asterisks for days when he was 'fuddled' with drink, but the fallout bites during the periods in which he was incapable of work due to alcohol-induced illness. Perennially bereft of money, though hanging on to the coattails of the highest ranks of Westmorland society, Hilton kept an accurate record of his expenditure for a week, usually in the region of six to ten shillings when at home. An outlay of £1.15.0 in the week beginning 16 October 1704 underlines the degree of drunkenness and it must have been slim comfort to review his outgoings for the following week:

Monday 23 October 1704. Att Beathom Hall and not out of my house all day being very sick & not able to sturr   0.0

Tuesday. Att Beathom Hall not abroad this day extreamly sick not out of bed   0.0

Wedensday. Att Beathom Hall not abroad this day   0.0

Thursday. Att Beathom Hall went in the morning to Levings with John Johnson came home mighty sick   0.0

Friday. Att Beathom Hall not well in bed all day   0.0

Saterday. Att Beathom Hall not abroad all day   0.0

Sonday. Att Beathom Hall not abroad all this day   0.0

This weeks expenses   0.0[88]

The previous week's binge leaves Hilton characteristically indisposed and unable to leave his bed. On Thursday it appears that he gamely rallied, visiting one of his numerous dining companions, Colonel Grahame, at nearby Levins. If he turned to the Withdrawal-Relief mode of recovery, as is more than likely, the visit seems only to have prolonged his physical symptoms.

Hilton's aspiration to maintain the habits of a bachelor gentleman says much about the indolence associated with that figure during the long eighteenth century. The journal is punctuated by remorseful passages in which Hilton commits to reform for numerous reasons, but mostly financial: he promises 'upon my knees night and morning' to

87   *The Rake's Diary: The Journal of George Hilton*, ed. Anne Hillman (Berwick-upon-Tweed: Curwen Archives Trust, 1994), p. xxxv.

88   Hilton, *Rake's Diary*, p. 62.

pray for the will to reform having 'had the misfortune to spend this quarter vizt from the 13th of May 1700 to the 5th of August (1700) £12 for pocket expences'.[89] Pocket expenses primarily meant outlay on alcohol. Before beginning his diary for 1702, Hilton drafted a list of resolutions amongst which was his oath to forswear 'lazinesse': 'That I will spend more time in my study than hitherto I have done [and] will for the futour be more circumspect how I dispose of that erepairable loss.'[90] Prudence was coupled to diligence for Hilton and lost time and lost money went hand in hand. The biggest tax on both was alcohol: 'I am most passionately resolved to have soe punctuall a guard over my inclynacions as never to loose my reason by immoderate drinking.' Unfortunately, by Friday 14 February he confesses, 'broake 3 of my resolucions vizt eate flesh laid with a woman and up till 2 o'clocke in the morning'. It is a better result than his attempts the same year 'not to drinke a dropp of strong liquor this Lent', which evidently lasts just two days.[91]

Hilton embodies the kind of flawed model of masculinity that, for many moralists, indolent unmarried men seemed prone to adopt, although the bachelor figure that was most frequently taken to task for stewing in bed till noon was one from whose advantages Hilton was debarred: the student. Hence, Robert Lloyd's 'The Law Student' (c. 1760) introduces the caricature drunken bachelor, who 'In purple slippers, and silken gown' (30) makes 'Last night's debauch, his morning conversation' (31).[92] Likewise, Jack Chace in Francis Coventry's *The History of Pompey the Little* (1751) boasts 'whenever he met you', about 'his last Night's Debauch or related the arrival of a new Wh – re upon the Town'.[93] Students were continually reminded of the dangers of 'giving themselves up to idleness and debauchery' and of their civic and social duty in manuals such as Daniel Waterland's *Advice to a Young Student with a Method of Study for the First Four Years* (1755). As Sir Joshua Reynolds argued in *A Discourse Delivered to the Students of the Royal Academy on the Distribution of Prizes, December 10, 1769*, 'Excellence is never granted to man, but as the reward of labour.'[94]

89   Hilton, *Rake's Diary*, p. 13.
90   Hilton, *Rake's Diary*, p. 28.
91   Hilton, *Rake's Diary*, p. 31.
92   Robert Lloyd, *The Poetical Works* (London: printed for T. Evans, 1774).
93   Francis Coventry, *The History of Pompey the Little: or, the Life and Adventures of a Lap-Dog* (London: printed for M. Cooper, 1751), p. 182.
94   Daniel Waterland, *Advice to a Young Student with a Method of Study for the First Four Years* ... (Oxford: Richard Clements, 1755), p. 13; Sir Joshua Reynolds, *A Discourse*

Waterland feared that the dissolute student would never be able to shake his youthful habits. In satirical vein, Jonathan Swift's 'The Answer to "Paulus"' (1754) similarly suggests the debauchery of the undergraduate is good training for professional life. A characteristic morning sees the lawyer hungover,

> With early clients at his door,
> Though he were drunk the night before,
> And crop-sick with unclub'd for wine,
> The wretch must be at court by nine:
> Half sunk beneath his brief and bag,
> As ridden by a midnight hag. (71–76)[95]

Aiming to guard against the acquisition of such pernicious habits, the third satire of Persius – a Latin poem which gained popularity because it spoke to Georgian anxieties about indolence – depicts a bachelor student as lazy and doltish, unashamedly idling away his financial and social opportunities. John Dryden produced a modern translation of the satires of Aulus Persius Flaccus in 1693 where the opening of the third satire faithfully rendered Persius's hungover youth struggling to attend to his studies with a head dulled by the aftermath of a drinking bout:

> Is this thy daily course? The glaring Sun
> Break in at ev'ry Chink; the Cattel run
> To Shades and Noon-tide rays of Summer shun
> Yet plung'd in sloth we lie; and more supine
> As fill'd with fumes of undigested Wine. (III, 1–5)[96]

Dryden retains the pastoral setting of the original. In contrast, Edward Burnaby Greene, when translating the satires in 1779, was more candid in proclaiming that Persius's third satire was an attack on 'yawning Indolence, the insipid character of the present age'. Greene's translations were consequently 'Adapted to the Times'.[97] He makes pointed and

---

delivered to the students of the Royal Academy on the Distribution of Prizes, December 11, 1769, by the President (London: Thomas Davies, 1769), p. 16.

95   Jonathan Swift, *The Complete Poems*, ed. Pat Rogers (New Haven, CT and London: Yale University Press, 1983).

96   *The Works of John Dryden*, ed. Vinton A. Dearing and H. T. Swedenberg, 20 vols, vol. IV: Poems 1693–1696, ed. A. B. Chambers and William Frost (Berkeley, Los Angeles, London: University of California Press, 1974).

97   Edward Burnaby Greene, *The Satires of Persius Paraphrastically Imitated, and Adapted to the Times* (London: T. Spilsbury for J. Dodsley, 1779).

colourful attacks on the contemporary lifestyle of the recently qualified
bachelor lawyer:

> Well! Now at length I see my stripling hurl'd
> From Books to Men, from College to the World!
> But whence those lids, from scenes of evening gay,
> Clos'd till thy windows dart the noon-tide ray?
> Life's modish drama! Supping where we dine!
> Exhausted spirits gain the gift of wine.
> Alike 'tis Pleasure's maze, 'tis Lux'ry's treat;
> Ev'n when the Dog-Star rules the realms of heat!
> Alike in *downy* doze supinely lays,
> While *sager* Beasts, recline in air, and shade.
>
> 'Away the cens'ring song! If scarce alive
> Noon gives me breakfast, Morn gives sleep at five.
> Ne'er earlier sought!' Tom – Dick – above, below!
> Thy Voice – *crack'd* Trumpet of a Puppet-show.
> At once the Papers' feast thy look pursues,
> The convers of the day well fram'd from News;
> With *Orb* half-clos'd, with nicely-pasted hair;
> Some loose *French* novel soothes thy *studious* care
> La Peigne appears! in broken-English way,
> 'Mi-Lady carte! Invitant to de Play!'
> Quick for an Answer! When, (oh! wretched lot!)
> Pens cramm'd with ink the guiltless paper blot.
> Water! – the *Sable* stream exchang'd to *White*,
> No mark can settle, and no pen can write;
> Letter by letter slowly shap'd at last,
> Smiles the fond Billet, ere two hours are pass'd.
> Hail! Dissipation, bliss of night, of day!
> Hurry not action! Without spirits gay! (III, 1–28)

Many of the themes associated with indolence in the Georgian age recur,
including diurnal disorder – bed at five in the morning and breakfast
at noon – even in the oppressive heat of summer. In classical astrology,
the rising of Sirius was often associated with periods of drought as well
as lethargy and bad luck: the reference prepares the way for Greene's
depiction of the young man with his voice left hoarse from dehydration.
Dryden's translation stays true to Persius in depicting the student's
frustrated attempts to pursue his studies – hands shaking, fine motor
skills impaired – but Greene's youth has abandoned any pretence of

diligence. His irritation is instead focused on the ineffective pen that prevents his reply to another social invitation. Congealed with ink, crying out for water, the pen symbolises the hangover as a period of incapacity and idleness, a violation of the norms of male occupation and productivity. His remedies are dubious French novels, the comb and pomade. Only the prospect of the next carouse stirs the broken 'stripling' – a term signalling juvenility – into action. Despite his sluggishness, Greene's idle youth gives little thought to the consequences of inebriety and inactivity.

Lacking occupation, the parody Georgian student turned to drink that, in its turn, increased the unlikelihood of profitable activity. The archetype of the inactive student, Hamlet, was undone by a different brand of lassitude, but in the eighteenth century even the great speeches of Shakespeare were repurposed as a commentary on the 'insipid character of the present Age'. John Lund's *Collection of Oddities* (1780?) includes a parody of Hamlet's 'To be, or not to be' soliloquy, which debates the pros and cons of the drinking career and provides a final interesting example of a Georgian hangover. 'To drink, or not to drink, – that is the question' (1) posed by Lund's sottish bachelor.[98] So rather than face the 'slings and arrows of outrageous fortune' (3, i, 58),[99] his speaker contemplates 'The rage, and torment of dry parching thirst' (3). In place of thoughts of mortality and suicide he envisages 'large draughts' (4) to 'cure the gasping evil, / And ease the panting gullet' (4–5). As Hamlet imagines 'what dreams may come' in 'that sleep of death' (3, i, 66), so the drunken philosopher reflects: 'for in that state of insensibility / What hazards do we run, when we have shuffled off / Our reason, must give us pause' (10–12). Hamlet ponders 'the respect / That makes calamity of so long a life' (68–69). In Lund's parody 'in most respects / Sobriety embitters life' (12–13). It is not the 'pangs of disprized love' (3, i, 72), 'the law's delay' (3, i, 72) or 'the proud man's contumely' (3, i, 71) that affects him so much as the 'toper's spurns' (14), 'the landlords disdain' (15) and the 'bachanals contumely' (15). Ultimately, the hangover is equated with death as the 'undiscovered country from whose bourn / No traveller returns' (3, i, 79–80) is recast as 'that crop sick plague / From which no toper's free but by being drunk again' (21–22), and the mirth achieved through inebriation subsides into the melancholy of the hangover:

98   John Lund, *Collection of Oddities* (Doncaster: C. Plummbe, 1780?).
99   William Shakespeare, *Hamlet*, ed. Philip Edwards (Cambridge: Cambridge University Press, 1985), p. 146.

> Thus maudlin thoughts makes cowards of us all;
> And thus the jolly toper's sparkling face
> Is sullied o'er with drinking small pale beer;
> And mirth and frolics of great pith and moment
> In this respect must certainly subside,
> And vanish with sobriety. (25–30)

Nursing his hangover and his small beer, the poem evidently reflects back upon the speaker's own feelings of contrition.

Hamlet is, of course, eventually roused to action. Not so the hungover law student, unless that action involves the hair of the dog, who is emblematic of a breed of irresponsible young men. But he is also representative of the larger Georgian concern with idleness and indolence in all walks of life, particularly of the self-induced variety that I have traced here. If hangovers reappraise an individual's capacity to protect a society's moral norms, then in the long eighteenth century this reappraisal was focused on debates about work and productivity, specifically the impact of the drinker's lack of occupation on the maintenance of civic and familial order. As we have seen, the spirit drinker was the most conspicuously hungover figure of the period, and the pernicious effects of gin were routinely envisaged as a communal, working-class hangover, but other elements of society were not exempt from condemnation for their drinking habits.

Taken together, the examples of hangovers in the long eighteenth century that I have analysed demonstrate that their representation was deeply embedded in moral and political debates about Britain's economic prospects as a newly self-conscious trading nation. Taken together, they also enable me to restate with increased conviction one of the larger concerns of this book, which is that the hangover is as much a response to the values of a socio-cultural context as it is to the consumption of alcohol. Examples from the eighteenth century enrich our understanding of what Kingsley Amis called the hangover's 'superstructure'. In the next chapter, which covers hangovers in the Romantic period, I take the opportunity to return, equipped with our better understanding of this socio-cultural superstructure, to the terrain of Chapter 1. We will retain a strong awareness of the moral appraisal of drinkers' alcohol use, but this is combined with an invitation to scrutinise more closely the complications of explaining the reaction – the interrelation of cognition, emotion and sensation – to those appraisals.

Chapter 4

Odes to Dejection: Romanticism and the Melancholy of Self-knowledge

Introduction

The title to this chapter may be a little misleading. It goes without saying that the Romantic hangover is not confined to the formal Ode, but the poetics of dejection, or its close neighbours, despondency, melancholy and care, that commonly feature in Odes, give us a starting point in introducing the hangover to our critical discussions of drunkenness and intoxication in literature of the Romantic period. Romantic literature celebrates alcohol – hence we find Thomas Moore demanding 'Come, Send Round the Wine' (1808) and a riotous Robert Burns dismissing the consequences of drinking, 'The cock may craw, the day may daw, / And ay we'll taste the barley bree' ('Willie Brew'd a Peck o' Maut' [1789] [7–8]),[1] – but also cautions against its consumption. As Anya Taylor has argued, there is a literary revival of Renaissance Dionysianism at precisely the same time that 'alcoholic realities' were being explored in medical literature produced by the likes of Arthur Stone, Thomas Trotter, Robert MacNish and Anthony Fothergill, and in moral tracts by reformed drinkers such as Basil Montagu's *Some Enquiries into the Effects of Fermented Liquors by a Water Drinker* (1814).[2] These concerns found literary outlet in Charles Lamb's coruscating account of alcoholic addiction 'Confessions of a Drunkard' (1813) and cautionary tales about the effects of alcohol on the rural and urban poor such as William Wordsworth's *The Waggoner* (1819) and 'The Two Shoemakers' from Hannah More's *Cheap Repository*

---

1   *The Poems and Songs of Robert Burns*, ed. James Kinsley, 3 vols (Oxford: Clarendon Press, 1968), I. All references to Burns's poetry are to this edition unless stated. The most recent study of Romantic drinking and fellowship is Ian Newman's *The Romantic Tavern: Literature and Conviviality in the Age of Revolution* (Cambridge: Cambridge University Press, 2019).

2   See Anya Taylor, *Bacchus in Romantic England: Writers and Drink, 1780-1830* (Houndmills: MacMillan, 1999), pp. 11–28.

Tracts (1795–97), early examples of the kind of temperance tales that became more common in the Victorian period.

The most regularly invoked motif of dejection in Romantic poetry is that found in Wordsworth's 'Resolution and Independence' (1807) where it is a way of processing social disenchantment – 'We poets in our youth begin in gladness; / But thereof come i' th' end despondency and madness' (48–49)[3] – that leads to a compensatory 'turn within' to the life of the mind. Jerome McGann identifies a general 'dialectic of gladness and despondency' in Romantic literature, but Taylor finds this is particularly problematic in Romantic drinking verse in which 'drinkers tinge ... classical joy with melancholy; whilst shouting *"carpe diem"*, they look anxiously ahead at the void'.[4] James Nicholls has similarly argued that 'in turning away from the convivial and the light-hearted, Romantic writers were able to mine the interiority of the ... drinker to an extent not previously attempted'.[5] However, neither Nicholls nor Taylor has openly addressed the topic of the hangover, which is the aspect of drinking that my study has suggested is most associated with increased levels of dejection and, potentially, self-awareness. The hangover needs incorporating into accounts of alcohol use in the Romantic period because it not only increases our knowledge of socio-cultural attitudes to alcohol, but also adds to our critical understanding of a host of issues concerned with Romantic introspection. These include the representation of the mind and imagination, the regulation of the emotions and the levels of moral accountability felt by the Romantic poet. In this chapter I will take the idea that the hangover is one of the foremost ways to mine interiority and explore what kinds of self-knowledge it brings.

The chapter focuses largely on poetry, alongside the correspondence of poets, as it is here that interesting shifts occur in the representation of hangovers that have an impact on the way that we view what I have formerly referred to as a Traditional-Punishment reaction. That is the hangover response wherein, as S. P. Garvey puts it, the conscience 'prompts the self to try to make amends for wrong doing'.[6] One of the purposes of this book is to demonstrate how analysis of hangover

---

3   William Wordsworth, *The Major Works*, ed. Stephen Gill (Oxford: Oxford University Press, repr. 2000). All references to Wordsworth's poetry are to this edition unless stated.

4   Jerome McGann, *Byron and Romanticism*, ed. James Soderholm (Cambridge: Cambridge University Press, 2002), p. 270; Taylor, *Bacchus*, p. 10.

5   James Nicholls, *The Politics of Alcohol: A History of the Drink Question in England* (Manchester: Manchester University Press, 2013), p. 78.

6   S. P. Garvey, 'Can Shaming Punishments Educate?', *University of Chicago Law Review*, 65.4 (1988), p. 766 (pp. 733–94).

literature makes such terms more meaningful. This chapter shows how the Romantics sought other ways of surmounting a Traditional-Punishment response than the perennial option of reaching again for the bottle, but that these do not come without their own problems. We begin with the first-generation Romantics – Burns, Wordsworth and Samuel Taylor Coleridge – before proceeding to examine the alcohol hangover and the hangover used more generally as metaphor for the loss of pleasure in the second-generation Romantics, John Keats and Lord Byron. The final section of the chapter considers the construction of apologies and the Romantic confession, returning briefly to Burns – whose representation of the hangover is so influential in the period – and then offering a reading of Lamb's 'Confessions'.

The Romantic period shows continuities, but also contrasts, with hangover literature of earlier periods. On many occasions Romantic literature is reminiscent of the kind of Protestant self-interrogation that we saw in the seventeenth-century 'culture wars', and there is a flavour of penitent's rhetoric in Romantic hangover descriptions. But, while framed by similar issues of guilt, penitence and remorse, Romantic hangovers also enable a finer-grained study of the rhythms of hangover consciousness and the perplexities of perception. When Robert Burns writes to Agnes McLehose, who corresponded with Burns using the name Clarinda, about 'fasting, except for a draught of water or small-beer', 'sick' and with 'low-spirits' following a night of 'savage hospitality', he remarks that hangovers are always likely to put him in the mood for self-reflection: 'Nothing astonishes me more, when a little sickness clogs the wheels of life, than the thoughtless career we run, in the hour of health.'[7] In that sense, the hangover is an occasion for rumination and, potentially, insight, not unlike the opportunity presented by the 'melancholy fit' (11) that Keats depicts in his Ode on that subject.[8] However, the experience of Romantic dejection is dialectical and, while it may produce a reflective state of 'poetically productive melancholy', it might just as easily result in a 'mute or incoherent mood', as David Riede expresses it, reminiscent of the 'deep sense of breakage' that was a significant part of my analysis of hangover consciousness in Chapter 1.[9] In Romantic literature, we are reminded of some of the

7   *The Letters of Robert Burns*, ed. G. Ross Roy, 3 vols (Oxford: Clarendon Press, 1985), I, p. 252.

8   *Keats's Poetry and Prose*, ed. Jeffrey N. Cox (New York and London: Norton, 2009). All references to Keats's verse are to this edition.

9   David G. Riede, *Allegories of One's Own Mind: Melancholy in Victorian Poetry* (Columbus: Ohio State University Press, 2005), pp. 1–2.

problems that inhere in rationalising, or coming to terms with, the feelings of a hangover and the fact that the stresses put upon the body that combine with awareness of moral failure or social stigma can complicate a Traditional-Punishment response or prompt drinkers to look for alternative forms of compensation to alleviate their dejection.

Penitent's Rhetoric or the Proper Purpose of Amendment

Melancholy and dejection are integral rather than incidental to the experience of Romantic intoxication and the myths surrounding it as the poetry and correspondence of Robert Burns makes abundantly clear. If despondency is sometimes relieved by alcohol, it can also be intensified by it. Burns had a great reputation for carousing and will forever be associated with whisky (although he preferred port wine).[10] The Kilmarnock edition of his *Poems, Chiefly in the Scottish Dialect* (1786), introduces readers to an array of lyrics and songs championing drunken merriment, extolling the virtues of 'John Barleycorn'. It is important, however, not to overlook the amount of expressions of regret and remorse interspersed throughout the collection. It is difficult to read poems such as 'Despondency: An Ode' and 'Man was Made to Mourn', for example, without thinking of the moral reappraisal we have previously seen associated with hangovers. Away from company, the poet is a figure who sighs out his cares and regrets for folly and indiscretion:

> Dim-backward as I cast my view,
>   What sick'ning Scenes appear!
> What Sorrows *yet* may pierce me thro',
>   Too justly I may fear!
>   Still caring, despairing,
>   Must be my bitter doom;
>   My woes here, shall close ne'r,
>   But with the *closing tomb!* ('Despondency: An Ode', 7–14)

---

10   The amount Burns drank is disputed by scholars, but there is no doubt that he was associated with heavy drinking in the earliest biographies, such as James Currie's of 1800, from which other Romantic writers would have had knowledge of Burns's life. His high spirits when intoxicated and some conspicuous examples of drunken indiscretion, along with the frequent mentions of alcohol in his verse, were more than enough to cement the associations in the public consciousness and in the minds of other writers. See Richard Hindle Fowler, *Robert Burns* (London: Routledge, 1988), pp. 237–38.

Nausea, as in the seventeenth-century sermon, is a state of mind as much as body and poems like this remind us that Burns lived in rigidly moral, Presbyterian Scotland. While others are happy with the 'bustling strife' (16) of work, Burns's speaker confronts every 'joyless morn the same' (24), enduring 'each grief and pain' (26), paralysed by inaction 'listless, yet restless' (27), sensations familiar to a student of the eighteenth-century hangover.

Naturally, Burns's feelings of regret cannot be sourced to specific acts committed whilst drunk in such poems, but they undoubtedly partake of the aesthetic of penitence and personal failure that we find in his letters describing hangovers and can be grouped together with them. Richard Hindle Fowler identified 36 separate occasions on which Burns corresponded drunk, 'fou', or with a hangover.[11] These letters range from short expressions of defiance to apologies and lamentations for weakness of the sort that emerge in the verse quoted above. They are multifarious, providing opportunity for flights of fancy, a chance for jaded witticism, or prompts for a declaration of passion, particularly in the flirtatious correspondence with Clarinda.[12] One hangover of severe physical proportions sends Burns's mind into wistful territory, hoping that his and Clarinda's bodies might one day be 'free from pain and the necessary supplies for the wants of nature, at all times and easily within our reach'.[13] Nevertheless, these accounts give the shared impression of Burns's difficulties in processing, and deriving a sense of a better self from, the experience of his hangovers.

In the same letter to Clarinda, for instance, Burns rephrases his view that 'There is no Philosophy, no Divinity, comes half so home to mind' as the reminder of mortality during his hangovers: his body never feels so close to death, which prompts a short accompanying lyric of dejection, reminiscent of 'Despondency: An Ode', half ironic, though not insincere:

> Sick of the world, and all its joy,
>   My soul in pining sadness mourns:
> Dark scenes of woe my mind employ,
>   The past and present in their turns.[14]

---

11   Fowler, *Robert Burns*, p. 241.
12   Adopting a comic lowland voice, for instance, Burns admits to William Nicol that he cannot write a long epistle as, 'Gude forgie me, I gat myself sae notoriously bitchify'd the day after kail-time that I can hardly stouter but and be' (Ross Roy [ed.], *Burns's Letters*, I, p. 120).
13   Ross Roy (ed.), *Burns's Letters*, I, pp. 120, 214.
14   Ross Roy (ed.), *Burns's Letters*, I, p. 212.

Sickness is projected onto the world, but, as a product of the hangover, this dejection is also about personal dissatisfaction and regret of the sort that we similarly find in a hangover letter to Gavin Hamilton of 7 January 1787 in which Burns confesses a Don Birnamesque 'miserable blank in my heart', or when he quotes *Proverbs* 23: 29–30: 'who hath wo [*sic*] – who hath sorrow? They that tarry long at the wine; they that go to seek mixed wine.'[15] At these moments, the mind relentlessly inspects the 'Dark scenes' of past actions and worries about the present and future.

In a hangover letter written to Robert Ainslie in 1791, Burns gives fuller rein to his suffering, attempting to capture the kind of messy experience of a hangover, whereby troubling sensations and emotions are interleaved with self-rebuke for social ills, self-inflicted humiliation, listlessness and lost time, which tells us more about their profound impact upon him:

> Can you minister to a mind diseased? Can you, amid the horrors of penitence, regret, remorse, headache, nausea, and all the rest of the d – d hounds of hell that beset a poor wretch who has been guilty of the sin of drunkenness – can you speak peace to a troubled soul?
>
> *Miserable perdu* that I am, I have tried everything that used to amuse me, but in vain: here must I sit, a monument of the vengeance laid up in store for the wicked, slowly counting every click of the clock as it slowly, slowly, numbers over these lazy scoundrels of hours, who, d – n them, are ranked up before me, every one at his neighbour's backside, and every one with a burthen of anguish on his back, to pour on my devoted head – and there is none to pity me. My wife scolds me, my business torments me, and my sins come staring me in the face, every one telling a more bitter tale than his fellow. When I tell you even *** has lost its power to please, you will guess something of my hell within, and all around me.[16]

Burns reminds us that hangover consciousness can take the form of a particularly uncomfortable coaction of body and mind. Here, the hangover is a good example of the Romantic focus on 'the tremulous body of sensibility', as Stephen Ahern phrases it, which has the potential

---

15   Ross Roy (ed.), *Burns's Letters*, I, pp. 78, 192.
16   Ross Roy (ed.), *Burns's Letters*, II, p. 121.

to overwhelm cognition.[17] Physical sensations set off or exacerbate the pangs of conscience and memories of actions for which the sufferer cannot initially atone. Burns writes of the 'mind diseased' to which physical remedies – such as habitual 'amusements' and even sex – cannot administer unction. This is first and foremost mental anguish, even if the body is invoked throughout.[18] Burns's sense of accountability and desire for atonement – 'devoted head' – are paramount to begin with, and he focuses on dimensions of a Traditional-Punishment reaction, which we have witnessed in previous eras, such as sinfulness or concerns about work and domestic responsibility. However, his reaction is difficult to pin down, drifting melodramatically between self-pity on the one hand and an emergent feeling of defiance on the other. Burns's admission of sin is even perhaps complicated by a lingering perception of injustice: the two impressions are not easily reconciled within the same letter.

The torment of such consciousness is set against the backdrop of the ticking clock: Burns's hyperawareness of passing time underlines how his perception is disordered. The hungover mind is manifestly not a place of dejected recompense as in the customary model of Wordsworth's 'Resolution and Independence', but of torment. Equally, far from being a poetically productive form of dejection, as is commonly the case with Romantic introspection, hangover anxiety, or 'hangxiety', prevents the poet's efforts at composition. Eventually, reading a letter from his correspondent allows Burns to 'breathe a little' and, perhaps most significantly, feel again, or at least regain intimations of pleasurable emotion:

> I began *Elibanks and Elibraes*, but the stanzas fell unenjoyed and unfinished from my listless tongue: at last I luckily thought of reading over an old letter of yours, that lay by me, in my bookcase, and I felt something, for the first time since I opened my eyes, of pleasurable existence. Well – I begin to breathe a little, since I began to write to you.[19]

The impression of recovery does not, however, detract from the twinning of the overburdened senses and conscience that make the poet's experience a deeply troubling one. Noticeably, throughout his account

---

17 Stephen Ahern, 'Diagnosing Romanticism', *ESC*, 31.2–3 (June/September 2005), p. 70 (pp. 69–76).

18 Burns was often depressed, but hangovers had a significant impact on his moods and he knew this, as when he complains to Agnes of 'an incessant head-ache, depression of spirits, and all the truly miserable consequences of a deranged nervous system' (Ross Roy [ed.], *Burns's Letters*, II, p. 10).

19 Ross Roy (ed.), *Burns's Letters*, II, p. 121.

of the hangover, Burns has recourse to an elevated discourse of sin and wickedness, redolent of Protestant conversion narratives. Self-pity finds outlet through the penitent's rhetoric, which is typically grandiose: guilt, that prohibits inner 'peace', is depicted as hell on earth; 'Hell within' – a reference to Milton's Satan – emphasises the piquancy of self-inflicted melancholy, distinguishing the Romantic hangover from other forms of dejection.

Evoking the Puritan sermon, it is not uncommon to find Burns associating guilt or shame with theatrical references to Hell. In 'Remorse', first included in his 1783 *Commonplace Book*, he delineates the 'burning hell' (14) or agonies of a mind haunted by vague impressions of indiscretions:

> Of all the numerous ills that hurt our peace,
> That press the soul, or wring the mind with anguish
> Beyond comparison the worst are those
> By our own folly, or our guilt brought on. (1–4)

He elaborates on the 'gnawing consciousness of guilt', recalling the same feelings that dog him in the letter to Ainslie, which burden the conscience. Physical and mental signs of torment overlap confusingly. The 'bitter horrors' (17) and 'agonizing throbs' (18) of heart redolent of nausea and tachycardia distract from, but ultimately lend greater weight to, the 'jarring thoughts' (20). Yet, a 'proper purpose of amendment' (21), which we have often found in Traditional-Punishment reactions in earlier periods, appears to be as much an aspiration as an attainment.[20]

The imagery of 'Remorse' indicates heightened awareness of sensations, as we usually find in representation of hangover consciousness, which are first perceived as evidence of punishment. However, if the experience ought to promote what Burns calls, in an accompanying notebook entry, a 'proper penitential sense of our misconduct',[21] then it also produces the impression of helplessness, evoking the man listening to the infernal ticking clock. The speaker is locked, as Nash and Kilday put it, 'into a cycle of guilt, remembering the consequences of transgression or anxiously awaiting future social failures with foreboding'.[22] Like 'Despondency: An Ode', where the glance backward is matched by

20   Raymond Lamont Brown (ed.), *Robert Burns' Commonplace Book* (Wakefield: S. R. Publishers Ltd, 1969), p. 7.
21   Brown (ed.), *Commonplace Book*, p. 7.
22   David Nash and Anne-Marie Kilday, *Cultures of Shame: Exploring Crime and Morality in Britain 1600–1900* (New York: Palgrave MacMillan, 2010), p. 5.

anticipation of 'What sorrows *yet* may pierce [him] thro'', moral amendment appears to be hindered by a hangover that proffers, but fails to deliver with clarity, greater self-knowledge.

Burns's hangovers are undoubtedly framed by the language of penitence and sin, although specific details of wrongdoing are left vague or unexpressed both in the letter to Ainslie and 'Remorse'. It appears that the penitential emphasis that we found in the early modern sermon, which might be expected to prompt a Traditional-Punishment reaction, is complicated by Romantic uncertainties about the self. Exaggeration and the potential for self-pity or egotism are poetically productive, but they emerge from a kind of mental incoherence: 'Lives there a man so firm ... / Can *reason* down [guilt's] agonizing throbs' ('Remorse, 16–17)? Presented in the tones of confession, the penitent poet reveals everything and yet strangely very little aside from 'the miserable blank in my heart' and a heightened awareness of the interconnection of his bodily and mental suffering. The blank is another way of expressing what Olivia Laing calls the 'deep sense of breakage' of the drinker, where the language of emotion or feeling discloses the self's capacity to feel whilst also inhibiting any fuller explanation for its condition. It is a peculiar kind of self-knowledge.

The water-drinking Wordsworth discerned in 'Despondency, An Ode' a depth of feeling that he could never read 'without the deepest agitation', described in a letter to Coleridge of 1799,[23] which Anya Taylor has convincingly linked to Wordsworth's feelings about Burns's legendary drinking. Wordsworth only left us one depiction of a hangover, but much is gained from contrasting it with those of Burns. In *The Prelude* (1805), Wordsworth describes the feelings of disgrace he experienced as a Cambridge student when he participated in a drunken party in the Christ's College rooms reputed to have once belonged to John Milton. Wordsworth recalls drunken antics and the subsequent hangover, which become a prominent example of disgrace or Bunyanesque backsliding. Unlike Burns, however, the hangover threatens but is eventually incorporated into the mythopoeia of the growth of the poet's mind:

> O temperate Bard!
> One afternoon, the first time I set foot
> In this thy innocent Nest and Oratory,
> Seated with others in a festive ring
> Of common-place convention, I to thee

---

23   Letter of February 1799, in *The Early Letters of William and Dorothy Wordsworth*, ed. Ernest de Selincourt, 5 vols (Oxford: Clarendon Press, 1935), I, p. 222.

Poured out libations, to thy memory drank,
Within my private thoughts, till my brain reeled,
Never so clouded by the fumes of wine
Before that hour, or since. Thence forth I ran
From that assembly, through a length of streets,
Ran, Ostrich-like, to reach our Chapel Door

...

Upshouldering in a dislocated lump,
With shallow ostentatious carelessness,
My Surplice, gloried in, and yet despised,
I clove in pride through the inferior throng
Of the plain Burghers, who in audience stood
On the last skirts of their permitted ground,
Beneath the pealing Organ. (III, 299–309, 316–22)

Wordsworth begins in retelling the festive occasion, but libations made to Milton quickly come to seem inappropriate and he reminds us that his precursor was a 'temperate Bard', famed for eschewing pleasure. Wine has a physical impact, producing ungainly 'Ostrich-like' movement, intoxicating the mind, in addition to prompting 'ostentatious carelessness' that leads him to attend chapel despite his drunkenness. Pride revealed by that transgression is less burdensome, however, than the recollection that Wordsworth has overstepped his mark in relation to the great poet of English epic. If *The Prelude* is ultimately designed to show that Wordsworth is 'a chosen Son' (III, 82), the censorious pealing organ – an instrument often associated with Milton's blank verse[24] – is represented as a rebuke to the youthful poet not to squander his time in foolish drunken behaviour.

Confessing to his indiscretion, Wordsworth differs from Burns in being able to pardon himself through reflecting on self-knowledge acquired through drinking. He makes amends by demonstrating in his later verse how the lesson enabled him to first understand and then set out his personal identity as a poet in the Miltonic moral and visionary tradition. When Wordsworth depicts a hangover, it is long after the event, and penitence is not primarily a moral issue, as the poet turns within to a new form of imaginative self-validation, of the sort also found in 'Resolution and Independence', which side-steps social accountability. He

---

24 See Milton's 'pealing organ' (161) in *Il Penseroso, Complete Shorter Poems*, ed. John Carey (London: Longman, 1971).

gives us a quite different version of the Romantic hangover from Burns, where imaginative gains replace 'the imperatives of "society," "family" and "duty"' with which drunkards are ordinarily required to reconnect in a Traditional-Punishment hangover.[25]

If Wordsworth felt a palpable sense of conflict when it came to Burns's reputation for heavy drinking then, as Taylor indicates, he was able to resolve the knowledge of his precursor's waywardness with his veneration of the poet by compromising on some of his natural antipathy towards alcohol.[26] Amends for Burns's 'uncontrolled propensities', that included both drunkenness and lechery, might be made through understanding that 'vice leads to misery' and, in the case of alcohol, a hangover, as Burns appeared to suggest by placing poems such as 'Despondency, An Ode' amongst his other rakehelly lyrics.[27] Taylor proposes that Wordsworth's views were also influenced by Samuel Taylor Coleridge's praise of Burns's genius in an 1812 edition of the *Friend*. Likewise, in narrating his own shameful memories of drunkenness in *The Prelude*, Wordsworth appealed not only to Milton, but to Coleridge – the addressee of *The Prelude* – although he well knew of Coleridge's own struggles with alcohol that recall the agitation of Burns.

Taylor recognises Coleridge as 'an aesthetician of Dionysian energy',[28] discernible in a series of drinking songs, but he is particularly insightful on the hangover, as indicated by prescient comments made in a schoolboy essay titled 'Temperance': 'Alas! at the moment we contract a habit [of drinking] we forego our free agency. The remainder of our life will be spent in making resolutions in the hour of dejection.'[29] 'Coleridge predicts his own dejection and loss of free agency', as Taylor notes, but, as with Burns, we must distinguish such dejection that derives from disappointed hopes of the world from that characteristic of the hangover.[30] Where the one queries social and cultural values or expresses disappointment at an imperfect world – as, for instance, in the domestic unhappiness that prompts Coleridge's 'Dejection: An Ode' (1802) – the other looks within at the reasons for the transgression of orthodox social values

25   Steven Earnshaw, 'Drink, Dissolution, Antibiography: The Existential Drinker', in *Biographies of Drink: A Case Study Approach to our Historical Relationship with Alcohol*, ed. Mark Hailwood and Deborah Toner (Newcastle-upon-Tyne: Cambridge Scholars, 2015), p. 204 (pp. 204–22).

26   Taylor, *Bacchus*, pp. 53–54.

27   Owen and Smyser (eds), *Wordsworth Prose*, III, p. 124.

28   Taylor, *Bacchus*, p. 93.

29   Samuel Taylor Coleridge, *The Collected Letters*, ed. Earl Leslie Griggs, 6 vols (Oxford: Clarendon Press, 1957–71), VI, p. 934.

30   Taylor, *Bacchus*, p. 115.

and, in doing so, focuses on the speaker's problematic reaction to having breached them.

Coleridge was notorious for his intake of laudanum and, as with many other Romantic writers, opium certainly contributed to the physical symptoms of hangovers recorded in his correspondence.[31] However, he takes as his subject the 'hour of dejection' subsequent to social drinking, and the cycle of making and unmaking resolutions to reform, in 'Honour' (1791). It at first appears to be a lightweight comic poem, but that is largely due to tone. 'Honour' is a mock-heroic account of the habits of a pleasure-seeking Georgian gambler that owes much to Pope's introduction of Belinda in *The Rape of the Lock*. Unlike Belinda, Coleridge's Philedon has no guardian sylph to shield his 'balmy rest' prolonged until noon – the hour of social shame throughout the eighteenth century as discussed in the previous chapter – as the poem opens with a description of his physical impairment:

> The fervid Sun had more than halv'd the day,
> When gloomy on his couch Philedon lay;
> His feeble frame consumptive as his purse,
> His aching head did wine and women curse;
> His fortune ruin'd and his wealth decay'd,
> Clamorous his duns, his gaming debts unpaid. (1–6)[32]

Recalling a number of depictions of hungover bachelors discussed in Chapter 3, Philedon assigns his aching head to the social maladies of wine, women and the club. The hazards of the gaming table lead to penury and he feels the imperative of a Traditional-Punishment response to the hangover kick in, contemplating ways to make amends for wrongdoing, which leads to a pledge of reformation scribbled with 'moral quill' (8) on the reverse of his 'tailor's bill' (7). This ushers in a satirical diatribe against contemporary notions of 'Honour' and gentlemanly conduct that led Philedon astray: 'Profuse of joy and Lord of right and wrong, / Honour can game, drink, riot in the stew, / Cut a friend's throat: – what cannot Honour do?' (38–40).

However, Philedon's aspiration for amendment is as ephemeral as the hastily composed note on a mislaid piece of paper. Reflections on the theme of honour turn rather quickly to the seductive influence of

31   See Virginia Berridge, *Demons: Our Changing Attitudes to Alcohol, Tobacco, and Drugs* (Oxford: Oxford University Press, 2013), pp. 52–53.

32   Samuel Taylor Coleridge, *The Complete Poems*, ed. William Keach (London: Penguin, 2004). All references to Coleridge's poetry are to this edition.

the Withdrawal-Relief method of recovery, because alcohol has a more immediate capacity to offset physical and emotional hangover symptoms with its armoury of pleasurable affects. Philedon departs into a reverie: 'But see! young Pleasure, and her train advance, / And joy and laughter wake the inebriate dance; / … For the gay grape joys celestial can move, / … With such high transport every moment flies' (49–55). This is the rhapsodic language of Romantic intoxication that Moore adopts and that Keats utilises in describing the awakening of Glaucus and Scylla in *Endymion* (1818), 'two deliverers' who 'tasted a pure wine / Of happiness, from fairy press oozed out' (III, 806–807) becoming 'Distracted with the richest overflow / Of joy that ever pour'd from heaven' (810–11). Coleridge's Philedon turns to similar pastoral and celestial imagery in an attempt to render the feelings of intoxication, but we must remember that he speaks as a man hungover and, at the very peak of his trance, the dejection induced by his hangover returns: 'I curse Experience that he makes me wise; / For at his frown the dear deliriums flew, / And the changed scene now wears a gloomy hue' (56–58). Recalling Burns's Nannie in 'Tam O'Shanter' (1791), the 'Enchantress Pleasure' (59) is transformed into a 'hideous hag' (59) and Philedon's 'joys appear but feverous dreams' (60), suggesting that the cold light of day reveals that lustful behaviour incited by drink has imbruted rather than ennobled the speaker.

In the hour of dejection, the conditional nature of the inebriate's desire to reform his ways and fluctuation between a Traditional-Punishment and Withdrawal-Relief reaction is encapsulated in the line 'The vain resolve still broken and still made' (13). External factors that eventually break the cycle of inaction underline the drinker's broken will and inability to maintain what Burns called a 'proper penitential' state:

> Such lays repentant did the Muse supply;
> When as the Sun was hastening down the sky,
> In glittering state twice fifty guineas come, –
> His Mother's plate antique had rais'd the sum.
> Forth leap'd Philedon of new life possest:
> 'Twas Brookes's all till two, – 'twas Hackett's all the rest! (65–70)

Life is restored with money and the moral dilemma serves a comic outcome, but Coleridge is as earnest about the subject of foregoing free agency as he was as a schoolboy.

Coleridge's mock-heroic mode helps to evoke the rising and plunging motions of hangover consciousness, particularly the drinker's susceptibility to the seductive pleasures of intoxicating liquor. If this recalls

Augustan verse, the psychological precision and evident self-doubt places it in the Romantic period. In like manner, 'Progress of Vice' (1790) shares the pastoral flourishes and aureate diction, Augustan couplets and mock-heroic idiom, of 'Honour' that combine with the intensity of Romantic consciousness of mental states, particularly suited to capturing self-induced melancholy, evoking anxiety, nerviness and recrimination:

> Deep in the gulph of Vice and Woe
> Leaps Man at once with headlong throw?
> Him inborn Truth and Virtue guide,
> Whose guards are Shame and conscious Pride.
> In some gay hour Vice steals into the breast;
> Perchance she wears some softer Virtue's vest.
> By unperceiv'd degrees she tempts to stray,
> Till far from Virtue's path she leads the feet away.
>
> Then swift the soul to disenthrall
> Will Memory the past recall,
> And Fear before the Victim's eyes
> Bid future ills and dangers rise.
> But hark! the Voice, the Lyre, their charms combine –
> Gay sparkles in the cup the generous Wine –
> Th' inebriate dance, the fair frail Nymph inspires,
> And Virtue vanquish'd – scorn'd – with hasty flight retires.
>
> But soon to tempt the Pleasures cease;
> Yet Shame forbids return to peace,
> And stern Necessity will force
> Still to urge on the desperate course.
> The drear black paths of Vice the wretch must try,
> Where Conscience flashes horror on each eye,
> Where Hate – where Murder scowl – where starts Affright!
> Ah! close the scene – ah! Close – for dreadful is the sight. (1–24)

Coleridge shares the remorseful sentiments we find in Burns's verse and letters, typified by anxiety for past indiscretion ('Will Memory the past recall') and foreboding ('future ills and dangers'). Coleridge's drunken pleasure seeker rehearses the possibility of punishment, imbued with feelings of remorse, that might curb his excesses, a reminder that 'Truth and Virtue' are inborn and 'Vice' is a departure from 'Virtue's path', recalling Wordsworth and his debt to Milton and Bunyan. Shame initially functions as a deterrent to further drunkenness but, in the language of Burns, it also noticeably 'forbids return to peace', or a full restoration of equilibrium. The tone of defiance or injustice discerned in Burns is absent here, but the hangover's superstructure has a similar nebulousness, an impression of free-floating guiltiness, which mingles with more recognisable reasons for shame. All of these factors prevent the drunkard, despite claiming devotion to vice is an aberration in the first stanza, from restoring emotional norms or social standards, leaving him locked in a cycle of inaction.

As with Burns's 'Remorse', when it comes to admitting his crime, precision is markedly lacking and a non-specific 'gay hour' is 'Perchance' the source of disquiet. Memory loss may be something to which Coleridge gestures: the poem deflects the reader's attention from specific detail, which might include an array of actions associated with drunken vice such as whoring and gambling, and focuses instead on the degree of the psychological and physical torment. There is a hint that the capacity to feel – to feel pleasure and subsequently overwhelming dread in this case – makes the drunkard vulnerable to the 'urge' to drink more in order to quiet the conscience.

In earlier periods, we saw such a Withdrawal-Relief mode of recovery adopted as an act of defiance against moral judgement. Even during the hangover – or perhaps especially, recalling the words of Birnam in *The Lost Weekend*: 'that's when you need it most'[33] – Coleridge depicts alcohol as the best remedy for the ills it causes. Yet, here defiance does not seem to be the dominant issue. If stanza two strikes an alluring tone, the third stanza is imbued with the language of addiction rather than intoxication: 'stern Necessity will force / Still to urge on the desperate course.' The aftershocks of alcohol are captured in the disjunction between hyperbolic imagery and a passive voice that suggests the absence of the drinker's agency in the overwhelming assault of pleasure and pain on his emotional life. The results of heavy drinking are laid bare, although the self's capacity to feel, registered physically in the conscience discernible in the eye, even as the drunkard self-medicates with alcohol, has been perverted. Ultimately, Coleridge evokes denial rather than the acquisition of self-knowledge through presenting a dialectic of gladness and dejection particular to the subjective experience of a hangover.

---

33   This line is actually from the screenplay: Charles Brackett and Billy Wilder, *The Lost Weekend* (Berkeley, Los Angeles, London: University of California Press, 2000), (B-5) p. 33.

Glutting Sorrow with Blunted Affect

In his drinking verse Coleridge reveals himself to be an aesthetician of hangovers that lurch between images of deterrence and further enticement to drink, where the Withdrawal-Relief response is as much a coping strategy as an act of defiance. Burns represents the misery of attempting to find ways to make amends and the desire to justify his actions as well as accept his punishment. Both poets find amendment for their awareness of moral shortcomings a more problematic issue than the reflective Wordsworth. But, as I indicated in this chapter's introduction, Wordsworth shifts the possibilities of what Anthony Cascardi calls purposive 'self-transformation' from moral conduct, which would signal a normative Traditional-Punishment response, to poetic or imaginative growth, which distinguishes his own hangover story in *The Prelude*. Burns and Coleridge depict drunkards who are not offered the same compensatory outlet.[34]

The hangovers that we find in the verse of some of the second-generation Romantics, Keats and Byron, share superficial similarities with the anxieties expressed by Coleridge, and yet also owe much to Wordsworth's imaginative recalibration of the ways in which personal worth and coherence are judged. In the case of these writers, however, the issue at stake is, I would suggest, feeling rather than imagination. Romantic literature and culture are conspicuously concerned with the business of feeling or emotion as a way of gauging self-worth as Joel Faflak and Richard Sha have recently argued.[35] When Keats and Byron model an aesthetic of the hangover, they tend to attribute self-awareness and self-knowledge to the capacity to feel loss acutely.

One problem with such an alternative model of recompense for the loss of the pleasures of intoxication was, however, that if intoxicants elevated the mind, as the period's medical literature was showing, they had the corresponding consequence of blunting affect or, at the very least, throwing the capacity to feel into doubt, once drunkenness wore off. In *The Anatomy of Drunkenness* (1827), for example, Robert MacNish explained intoxication as a result of alcohol's overstimulation of the nervous system. 'The mental manifestations produced by [intoxicating agents] depend almost entirely upon the nerves.' He continues:

34   Anthony Cascardi, *The Subject of Modernity* (Cambridge: Cambridge University Press, 1992), p. 7.
35   Joel Faflak and Richard C. Sha (eds), *Romanticism and the Emotions* (Cambridge: Cambridge University Press, 2014), p. 3.

The power of exciting the feelings inherent in these principles, can only be accounted for by supposing an intimate relation to subsist between the body and the mind. The brain, through the medium of its nervous branches, is the source of all this excitement ... there can be little difficulty in apprehending why intoxication produces so powerful a mental influence. This must proceed from a resistless impulse being given to the brain, by virtue of the peculiar action of inebriating agents upon the nerves.[36]

Intoxication draws together body, mind and nervous system in affective reciprocity. A long history of scientific investigation into the nerves in the eighteenth century, which is well set out by G. J. Barker-Benfield,[37] lies behind MacNish's remarks and demonstrates how much he owed to the Edinburgh medical school of William Cullen and John Brown. In a notebook entry, Coleridge similarly records that alcohol 'excite[s] the sensations' and acts on the 'nervous system', heightening emotional intensity.[38] Increased circulation was also an important factor in understanding the way that alcohol intoxicated body and mind and, as Taylor notes, the 'tipsy Joy' (86) that Coleridge describes in 'The Nightingale' (1798) recalls medical theories of pleasurable physical sensation. Coleridge's tipsiness 'courses along the blood ... stimulating to excitement whether as rapidity of movement, of perception, or of thought'.[39]

'But', as MacNish cautions, the brain's 'energies, like those of any other part, are apt to be over-excited' by alcohol, after which the physical and emotional consequences of a hangover follow: 'When this takes place, the balance is broken; the mind gets tumultuous and disordered, and the ideas inconsistent, wavering, and absurd. Then come the torpor and exhaustion subsequent on such excessive stimulus.'[40] The mind, unbalanced by alcohol in the state of drunkenness, eventually undergoes its aftershocks, falling into the torpor of the hangover. Perhaps the most notable consequence is that the capacity to feel, which was at first unnaturally increased, is proportionally diminished through

---

36   Robert MacNish, *The Anatomy of Drunkenness* (New York: Appleton, 1827), pp. 89–90.

37   G. J. Barker-Benfield, *The Culture of Sensibility: Sex and Society in Eighteenth-Century Britain* (Chicago, IL and London: University of Chicago Press, 1996), pp. 1–36.

38   Cited in Taylor, *Bacchus*, p. 116.

39   Taylor, *Bacchus*, p. 104.

40   MacNish, *Anatomy*, p. 91.

what MacNish identifies as a 'languor corresponding to the previous excitation'.[41]

It is this kind of languor that Keats and Byron attempt to capture in their hangover literature. Whether it is a product of alcohol specifically, other stimulants like opium, or just heightened sensory and emotional experience in general, Keats expresses loss as a numbing of sensations and emotional activity analogous to a hangover. The prime example of this is *Endymion*, which tells the tale of the shepherd boy who loses his vision of the moon goddess, Cynthia. Noticeably, his willingness to give way to emotion and indulge in self-pity is described as a type of hangover following an erotic experience:

> The lyre of his soul Eolian tuned
> Forgot all violence, and but communed
> With melancholy thought: O he had swooned
> Drunken from pleasure's nipple; and his love
> Henceforth was dove-like. Loth was he to move
> From the imprinted couch, and when he did,
> 'Twas with slow, languid paces, and face hid
> In muffling hands. (II, 875)

The loss of pleasure corresponds to a hangover and borrows its imagery. Endymion's level of despondency is depicted as the consequence of intoxication, demonstrating that dejection is his failing. Yet, atonement is now not so much a matter of self-reliance as it was in Wordsworth, or the struggle to express or admit moral failure as in Coleridge and Burns, as the willingness of the subject to turn within and find a corresponding capacity to suffer deeply. The damaging impact of intoxication on the body – primarily sluggishness and disorientation – proves the authenticity of the feelings or the inner life. Even so, Endymion's inability to recover from his despondency testifies only to his capacity to feel, which isolates him from his sister and other companions as he drifts into egotistical reveries.

Likewise, the Indian maiden with whom Endymion becomes enraptured sings an 'Ode to Sorrow' that follows an encounter with 'Bacchus and his kin' (IV, 201). Estranged from the god of wine, who abandons her in the forest – there is undoubtedly a symbolic hangover in play here – she is 'Sick hearted, weary' (271) and enraptured with feelings of grief:

41   MacNish, *Anatomy*, p. 91.

Come then, Sorrow!
Sweetest Sorrow!
Like an own babe I nurse thee on my breast:
  I thought to leave thee
  And deceive thee,
But now of all the world I love thee best. (281–86)

As with Endymion, hangover sensations are an outlet for the mind.
Taylor describes Keatsian intoxication as a feeling of 'intense sorrow
pulsing at the centre of intense joy'.[42] This is rendered most beautifully in
the image from the *Ode on Melancholy* (1820), in which 'aching Pleasure'
(23) turns to 'poison while the bee-mouth sips' (24). Both in the Odes
and *Endymion*, Keats captures the unnatural elevation of spirits that
constitutes intoxication, but also acknowledges the subsequent hangover
that mixes poisonous symptoms with remaining traces of elation. As
Michael G. Cooke observes, the word intoxication includes the word
'toxic' and has a much longer association with 'The poisoning of moral
and mental faculties' than 'with the action or power of exhilarating the
mind' (*OED*). 'The very idea of *in-toxic-ation* entails self-contradiction:
elation it affords, but while its subject is in elation, its poison is in him.'[43]
    The sensations of this experience are likewise contradictory and hard
to render. Differentiating hangovers from Wordsworthian dejection,
alcohol seemingly has the confusing ability to both intensify *and*
blunt affect, through what Cooke terms 'the self-reactive tendency
of intoxication'.[44] Like Burns in a hangover letter to Clarinda, who
desperately wishes to feel pity for another – 'Give me to feel "another's
woes"'[45] – Keats memorably indicates the 'gravitational force opposing
elation', which puzzlingly retards feeling or indicates its loss in *Ode to a
Nightingale* (1819).[46] Keats's speaker experiences first a rapturous yearning
for alcohol followed by an image of intense loss that partakes of the
hangover's interconnected physical and emotional dimensions:

O for a draught of vintage, that hath been
Cool'd a long age in the deep-delved earth,
Tasting of Flora and the country green,

42   Taylor, *Bacchus*, p. 157.
43   Michael G. Cooke, 'De Quincey, Coleridge, and the Formal Uses of Intoxication',
      Yale French Studies, 50 (1974), p. 27 (pp. 26–40).
44   Cooke, 'Formal Uses', p. 29.
45   Ross Roy (ed.), *Burns's Letters*, I, p. 218.
46   Cooke, 'Formal Uses', p, 29.

Dance, and Provencal song, and sunburnt mirth!
O for a beaker of the warm South,
Full of the true, the blushful Hippocrene,
With beaded bubbles winking at the brim,
And purple-stained mouth:
That I might drink and leave the world unseen,
And with thee fade away into the forest dim:

Fade, far away, dissolve, and quite forget
What thou among the leaves hast never known,
The weariness, the fever, and the fret
Here, where men sit and hear each other groan. (11–24)

Keats's speaker experiences profound depression of spirits, expressed through feverishness, fretfulness and incoherent groans, but accompanied by inarticulacy or the mute incoherence Riede finds in Romantic poems of dejection. The speaker impresses his capacity to feel acutely the absence of the 'draught of vintage', but through a type of numbness. Beyond that he is debarred from self-knowledge that he can express.

What is missing from the hangover literature of the second-generation Romantics is the punitive or penitential superstructure that Burns invokes and with which Coleridge's drunkards wrestle. The Traditional-Punishment context has arguably been replaced by the cultivation of negative affect for its own sake, just as in the *Ode on Melancholy* Keats urges his reader to 'glut thy sorrow on a morning rose' (15). A 'post-visionary hangover', as Arthur Ward suitably expresses it, leaves the speaker of the Nightingale Ode bereft of the bird's song, although it is worth noting that the fact that the 'remedy sounds suspiciously like the ailment' – even though 'Bacchus and his pards' (32) are dismissed in favour of poesy – gives an inkling that alcohol is implicated in his recovery.[47] The speaker seeks further intoxication of the brain that is otherwise 'dull' or 'retards' (34) feeling and Keats finds it hard to conceive of mental stimulation without the Bacchic language and imagery that his speaker ostensibly discards. Nor can he conceive of the subject of loss, it would appear, without recourse to the motif of the hangover.

The problem I am raising in analysing the rich emotional and sensational content that Keats produces through mixing the diction of intoxication and the hangover is twofold. First, the hangover as MacNish

---

47   Arthur Ward, *Death and Eroticism in the Poetry of Keats and Tennyson* (Los Angeles: University of California Press, 1975), p. 73.

describes it, and as Keats relays it, deadens or retards physical sensation, dulling the brain and fraying the nerves. This means feeling becomes a rather unsteady way to evaluate self-worth or set out an identity that affirms compensation for the experience of loss (whether it be loss of the experience of drunkenness or pleasure more largely). Second, and by way of contrast, 'excessive self-examination coupled with a preoccupation with the feeling body can encourage self-absorption, skepticism, neurosis', as Ahern puts it.[48] There is a danger that the poetics of the hangover produces a discourse of feeling that drifts into exaggerated self-pity, analogous to the hyperbole of Burns's penitent's rhetoric, throwing the authenticity of that feeling into doubt.

Adding Sigmund Freud's work on melancholy and mourning to the Romantic medical discourse of intoxication is one way in which we might approach the muddle of the hangover's coupling of excessive feeling with its absence. Endymion and the Indian maiden are figures who experience grief so acute, or what Lynn Enterline, explaining Freud's theory, calls a 'sense of loss that exceeds all compensation', that it proves physically disabling and so the ego turns inward, yet, because the source of discomfort is nebulous, the intensity of affect seems 'in excess of its occasion'.[49] Different types of affect, some quantifiable, others examples of untethered hangxiety, appear to coexist to a greater degree than in the hangover literature of earlier periods, while feeling has the potential to overwhelm cognition. In the language of the hangover used by Keats to puncture elation in *Endymion* and the Odes, the effect is to render the impression of an unformulated, existential, problem that outstrips that disclosed or attributed to the absence of drink or other kinds of pleasure.

The same effect is apparent in Byron's *Childe Harold's Pilgrimage* (1812–18) wherein the hero's heightened susceptibility to his self-inflicted discontents puzzlingly blunts affect. Imprisoned within himself by self-disgust, Byron's Childe Harold, not unlike Endymion, 'Apart ... stalk'd in joyless reverie' (I, 50), rehearsing his regrets, before departing his homeland with the reverberations of once pleasurable excess sounding tinny in his ear.[50] 'Sore sick at heart' (I, 46), Harold's gloom is attributed to 'fellow bacchanals' (47) who have 'condemn'd to uses vile' (59) the once 'venerable pile' (56) of his father's home, where 'Paphian girls' (61) have replaced 'holy men' (63). Even in his 'maddest mirthful mood'

48   Ahern, 'Diagnosing Romanticism', p. 70.
49   Lynn Enterline, *The Tears of Narcissus: Melancholia and Masculinity in Early Modern Writing* (Stanford, CA: Stanford University Press, 1995), pp. 1–3.
50   Lord Byron, *The Complete Poetical Works*, ed. Jerome J. McGann, 7 vols (Oxford: Clarendon Press, 1980–93), II. All further references to Byron's works are to this edition.

(64), we are told, 'Strange pangs would flash along Childe Harold's brow' (65), physical signs of his tormented conscience for which, the narrator tells us, he cannot or will not make 'atonement' (38).

Instead, Byron cultivates a world-weary aesthetic out of hangover sensations to express Harold's curious capacity to express feeling and yet claim the inability to feel, mingling remorse with defiance: ''Tis said, at times the sullen tear would start, / But Pride congeal'd the drop within his ee' (I, 48–49). Overburdened with an apparently free-floating sense of guiltiness, Harold's reaction to hedonism also produces a 'dull satiety which all destroys' (IV, 1070) – like Keats's retarded feelings – most particularly the power to experience and express emotion. Where Endymion indulges in self-pity, Harold defiantly dismisses it, but both characters hint at incomprehensible causes that outstrip the immediate occasion of drunkenness or maddest mirthful moods. That is not to say that the narrator does not propose reasons for Harold's self-torment. Crimes attributed to Harold's experience of 'Sin's long labyrinth' (I, 37) take in a lost love who escaped 'from him whose kiss / Had been pollution unto aught so chaste' (I, 41–42) – anticipating the themes Byron later explored in *Manfred* (1817) – and rumours of 'some deadly feud / Or disappointed passion' (I, 66–67). Nevertheless, the overtaxed nervous system mainly produces an impression of loss where, as Freud has it, 'one cannot see clearly what it is that has been lost'.[51]

Assignable symptoms of hangovers infiltrate the poem's language of loss and grief, particularly nausea and dryness of mouth in the fourth canto: 'we gasp away – / Sick, sick; unfound the boon, unslaked the thirst' (1108–1109). The narrator imagines 'young affections' (1072) turning to 'trees whose gums are poison' (1077), in similar fashion to the poison that Keats references in *Ode on Melancholy*. Both poets intuitively express the toxicity at the heart of intoxicants. However, these are experiences that highlight nebulous feelings of sorrow and guilt that cannot be readily sourced to personal indiscretion or bodily suffering, yet nevertheless find expression through the language of the hangover. They leave impressions of some dreadful deed – what Taylor calls an 'objectless dread that rises from within'[52] – to which, to return to the words of Charles Jackson that I cited in Chapter 1, the Romantic sufferer 'cannot bear witness' and which cannot be adequately verbalised.

---

51 Sigmund Freud, *The Standard Edition of the Complete Psychological Works of Sigmund Freud*, trans. James Strachey, 24 vols (London: Hogarth Press, repr. 1963), XIV, p. 245.
52 Taylor, *Bacchus*, p. 73.

We are firmly in the territory of one of this book's major concerns which is how hangovers confront sufferers with Laing's 'deep sense of breakage'. From where do these feelings arise? The greater presence of nebulous dejection in these Romantic hangovers, compared with those we have seen in earlier periods, reminds us that not only does Romantic poetry make the introspective self a proper subject of inquiry, but also that interpreting feeling became a more complicated business in the late eighteenth and nineteenth centuries. As Thomas Dixon has demonstrated, it was during the Romantic period that centuries-old moral distinctions between the higher 'affections' and the lower 'passions' and 'appetites' finally broke down,[53] making it unclear whether negative affect was symptomatic of morally inappropriate behaviour as it had been in, for example, the seventeenth-century sermon.

Uncertainties about the self are particularly evident in Byron's hangover descriptions. *Childe Harold* projects an impression of dejection that is induced or exacerbated, rather than relieved, by alcohol, but the problem of blunted affect and the struggle to account for the hangover's miserable superstructure were also a notable feature in Byron's accounts of his own hangovers. Although he periodically felt the kind of remorse that ordinarily leads drinkers to make amends, as in the account of his anxiety at having offended his friend Thomas Moore at a drinking party at the Cambridge Whig Club,[54] it is more common, and in keeping with the hangover poetics of *Childe Harold*, to find Byron anxiously puzzling over his emotional unpredictability, hinting at and yet masking the 'elusive core of his person'.[55] In his Ravenna journal, Byron gives one particularly melodramatic account of the after-effects of a dinner party with the Gambas when he consumed a bottle of Imola wine and some cockles, before quaffing several large glasses of spirits on his return home. Byron's attention to physical consequences quickly shifts to the subject of his emotions:

> All was pretty well till I got to bed, when I became somewhat swollen, and considerably vertiginous. I got out, and mixing some soda-powders, drank them off. This brought on temporary relief.

---

53   Thomas Dixon, '"Emotion": The History of a Keyword in Crisis', *Emotion Review*, 4.4 (Oct. 2012), pp. 338–44.

54   He writes that he had been 'insane with the fumes of wine'. Fearing he had insulted Moore, Byron wrote to him a note of apology that indicates shame – 'I really thought … that I had said – I know not what – but something I should have been very sorry for, had it, or I, offended you' (Leslie A. Marchand [ed.], *The Letters and Journals of Lord Byron*, 12 vols [London: John Murray, 1973–82], I, p. 158).

55   Taylor, *Bacchus*, p. 74.

I returned to bed; but grew sick and sorry once again. Took more soda-water. At last I fell into a dreary sleep. Woke, and was ill all day, till I had galloped a few miles ... I remarked in my illness the complete inertion, inaction, and destruction of my chief mental faculties. I tried to rouse them, and yet could not – and this is the *Soul!!!* I should believe that it was married to the body, if they did not sympathise so much with each other. If the one rose, when the other fell, it would be a sign that they longed for the natural state of divorce.[56]

We can infer that Byron experienced quite a number of physical consequences: sickness indicates nausea and he admits to a period of vertigo, as he slakes his raging thirst with soda water. Byron may have been less knowledgeable than Keats when it came to contemporary medical writing, but his account of physical sensations echoes those of the likes of Thomas Trotter and Arthur Stone who, in *A Practical Treatise on the Diseases of the Stomach and Digestion* (1806), notes symptoms of hangover include 'torpor of the limbs', 'palpitations' and 'sleeplessness', all of which Byron experiences.[57]

During his hangovers Byron occasionally responds in ways that suggest penitence and even evidence of resolutions – if not quite for moral amendment then certainly as a form of self-improvement. Strenuous exercise makes the body a site of punishment or self-flagellation. In this case Byron goes horse riding, at other times he exercised through swimming or a period of self-imposed abstinence, 'temperance and exercise', which he claims 'I have practiced at times, and for a long time together vigorously and violently'.[58] Byron's consumption of soda-water in Italy, mixed from salts that he often requested be sent from England, could qualify, on the other hand, as a brand of Withdrawal-Relief and he described their effect as that of 'a temporary inebriation, like light champagne'.[59] However, if both reactions feature in Byron's account of his hangover, his oscillation between the two – recalling Coleridge's 'Progress of Vice' – is less troubling to him than the lack of correlation between sensation and the perception of punishment that is a major part of his experience of dejection. All that can be said is that his feelings outstrip ordinary

56   Marchand (ed.), *Byron's Letters and Journals*, VIII, p. 51.
57   Arthur Daniel Stone, *A Practical Treatise on the Diseases of the Stomach and Digestion* (London: Cadell and Davies, 1806), pp. 109–10.
58   Marchand (ed.), *Byron's Letters and Journals*, VIII, p. 15.
59   Marchand (ed.), *Byron's Letters and Journals*, VIII, p. 16.

dejection and seem to derive from obscure personal failings rather than external sources.

In the description of his Ravenna hangover, it is not clear whether the word 'ill' relates to body or mind. Equally, the sorriness that accompanies Byron's sensations of sickness does not appear to be remedied as straight-forwardly as his thirst. In Chapter 1, I argued that, far from uncloud the intoxicated mind, the hangover has its own irrationality. What most disturbs Byron is the claimed inertia of his 'mental faculties' – despite his black humour about the 'natural state of divorce' of body and soul – and a complete inability to raise his mood. Byron experiences an excessive depression, but the consumption of alcohol cannot wholly account for the degree of his emotional and bodily inertia. Neither does it lead to a conventional expression of penitence. The aftermath of the Gambas' party is part of a larger pattern. At the age of 32 Byron claimed that he nearly always woke in low spirits, 'which I have invariably done for many years'.[60] He knew that alcohol made him highly emotional, as when he wrote to Elizabeth Pigot about the choirboy John Edleston's departure from Cambridge 'with a bottle of Claret in my Head, & tears in my eyes', or admitted that wine and spirits often made him 'sullen and savage to ferocity'.[61] The effects of hangovers on his moods were more disturbing because he felt they revealed a level of dejection that he could not readily explain.

Writing in his journal he wonders whether this is all hypochondria; in other words, psychosomatic:

> I have been considering what can be the reason why I always wake, at a certain hour in the morning, and always in very bad spirits – I may say in actual despair and despondency, in all respects – even of that which pleased me over night. In about an hour or two, this goes off, and I compose either to sleep again, or, at least, to quiet. In England, five years ago, I had the same kind of hypochondria.[62]

Byron expresses 'languor corresponding to the previous excitation' of his nerves through alcohol that MacNish discerns in the hangover – what pleased overnight causes despair by morning – and yet this is not a complete correspondence and leaves open possibilities of a more nebulous source of suffering that, *pace* Freud, cannot be expressed other than perhaps in the moans and groans of Keats's man of suffering. If

---

60   Marchand (ed.), *Byron's Letters and Journals*, VIII, pp. 15–16.
61   Marchand (ed.), *Byron's Letters and Journals*, VIII, p. 16.
62   Marchand (ed.), *Byron's Letters and Journals*, VIII, p. 42.

the hangover provides Byron with an opportunity for self-reflection, self-knowledge, at least of a Wordsworthian kind, is not forthcoming or is, at best, provisional. Instead, Byron gives the impression of being imprisoned within himself unable to say exactly what is wrong, his increased sensitivity apparently demonstrating a peculiar absence of feeling. Hangover consciousness indicates the self's incapacity to find emotional compensation for alcohol's assault on body and mind and the likelihood of Byron glutting his sorrow on a morning rose is slim. Then again, blunted affect and apathy appear to be less problematic for inhibiting a proper penitential sense of guilt and remorse than for bringing to light self-inflicted obstructions to feeling.

Apologies: Confessors and Egotists

Keats and Byron represent hangovers that obstruct attempts to validate the self in ways other than those we have previously witnessed in a Traditional-Punishment response. Wordsworth is different, but then his reflections on the hangover are retrospective. All this does not mean that Romantic writers did not attempt to apologise for their drunkenness, and Coleridge's correspondence shows that he was no stranger to the written apology following nights of indiscretion. As Taylor notes, Coleridge often wrote letters of apology to the hosts of drinking parties whom he had offended, promising to make amends, vowing to Daniel Stuart, for example, 'entire abstinence from Spirits' in future, and owning to J. J. Morgan 'hauntings of Regret' for his 'sottish Despondency'.[63] Shame prompts Coleridge to attempt to make amends for wrongdoing and restore good social relations, but it was Burns who turned the letter of hungover apology into an art form. As a prelude to discussing the more formalised apology of the drunkard's confession adopted by Charles Lamb it is worth pausing over.

In the letter of 1791 to his drinking companion Robert Ainslie, quoted above, Burns demonstrates how expressions of penitence cannot always be neatly separated from contrasting reactions such as self-pity or excuse. The subjective response to social judgements on drinking is a complex business that might even throw the sincerity of expressions of contrition into doubt. This problem is set out more fully in a letter to Maria Riddel, composed at some point during the festive season of 1793/94. On this occasion, the source of Burns's anxiety is quite

---

63   E. L. Griggs (ed.), *Unpublished Letters of Samuel Taylor Coleridge*, 2 vols (New Haven, CT: Yale University Press, 1933), II, pp. 51, 57.

specific: at a party Burns was discussing the Rape of the Sabine Women and apparently acted it out to a horrified Elizabeth Riddel: 'rough behaviour', according to one euphemistic Victorian editor.[64] The letter Burns composed the following morning is presented as an epistle from the dead to the living, demonstrating the way that the anxiety and guilt that gnaws at his mind produces not only feelings of contrition but also hints at factors that might complicate both amendment and the acquisition of self-knowledge:

Madam, I daresay that this is the first epistle you ever received from this nether world. I write you from the regions of hell, amid the horrors of the damned. The time and manner of my leaving your earth I do not exactly know, as I took my departure in the heat of a fever of intoxication, contracted at your too hospitable mansion; but, on my arrival here, I was fairly tried, and sentenced to endure the purgatorial tortures of this infernal confine for the space of ninety-nine years, eleven months, and twenty-nine days, and all on account of the impropriety of my conduct yesternight under your roof. Here am I, laid on a bed of pitiless furze, with my aching head reclined on a pillow of ever-piercing thorn, while an infernal tormentor, wrinkled, and old, and cruel – his name I think is Recollection – with a whip of scorpions, forbids peace or rest to approach me, and keeps anguish eternally awake. Still, Madam, if I could in any measure be reinstated in the good opinion of the fair circle whom my conduct last night so much injured, I think it would be an alleviation to my torments. For this reason I trouble you with this letter. To the men of the company I will make no apology. Your husband, who insisted on my drinking more than I chose, has no right to blame me; and the other gentlemen were partakers of my guilt. But to you, Madam, I have much to apologize. Your good opinion I valued as one of the greatest acquisitions I had made on earth, and I was truly a beast to forfeit it. There was a Miss I too, a woman of fine sense, gentle and unassuming manners – do make, on my part, a miserable d-mned wretch's best apology to her. A Mrs. G – , a charming woman, did me the honour to be prejudiced in my favour; this makes me hope that I have not outraged her beyond all forgiveness. To all the other ladies please present my humblest contrition for my conduct, and my petition for their gracious pardon. O all ye powers of decency

---

64   *Poems Songs and Letters Being the Complete Works of Robert Burns*, ed. Alexander Smith (London: MacMillan and Co., 1868), p. 540.

and decorum! whisper to them that my errors, though great, were involuntary – that an intoxicated man is the vilest of beasts – that it was not in my nature to be brutal to any one – that to be rude to a woman, when in my senses, was impossible with me – but –

*****

Regret! Remorse! Shame! ye three hellhounds that ever dog my steps and bay at my heels, spare me! spare me! Forgive the offences, and pity the perdition of, Madam,

Your humble Slave, R. B.[65]

Once again, Burns's sentiments recall the association of the hangover with damnation in the Puritan sermon, or the purgatorial sense of a sinner awaiting judgement. He expresses penitence sincerely in parts, although there is such vividness and relish in the delivery that the authenticity of these expressions is rendered doubtful. There is also a social aspect to be considered: Burns only rehearses sentiments proper to a gentleman.

The mind, or 'Recollection' in this case, no doubt exacerbates physical torment, which Burns parades in exaggerated fashion. Self-flagellation and penitent's rhetoric join signs of deep humiliation to those of self-justification. Bodily suffering is deployed to prove his remorse, and yet that hints at literary flourishes that draw the expression of feeling into question in not dissimilar fashion to the examples I discussed in Keats's *Endymion*. The proper penitential sense of Burns's misconduct is expressed by his overt desire to make amends, to 'be reinstated in the good opinion of the fair circle whom my conduct last night so much injured', which is how the normative Traditional-Punishment response functions. Yet, that is not an amendment made without qualifications as Burns makes it clear that his apology does not apply to the men of the drinking party. Moreover, Burns's apology is further qualified by his tendency to dissociate himself from his misdemeanours: alcohol momentarily altered not only his customary behaviour but his character. The actions 'were involuntary ... not in my nature'.

Far from being a straightforward letter of apology written when hungover, Burns's epistle to Mrs Riddel suggests both prosaic and more existential problems in accounting for bodily and emotional suffering and moral inadequacy. The mixture of contrition and defiance hints at inconsistent, perhaps even irreconcilable, aspects in Burns's character

65   Ross Roy (ed.), *Burns's Letters*, II, pp. 271–72.

that qualify social reconnection. The idea that remorse expressed during the hangover is inauthentic, or only temporary, muddled by the tendency of intense self-reflection to drift into egotism, and that the hangover may even obstruct pledges of penitence, is a particular feature of Lamb's 'Confessions of a Drunkard'.

'Confessions' was first published as an anonymous essay in the *Philanthropist* magazine in 1813, before being reprinted a year later in Montagu's *Some Enquiries*. Here it was advertised as the composition of 'a Water Drinker', but Lamb finally put his name to the 'Confessions' in 1822, when the essay appeared in the *London Magazine*. He also added a disclaimer, in response to allegations published in the *Quarterly* that the account was autobiographical, that this was a work of fiction. The confession later became anthologised as one of the *Last Essays of Elia*. Charles Robert Leslie argued that the 'Confessions' 'greatly exaggerate[s] any habits of excess he may have indulged. The regularity of his attendance at the India House ... prove[s] that he never could have been a drunkard', although Lamb's reputation preceded him.[66]

In his correspondence Lamb often ponders his embarrassing behaviour when drunk. Following one invitation to dine at the house of the Reverend Henry Carey, the apparent earnestness of Lamb's tone makes his sentiments, and drunken actions, comical or at least difficult to condemn, his verboseness disarming any grudge:

> I protest I know not in what words to invest my sense of the shameful violation of hospitality, which I was guilty of on that fatal Wednesday. Let it be blotted from the calendar. Had it been committed at a layman's house, say a merchant's or manufacturer's, a cheesemonger's or greengrocer's, or, to go higher, a barrister's, a member of Parliament's, a rich banker's, I should have felt alleviation, a drop of self-pity. But to be seen deliberately to go out of the house of a clergyman drunk! A clergyman of the Church of England too![67]

This is penitent's rhetoric, but it is able to convey deep feelings of humiliation mixed with jokiness – 'the house of a clergyman drunk!' The letter serves the purpose of making amendment, written in the hope that it will reinstate Lamb in the clergyman's regard, but the hangover

---

66   Charles Robert Leslie, *Autobiographical Recollections*, 2 vols (London: John Murray, 1860), I, p. 54.

67   Charles Lamb, *Selected Writings*, ed. J. E. Morpurgo (New York: Routledge, 2003), p. 74.

gives a perspective on the drunken events that incorporates both shame and levity. As in the case of Burns, the hangover presents an experience that forces reappraisal of the individual but, in calling out for articulation, there is a pleasure in articulating it well and with precision.

E. W. Marrs records that 'throughout his manhood there were periods, often of stress, in which [Lamb] drank excessively'.[68] One such period led to a hangover recounted by Henry Crabb Robinson. Lamb had departed Enfield for Chancery Lane in 1832, having once more placed his sister Mary in an asylum. He 'drank more in one day than in any other in his life'. 'Having told [Edward] Moxon that, he ... implored Moxon to come out to restrain him. Lamb became drunk at a dinner party that included Emma [Moxon] and [Henry Crabb] Robinson at the Talfourds'.' Lamb attempted to employ Moxon as a chaperone, but the effort proved fruitless:

> He slept there in his clothes that night and the next and, not knowing what else to do, went to pound on Robinson's door on the two following mornings. 'Yet in the midst of this half-crazy irregularity,' Robinson recorded on May 28, 1832, 'he was so full of sensibility that speaking of his sister he had tears in his eyes – and he talked about his favourite poems with his usual warmth, praising Andrew Marvell extravagantly.'[69]

Lamb's tears and manic behaviour at Crabb Robinson's show a less controlled response to the hangover than in the letter to Carey. They give some flavour of his theatrical conduct, but mostly indicate his inability to control his emotions when drunk or hungover. Crabb Robinson's report depicts Lamb as a problem drinker whose hangovers led him to highly emotional, at times irrational, outbursts and unpredictability, but in 'Confessions' this kind of reaction is almost indistinguishable from the sense of perspective in the letter to Carey making it tortuously difficult to place the real sentiments of the confessor.

The aim of religious confession is atonement and pardon whereby the penitent comes to self-knowledge as a sinner. Susan M. Levin argues that in the Romantic period the purpose of confession became more secular in nature. Prompted by Rousseau's posthumously published *Confessions* (1782), attention is transferred from the search for absolution to an examination of past actions and 'an attempt to set out a personal

---

68   Intro. to *The Letters of Charles and Mary Lamb: Letters of Charles Lamb, 1796–1801*, ed. Edwin Wilson Marrs, 3 vols (Ithaca, NY and London: Cornell University Press, 1975), I, p. lvi.

69   Marrs (ed.), *Lamb Letters*, I, p. lvi.

identity' where 'in analysing what he has done wrong by examining his past and present existence, the confessor will' look for 'pardon through self-knowledge', but will come to understand that such knowledge is always provisional.[70] Lamb's 'Confessions' do not eschew the possibility of amendment, but they do dramatise the bodily and mental suffering that problematises statements of contrition and the drunkard's capacity, or willingness, to reform.

Lamb's drunkard pulls no punches in parading his bodily suffering. Drink has ruined his constitution and he is unable to stomach water: 'my waking stomach rejects it'. His thirst becomes a subject of dreams: 'I can sometimes fancy thy cool refreshment purling over my burning tongue.'[71] If his hangovers draw his attention firstly to somatic symptoms, however, they quickly come to signify problems of cognition:

> Twelve years ago, I was possessed of a healthy frame of mind and body. I was never strong, but I think my constitution (for a weak one) was as happily exempt from the tendency to any malady as it was possible to be. I scarce knew what it was to ail anything. Now, except when I am losing myself in a sea of drink, I am never free from those uneasy sensations in head and stomach, which are so much worse to bear than any definite pains or aches.[72]

The drunkard's resort to Withdrawal-Relief is a reaction to a cluster of negative pains that cannot be definitely assigned to the body and yet seem to find expression there. Free-floating impressions, or 'sensations', fill his hungover mornings with depression that leads to suicidal fantasies: 'the first feeling which besets me, after stretching out the hours of recumbence to their last possible extent, is a forecast of the wearisome day that lies before me, with a secret wish that I could have lain on still, or never waked'. Connected thought proves difficult, penning his confession an act of will that only serves as a 'poor abstract' of his condition.[73] The drunkard confesses to physical infirmity, frayed nerves and attributes this to his drinking and yet, like Byron, retains a sense of elusive reasons for such a heightened state of melancholy: 'I perpetually catch myself in tears, for any cause, or none.'[74]

70   Susan M. Levin, *The Romantic Art of Confession: De Quincey, Musset, Sand, Lamb, Hogg, Frémy, Soulié, Janin* (Columbia, SC: Camden House, 1998), p. 3.
71   Charles Lamb, *The Essays of Elia* (London: Grant Richards, 1901), p. 348.
72   Lamb, *Elia*, p. 349.
73   Lamb, *Elia*, p. 349.
74   Lamb, *Elia*, p. 350.

Social factors that exacerbate shamefulness include his inability to work effectively due to his increasingly nervous condition: 'Business ... now wearies, affrights, perplexes me.' Unable to control his moods he experiences paranoia: 'I fancy all sorts of discouragements.'[75] But most incapacitating of all is the drunkard's attempts to repent and reform, which produces a nightmarish vision of alcoholic withdrawal:

> Begin a reformation, and custom will make it easy. But what if the beginning be dreadful, the first steps not like climbing a mountain but going through fire? What if the whole system must undergo a change violent as that which we conceive of the mutation of form in some insects? What if a process comparable to flaying alive be to be gone through?[76]

What has hitherto not been stated sufficiently clearly about 'Confessions of a Drunkard' is that it is a document that demonstrates the impediments that the hangover places in the way of the drunkard's capacity to reform, rather than the prospect of the delights associated with inebriety. Lamb shifts the focus of confession from an expression of amendment to a study of the somatic and psychological pains of the hangover.

However, the process of composition undoubtedly entails something of an exaltation, rather than diminishment, of the self that suggests Romantic theatricality. During a period of penitence, writing with a hangover, with 'tears trickling down [his] cheeks', the drunkard asks not for forgiveness but for sympathy. If the drunkard finds his own capacity to feel destroyed, his pitiable condition begs sympathetic reciprocity in his reader: 'O pause, thou sturdy moralist, thou person of stout nerves and a strong head.' He entreats 'compassion' and 'human allowance'.[77] The ghastly physical mutation required for reform is too great for contemplation and, if he admits to 'a sense of shame', acceptance of responsibility is displaced onto his constitutional weakness as a 'nervous' man not blessed like those with 'robust heads and iron insides'. Fears at becoming 'an object of compassion' demonstrate a high level of shame-proneness and yet responsibility is further displaced onto the role that 'men of boisterous spirits' played in leading a man 'of no original indisposition to goodness' into self-destructive habits. When 'protesting friends, a weeping wife, and

75   Lamb, *Elia*, p. 349.
76   Lamb, *Elia*, p. 342.
77   Lamb, *Elia*, pp. 344, 342.

a reprobating world' are insufficient to instil the proper penitential sense, what remains is the simple confession of feeling or, and worse than this, the loss of feeling.[78]

Lamb shows how a drunkard is a figure of incongruous, at times irrational, elements. He might come to face such insurmountable emotional and physical suffering during his hangovers that he *cannot* make amends even if he can see full well that he has transgressed socially acceptable behaviour and values and understands this to be wrong. At the same time, the accountability expressed is continually rendered doubtful by the drunkard's havering character and penchant for flamboyant displays of emotion. The act of composition suggests a degree of self-control, verging on self-absorption, that the content of the confession belies. Pardon is partly an issue of increased self-knowledge, partly a result of engaging a sympathetic ear, partly an acknowledgement of wrongdoing, but manifestly not a reliable pledge of reformation.

Romantic depictions of hangovers show continuities with examples from earlier periods, particularly the rhetorical aspects that owe much to the Protestant hangover literature of the seventeenth century, but also significant differences. The factors that problematise Lamb's reconnection with social values and compound the drunkard's suffering demonstrate how a Traditional-Punishment hangover response is complicated by Romantic uncertainties about the self. These are affected by the complex interplay of heightened and diminished susceptibility to negative affect, a persistent impression of an abstract sense of dread and the usual somatic symptoms of a hangover. It is the kind of interplay to which literature can guide us that I earlier argued is largely missing from quantitative data research. In that sense, Lamb's 'Confession' should be considered as a product of Romantic attitudes to alcohol and to partake of the same kind of motifs of self-inflicted dejection that we find in the poetry of Burns, Coleridge, Keats and Byron. Romantic literature has taught us that hangovers are periods of dejection that encourage a heightened awareness of interiority, which can be productive of self-knowledge, although they just as regularly inhibit its communication. Hungover poets expressed alternative ways to validate their experience, although with different degrees of success, frequently drifting between seeming genuinely and inauthentically penitent. Romantic literature is characterised by the turn within, but the greater impression of abstract misery and irreconcilable complexities, distinguishes its hangovers and adds weight

---

78   Lamb, *Elia*, p. 346.

to the argument that this turn sometimes brings with it a nagging awareness of a deep sense of breakage rather than the compensation of greater self-knowledge.

Chapter 5

Moral Sensitivity and the Mind: Tired and Emotional Victorians

Introduction

The Victorian period is often remembered as a morally severe one, associated with rectitude, propriety and self-help. This was especially true when it came to alcohol. Issues of temperance and teetotalism dominated writing about alcohol in Britain and America as the nineteenth century progressed. Drunkards, such as those we find in George Cruikshank's *The Bottle* (1847), were demonised and moral judgements often carry the same force that we saw in the culture wars of the seventeenth century, another period notable for its austerity when it came to the subject of drink. As we might expect, the Victorian period is therefore a fertile one for hangovers that highlight a variety of reasons to feel ashamed for excessive drinking, including negligence of health and social duties, disregard of familial and professional obligations.

However, literature of the Romantic period, as we have just seen, had brought greater attention to the complexity of the inner life of the drinker, largely through the depiction of hangovers in poetry that muddied distinctions between sensation and perception. As the nineteenth century progressed, the realist novel, with its scope for lengthy description and psychological precision in characterisation, replaced poetry as the dominant form of literature and it is here we find Victorian writers developing their own insights into the constituents that make up what this book has referred to as a Traditional-Punishment response to a hangover. Informed by enhanced medical understanding of drunkenness, led by the research of Robert MacNish, which I examined briefly in Chapter 4, and subsequently Alexander Peddie and Norman Kerr, who demonstrated more clearly than before the damaging effects of heavy drinking on the body and nervous system, novelists such as Charles Dickens, Anne Brontë and George Eliot began to 'recognise and preserve the complex humanity of the alcoholic',[1] as Thomas Gilmore has it, as a response to the 'shift in the valence of alcohol ... from a register of intoxication to one of addiction'.[2] Very little attention has, however, been paid to how this was achieved through Victorian depictions of hangovers, even in the scholarly accounts of nineteenth-century drinking by the likes of Henry Yeomans and Thora Hands.[3] In this chapter, we will find that studying hangover literature enhances and refines our understanding of the psychological experience of Victorian drinkers.

However, even as Victorian medicine was clarifying the etiology of problem drinkers, it left gaps and indeterminacy when moving beyond the study of physiology, which is where I have argued hangovers become most personally and culturally interesting. Hence, in Brontë's *The Tenant of Wildfell Hall* (1848), when Helen Huntingdon upbraids her dissolute husband, Arthur, after an evening of riot and debauchery with his cronies, following which he is characteristically 'sick and stupid', she worries that, despite his promise that his drunken antics 'should never again be repeated', 'he is losing the little self-command and self-respect he once possessed' as he turns to the hair of the dog.[4] Brontë indicates that the reason for a drinker's loss of control around alcohol involves more than just feelings of sickness and stupidity: the hangover says something more deeply troubling about Arthur's character; about a loss of respect for the self that emerges from his particular habitus to which physical symptoms contribute but about which they cannot wholly speak. I will propose that analysing the hangovers of tired and emotional figures such as Arthur Huntingdon is one way of exploring the moral standards to which Victorian drinkers were held. I do not confine myself wholly to hangovers of characters who are losing control of their drinking habits like Huntingdon – the hangovers of the likes of Dickens's David Copperfield and Thomas Hardy's Jude Fawley that I analyse below belong to neophytes in comparison – but, in keeping with the age, the compulsive drinker takes centre stage.

---

1   Thomas B. Gilmore, *Equivocal Spirits: Alcoholism and Drinking in Twentieth-Century Literature* (Chapel Hill: University of North Carolina Press, 1987), p. 8.

2   Marty Roth, *Drunk the Night Before: An Anatomy of Intoxication* (Minneapolis and London: University of Minnesota Press, 2005), p. xiii.

3   Henry Yeomans, *Alcohol and Moral Regulation: Public Attitudes, Spirited Measures and Victorian Hangovers* (Bristol and Chicago, IL: Policy Press, 2014); Thora Hands, *Drinking in Victorian and Edwardian Britain: Beyond the Spectre of the Drunkard* (London: Palgrave Macmillan, 2018).

4   Anne Brontë, *The Tenant of Wildfell Hall*, ed. G. D. Hargreaves (Harmondsworth: Penguin, 1979), p. 291.

The chapter focuses first on some examples of moral sensitivity in the novels of Dickens, and related temperance narratives by Ellen Wood and T. S. Arthur, which are expressed through Traditional-Punishment responses that engage with early nineteenth-century medical understanding of alcohol's effects on the body. These help remind us of the ways in which a drinker's body is rarely just a physical body and carries with it social judgement. The chapter proceeds to argue that, by mid-century, new ideas concerning compulsive behaviour and the impact of alcohol on the mind saw Wood and Anne Brontë seek ways to express the emotional complexity of the drunkard, developing the sense of objectless misery or hangxiety we saw become increasingly prevalent in hangover literature in the Romantic period. In the final part of the chapter I will propose, through readings of Eliot's *Janet's Repentance* (1857) and Hardy's *Jude the Obscure* (1895), that, while the Victorian period is still often viewed as morally severe, its literature that tackled drunkenness was just as concerned with exploring the psychological impact of moral judgements on drunkards as in passing them.

Dickens, Medicalisation and the Moral Body

That drunkenness is a state frequently associated with loss of self-awareness and self-control, particularly regarding the mind's ability to coordinate the body, almost goes without saying. Slurred speech and stumbling are twin hallmarks of the comic drunken figure in literature stretching right back to the Sileni of Greek drama.[5] Cathy Shrank observes that drunkenness is commonly viewed as robbing humans of 'reason, speech and a conscience'.[6] Perpetuating the stereotype of the stumbling, stuttering drunkard, *Punch* magazine, in one of their series of *Letters to His Son*, mischievously counsels a young man to control his level of alcohol intake through reference to a kind of body/mind reciprocity: 'A man may be knee-drunk – hip-drunk – shoulder-drunk – nay chin-drunk; but the wine should be allowed to rise no higher.' Any further would affect the brain and therefore the 'fine fluency of speech'.[7]

5   See Helene E. Roberts (ed.), *Encyclopedia of Comparative Iconography: Themes Depicted in Works of Art* (Chicago, IL: Fitzroy Dearborn, 1998), p. 265.
6   Cathy Shrank, 'Beastly Metamorphoses: Losing Control in Early Modern Literary Culture', in *Intoxication and Society: Problematic Pleasures of Drugs and Alcohol*, ed. Jonathan Herring *et al* (London: Palgrave Macmillan, 2012), p. 195 (pp. 193–209).
7   Douglas Jerrold, *Punch's Letters to His Son, Corrected and Edited from the Mss. in the Alsatian Library* (London: Wm. S. Orr & Co., 1843), p. 136.

In *David Copperfield* (1850), Dickens depicts his titular character's first
drunken experience in which the wine rises a little too high, leading
to a hangover. Dickens is at pains to demonstrate the full array of
bodily and mental signs of disturbance as Copperfield loses his ability
to exert control over sensory and emotional discordance and the mind's
sovereignty is thrown into question by the experience of intoxication,
but more so by the excruciating hangover. Copperfield spends an evening
of excess with his friend Steerforth, during which he records recklessly
passing 'the wine faster and faster … continually starting up with a
corkscrew to open more wine, long before any was needed', which leads
to somatic and mental disarray. That the wine has gone beyond knees,
shoulders and chin and reached his intellectual faculties is underlined
when Copperfield announces (in two words) 'Steerforthyou'retheguidin
gstarofmyexis tence': a memorable example of slurred drunken speech.[8]
Dickens renders the feelings of disassociation as Copperfield loses control
of his executive functioning, failing to recognise himself in the drunkard
who leaves the festive group to take a breath of fresh air: 'Somebody was
leaning out of my bedroom window, refreshing his forehead against the
cool stone of the parapet, and feeling the air upon his face. It was myself.
I was addressing myself as "Copperfield", and saying, "Why did you try
to smoke? You might have known you couldn't do it."' Copperfield's eyes
have 'a vacant appearance', he looks 'pale' and is surprised to find 'my
hair – only my hair, nothing else – looked drunk'.[9] Intoxication inhibits
his ability to rationalise the experience and Steerforth eventually guides
Copperfield to bed, where the loss of bodily and mental control gradually
merges into a hangover.

Copperfield's hangover consciousness is of an acute variety, his
waking moments redolent of Feldman Barrett's theory of 'constructed
emotion':

> I stepped at once out of the box-door into my bedroom, where only
> Steerforth was with me, helping me to undress, and where I was
> by turns telling him that Agnes was my sister, and adjuring him
> to bring the corkscrew, that I might open another bottle of wine
> … somebody, lying in my bed, lay saying and doing all this over
> again, at cross purposes, in a feverish dream all night – the bed
> a rocking sea that was never still! How, as that somebody slowly
> settled down into myself, did I begin to parch, and feel as if my

8   Charles Dickens, *David Copperfield*, ed. Jerome H. Buckley (New York and London:
     Norton, 1990), p. 307.
9   Dickens, *Copperfield*, p. 308.

outer covering of skin were a hard board; my tongue the bottom of an empty kettle, furred with long service, and burning up over a slow fire; the palms of my hands, hot plates of metal which no ice could cool!

But the agony of mind, the remorse, and shame I felt when I became conscious next day! My horror of having committed a thousand offences I had forgotten, and which nothing could ever expiate – my recollection of that indelible look which Agnes had given me – the torturing impossibility of communicating with her, not knowing, Beast that I was, how she came to be in London, or where she stayed – my disgust of the very sight of the room where the revel had been held – my racking head – the smell of smoke, the sight of glasses, the impossibility of going out, or even getting up! Oh, what a day it was![10]

With returning sobriety – and the somatic aftershocks of inebriety – Copperfield signals resumption of his first-person narration as 'somebody' transitions into 'I'. Typically, the first things to tell the tale of the previous evening's indiscretions are the symptoms of the hangover assigned to the body in the form of dizziness and nausea. These modulate into thirst, sensations of heat and cold, headache and sickness, particularly at the smell of stale cigar smoke. They show that Dickens was undoubtedly largely influenced by his reading of MacNish, who gives a detailed account of what he calls the 'fit of drunkenness' and the subsequent hangover in *The Anatomy of Drunkenness* (1827).[11]

'When the drunkard is first put to bed', writes MacNish, 'then begins the "tug of war"',

> then comes the misery which is doomed to succeed his previous raptures. No sooner is his head laid upon the pillow than it is seized with the strongest throbbing. His heart beats quick and hard against the ribs. A noise like the distant fall of a cascade, or rushing of a river, is heard in his ears: sough – sough – sough, goes the sound. His senses now become more drowned and stupefied.

---

10   Dickens, *Copperfield*, pp. 309–10.
11   Makras Kostas has already demonstrated that Dickens's depictions of inebriates, such as Master Warden in *The Drunkard's Death* (1836) (one of the *Sketches by Boz*), closely follow the Scottish surgeon's accounts of the appearance of chronic drinkers. 'Dickensian Intemperance: The Representation of the Drunkard in "The Drunkard's Death" and *The Pickwick Papers*', *19: Interdisciplinary Studies in the Long Nineteenth Century*, 10 (2010), pp. 1–18. Nobody has previously noticed that Dickens's depiction of Copperfield's hangover also derives from MacNish.

> A dim recollection of his carousals, like a shadowy and indistinct dream, passes before the mind. He still hears, as in echo, the cries and laughter of his companions. His giddiness is greater than ever; and he feels as if in a ship tossed upon a heaving sea.[12]

Anticipations of Copperfield's experience of being in a 'feverish dream', the confusion of his state of mind, but also the way that unwelcome physical motion is rendered through the sound and movement of water are striking. In both cases boundaries between self and world, body and mind, are indistinct: MacNish's 'sough – sough – sough' and 'giddiness' is a physiological condition sometimes known as 'the spins', but is attributed to the bed – which is a 'rocking' or 'heaving' sea – rather than to its real cause which is disruption of the inner ear. The hangover follows in unmistakable fashion:

> In the morning he awakes in a high fever. The whole body is parched; the palms of the hands, in particular, are like leather. His head is often violently painful. He feels excessive thirst; while his tongue is white, dry, and stiff. The whole inside of the mouth is likewise hot and constricted, and the throat often sore. Then look at his eyes – how sickly, dull, and languid! The fire, which first lighted them up the evening before, is all gone. A stupor like that of the last stage of drunkenness still clings about them, and they are disagreeably affected by the light. The complexion sustains a great change: it is no longer flushed with the gayety and excitation, but pale and wayworn, indicating a profound mental and bodily exhaustion. There is probably sickness, and the appetite is totally gone. Even yet the delirium of intoxication has not left him, for his head still rings, his heart still throbs violently; and if he attempts getting up, he stumbles with giddiness.[13]

Somatic after-effects, combined with those experienced overnight, can be duly ticked off against Penning, McKinney and Verster's measure of hangover severity that I have previously cited (Fig. 1.2): Thirst, Dry mouth, Sweating, Headache, Apathy, Photo-sensitivity, Weakness, Dizziness, Balance problems, Vertigo, Reduced appetite, Nausea, Vomiting, Palpitations, Heart pounding. There is no self-command over gross – let alone fine – motor functions, as the body undergoes tremors. Even

---

12   Robert MacNish, *The Anatomy of Drunkenness* (New York: Appleton, 1827), pp. 22–23.
13   MacNish, *Anatomy*, p. 23.

standing up becomes problematic, while the major organs – brain, heart, liver, stomach – and the nervous system produce uncomfortable by-products from working overtime to reassert order.

MacNish gives the hangover a new diagnostic precision that it lacked in earlier medical writing. However, there is no doubt that Dickens develops his source material into an account replete with social and moral commentary, reminding us that the categories that science uses to measure hangover symptoms only reveal part of the experience. Dickens depicts the mind's struggle to rationalise sensations – its hangover consciousness – before they resolve themselves into recognisable feelings of shame and remorse. Along with feelings of illness, Copperfield experiences a powerful sense of personal diminishment, or loss of self-respect, in terms of his embarrassment for his loss of inhibition around Agnes Wickfield (who eventually becomes Copperfield's second wife). Just as drunkenness was manifested in a strange self-division, so, in his hangover, Copperfield addresses himself as the 'Other': 'Beast that I was', socially intolerable. Physical sensations eventually become an index of his self-disgust, forming part of an experience that is foundational in establishing Copperfield's understanding of the importance that self-worth, built upon self-reliance, will play in his social progress and in his future relationship with Agnes.

It is noticeable, however, that Dickens's choice of imagery subtly contests the suggestion of a full return to the self – that the conversion from the third to first person of the passage supposes – through references to a series of inanimate domestic objects: Copperfield's skin is a 'hard board', redolent of MacNish's drunkard's leathery hands, his tongue like the limestone furring up an unclean kettle and the palms of his hands 'hot plates of metal'. The description is not just about bodily suffering but about the twinning of physical and moral varieties of self-disgust – reminiscent of the hangover of Kingsley Amis's Jim Dixon – the latter reified in the unbearable filth of the room and glasses, which disavow Copperfield's ability to resume proper control of his person.

If anything, the hungover body is just as alien as it was on the previous night, it is only that the semantics are drawn from a different field. Dickens captures the unpleasant sensations of a hangover, but indicates they cannot be prised apart from the damage done to Copperfield's intellectual and moral faculties. Copperfield's physical suffering appears to be merited punishment for his shame concerning Agnes: thoughts on that topic run beyond his control, signalled by the kind of hyperbolic maudlin utterances about 'a thousand offences' and 'torturing impossibility' that we saw characterise the penitent's rhetoric of the Romantic period. Here, however, sincerity is not in doubt and Dickens shows that repairing the damaged ego involves making social amends, which can be just as momentous a job as embarking on a physical recovery.

MacNish noted that most drinkers he had studied found that hangovers prompted expressions of remorse and new regard for self-restraint of the kind we find in *David Copperfield*: '[The drinker] is sorry for his conduct, promises solemnly never again so to commit himself, and calls impatiently for something to quench his thirst.'[14] The Traditional-Punishment response is a reaction to a socio-cultural context where moral worth is measured by self-control. As Steven Earnshaw puts it, the drunkard of the nineteenth century is told they 'must re-connect' with a 'stable self', 'in reaction to the imperatives of "society," "family" and "duty"' if they are to reform.[15] But what constitutes a 'stable self' in this kind of context? As we learned in Chapter 4, the hangover raises issues of self-division and throws into doubt the mind's capacity to control the body, the inner life of the drinker suggesting a degree of emotional suffering that can make social re-connection an uninviting prospect.

Copperfield pulls through his trial, but Dickens showed elsewhere that the physical indisposition of a hangover, as Charles Lamb had previously demonstrated, might prevent penitence and the restoration of social values when it came to the complex topic of problem drinkers. The most pertinent example is perhaps the drunken father of Jenny Wren in *Our Mutual Friend* (1865). *Our Mutual Friend* is the novel in which Dickens shows most concern with the hangover, the metropolis recalling Lord Byron's 'cauldron' of 'misty mornings[s]' where all London seems to be viewed through '[a] drunken man's dead eye' (*Beppo*, 43).[16] The public house called the *Six Jolly Fellowship-Porters*, for example, is notable for the inscription on the door-posts, 'The Early Purl House', the narrator recording, 'it would seem that Purl must always be taken early.'[17] Purl was a hangover remedy in which beer was infused with gin, and Henry Mayhew gives an evocative description of the lives of the London 'purl men' in *London Labour and the London Poor* (1861–62).[18]

14   MacNish, *Anatomy*, p. 24.

15   Steven Earnshaw, 'Drink, Dissolution, Antibiography: The Existential Drinker', in Mark Hailwood and Deborah Toner (eds), *Biographies of Drink: A Case Study Approach to our Historical Relationship with Alcohol* (Newcastle-upon-Tyne: Cambridge Scholars, 2015), p. 204 (pp. 204–22).

16   Lord Byron, *The Complete Poetical Works*, ed. Jerome J. McGann, 7 vols (Oxford: Clarendon Press, 1980–93), IV.

17   Charles Dickens, *Our Mutual Friend*, ed. Stephen Gill (Harmondsworth: Penguin, repr. 1977), pp. 105–106.

18   Henry Mayhew, *London Labour and the London Poor*, 4 vols (London: Charles Griffin and Co., 1865), II, p. 108.

Jenny's dipsomaniac father is one of the victims of such drinking establishments. Dickens shows the way that drink inverts the customary hierarchy of the family as Jenny plays the role of mother or 'the person of the house' to her father whom she addresses as her 'bad child'. The old man skives and drinks, leaving Jenny to run the household and she scolds him for his lack of self-respect in scenes that evoke the spirit of the moral tracts of the temperance age:

> 'Go along with you! Go along into your corner! Get into your corner directly!'
> The wretched spectacle made as if he would have offered some remonstrance; but not venturing to resist the person of the house, thought better of it, and went and sat down on a particular chair of disgrace.
> 'Oh-h-h!' cried the person of the house, pointing her little finger, 'You bad old boy! Oh-h-h you naughty, wicked creature!'
> The shaking figure, unnerved and disjointed from head to foot, put out its two hands a little way, as making overtures of peace and reconciliation. Abject tears stood in its eyes, and stained the blotched red of its cheeks. The swollen lead-coloured under lip trembled with a shameful whine. The whole indecorous threadbare ruin, from the broken shoes to the prematurely-grey scanty hair, grovelled. Not with any sense worthy to be called a sense, of this dire reversal of the places of parent and child, but in a pitiful expostulation to be let off from a scolding.[19]

The wretched man is still crapulous, but the shaking that Dickens depicts is not just a feature of his drunkenness and gets worse when he cannot get hold of alcohol: 'the wicked old boy would whine and whimper, and would sit shaking himself into the lowest of low spirits, until such time as he could shake himself out of the house and shake another threepennyworth into himself'.[20] These tremors are accompanied by moments of delusion and paranoia, even hallucination, as the body shows the toll alcohol has taken on Jenny's father. If his moral faculties are just about intact – 'it was always on the conscience of the paralytic scarecrow that he had betrayed his sharp parent for sixty threepennyworths of rum'[21] – the physical torment of the hangover seems to

19   Charles Dickens, *OMF*, pp. 291–92.
20   Dickens, *OMF*, p. 782.
21   Dickens, *OMF*, p. 782.

no longer provide a curb to his appetites and indeed appears to reduce his capacity to make amends.

The tremors of Jenny's alcoholic father make it unclear where the ordinary physical symptoms of a hangover end and the more damaging signs of alcohol withdrawal begin. The distinction is often hazy, even in the sciences, and if the former is sometimes attributed to having too much alcohol in the system and the latter to having too little, recent medical research has proposed that the physical hangover is causally linked to withdrawal. Robert Swift and Deena Davidson explain that: 'When alcohol is removed from the body … the central nervous system and the portion of the nervous system that coordinates response to stress (i.e., the sympathetic nervous system) remain in an unbalanced "overdrive" state.' This results in '[s]ympathetic nervous system hyperactivity', which 'accounts for the tremors, sweating, and tachycardia observed in both hangover and AW [Alcohol Withdrawal] syndrome'.[22] MacNish observes that '[a] general tremor' is a consequence of the after-effects of drinking, which results from what he calls 'nervous irritability'.[23]

Unlike science, for the Victorian temperance advocate, recalling the gin prohibitionist of the previous century, a hazy division between the hangover and symptoms of more chronic withdrawal could be an advantage. Being unable to explain when one state began and the other ended, when the drinker actually lost control of his body's cravings for liquor, added to the impression, as the American temperance reformer Lyman Beecher put it, of 'the undefined nature of the crime [of drunkenness] in its early stages'.[24] Indistinctness helped to popularise the belief that one drink was one too many (it was always a problem of temperance advocates to prove that moderate drinking was as bad as habitual consumption). The notion that the hangover worsened, but was not qualitatively distinct from withdrawal, as drinking problems increased was a straightforward way of tethering the two together and suggesting that intolerance of the physical symptoms of a hangover, as Span and Earleywine have argued, might go some way to predicting addiction.[25]

22   Robert Swift and Deena Davidson, 'Alcohol Hangover: Mechanisms and Mediators', *Alcohol Health and Research World*, 22 (1998), p. 57 (pp. 54–60). See also G. Tsai, D. R. Gastfriend and J. T. Coyle, 'The Glutamatergic Basis of Human Alcoholism', *American Journal of Psychiatry*, 152.3 (1995), pp. 332–40.

23   MacNish, *Anatomy*, p. 116.

24   Lyman Beecher, *Six Sermons on the Nature, Occasions, Signs, Evils, and Remedy of Intemperance* (New York: The American Tract Society, 1827), p. 7.

25   S. A. Span and M. Earleywine, 'Familial Risk for Alcoholism and Hangover Symptoms', *Addictive Behavior*, 24.1 (Jan–Feb 1999), pp. 121–25.

It is in this sense that Dickens's depiction of Jenny's 'bad child' shares much with examples of hungover drunkards in temperance narratives. The difference lies in the fact that temperance authors generally have less interest in giving rounded psychological treatment to the drunkard – in acknowledging the complexity of their subjectivity – and more in using hangovers to chart moral deterioration. Wood's *Danesbury House* (1860), a temperance novel first written for entry into a competition run by the Scottish Temperance Society in 1859, is one such example. Robert Danesbury's encroaching alcoholism and associated moral shortcomings are traced through his worsening tremors and increasingly haggard appearance. The solicitor Mr St George, who functions as a moral commentator on the drinking of the well-heeled young men of the Danesbury family, provides an amateur rather than professional diagnosis. 'His looks and his shaking hands bespeak [addiction]. Besides, he could not be squandering away the money that he is, unless drink played its full share. I smelled it strong this morning when we were speaking to him', he tells his legal partner.[26]

Later in the novel, as alcohol takes increasing hold on his habits, Robert's hangovers noticeably worsen, as does his physical appearance and ability to conceal the shakes. Robert begins the novel as a rakish figure, but comes increasingly to disregard his personal appearance:

> Robert came in, his dress loose, and his gait slouching. Though three o'clock, it was his first appearance that day. His eyes were bloodshot, and his countenance bore the marks of his evil life. His slippers were down at heel, his coat dirty and torn, his pantaloons unbraced, and he had no collar on … Robert held his hat, which he had carried on his head into his chamber the previous night: he now essayed to place it on the table, but his hand shook, and it slipped on the floor.[27]

The shaking hand may be a less theatrical type of lost control than those associated with the often amusing stumbling of the character drunk, but it speaks volumes about the decline, in both physical and moral terms, of the drinker.

What Wood calls the marks of an 'evil life' of sustained alcoholic indulgence are similarly termed the 'corroborating signs of evil progress'

---

26   Mrs Ellen Wood, *Danesbury House*, ed. Curt Herr (Alfred, NY: Whitlock Publishing, 2009), p. 108.

27   Wood, *Danesbury House*, p. 194.

by T. S. Arthur in the temperance tale *Ten Nights in a Bar-Room* (1854).[28] Arthur's narrator, the commerical traveller Jacobs, recounts his time spent at intervals over a series of years in the American milltown Cedarville. He witnesses the deleterious effects of the new bar of Simon Slade on the inhabitants and hangover symptoms provide a way of connecting the 'Nights', explaining the declining fortunes of the landlord and other key characters such as the swindler Harvey Green. Jacobs is not privy to the harder drinking and gambling, over which a veil is drawn through the use of the bar's secret back rooms, but, like Mr St George's appraisal of Robert Danesbury, he uses the physical signs of hangovers to decipher the moral jeopardy of the inebriates:

> The landlord did not make his appearance on the next morning until nearly ten o'clock; and then he looked like a man who had been on a debauch. It was eleven before Harvey Green came down. Nothing about him indicated the smallest deviation from the most orderly habit ... he looked as if he had slept soundly on a quiet conscience.[29]

Significantly, the first act of Slade is 'to go behind the bar and take a stiff glass of brandy and water'. Green instead orders 'beefsteak and coffee for his breakfast'.[30] As MacNish remarks, 'There is nothing more indicative of health than a good appetite for breakfast; but confirmed topers, from the depraved state of their stomachs, lose all relish for this meal.'[31] MacNish notes that the greater the physical problems associated with drink, the higher the chances that a 'confirmed drunkard' will turn to Withdrawal-Relief to regain control of his body: 'When [he] awakes with a tremor, he immediately swallows a dram: the most violent shaking is quieted by this means.'[32] As his drinking worsens, so does Simon Slade's appetite and his shaking. Slade's lack of inhibition around the bottle makes him vulnerable to the more calculating Green as he turns to the hair of the dog to restore physical equilibrium.

Like Robert Danesbury, the hungover Slade's breath unmistakably attests to the nauseating taint of frequently imbibed liquor: 'His face had grown decidedly bad in expression, as well as gross and sensual. The

---

28   T. S. Arthur, *Ten Nights in a Bar-Room and What I Saw There* (Bedford, MA: Applewood Books, 2010), p. 113.
29   Arthur, *Ten Nights*, p. 134.
30   Arthur, *Ten Nights*, p. 134.
31   MacNish, *Anatomy*, p. 108.
32   MacNish, *Anatomy*, pp. 116–17.

odor of his breath, as he took a chair close to where I was sitting, was that of one who drank habitually and freely; and the red, swimming eyes evidenced, too surely, a rapid progress toward the sad condition of a confirmed inebriate.'[33] In his depiction of physical hangover symptoms, Arthur demonstrates that, like Dickens, he was familiar with the medical accounts of alcohol dependence of his day. MacNish observes: 'The breath of a drunkard is disgustingly bad, and has always a spirituous odour.' Redness of the eyes after drinking is a result of alcohol's dilation of the sclera – tiny blood vessels on the surface of the eye – that causes inflammation. It is another one of MacNish's 'corroborating signs' of the hangover that harks back to Proverbs 23:29: '[The eyes are] red and watery, and have an expression so peculiar that the cause can never be mistaken. This, and a certain want of firmness about the lips, which are loose, gross, and sensual, betray at once the toper.'[34] They betray Simon Slade on multiple occasions.

The Victorian temperance narrative is typically quick to reinforce the age's condemnation of familial, social and personal failings on chronic drinkers, but they also hint at reasons why those drinkers might lose control of their alcohol use. When Jenny Wren's father tries to give a reason for his drinking, he finds himself at a loss: '"Circumstances over which had no control," was the miserable creature's plea in extenuation.'[35] His recovery of a stable self – both physically and in terms of social reconnection – is inhibited by the severity of his hangover symptoms. It is not that he cannot understand right and wrong, but that he is no longer capable of doing right. Each night he battles his conscience, attempting to pull together the irreconcilable aspects of his character, in MacNish's 'tug-of-war': 'the bed on which Mr Dolls reposed was a bed of roses from which the flowers and leaves had entirely faded, leaving him to lie upon the thorns and stalks'.[36] The morning brings the tremors along with the 'lowest of low spirits'. But that is another matter to which my attention will now turn. Because, while the likes of Dickens and Arthur shared their knowledge of the latest medical research into the effects of drunkenness on the body, which allowed them to establish some of the socio-cultural dimensions of a Victorian hangover, others were exploring the limits of scientific inquiry when considering the effect that alcohol had on mental health.

33 Arthur, *Ten Nights*, p. 113.
34 MacNish, *Anatomy*, pp. 112, 113.
35 Dickens, *OMF*, p. 292.
36 Dickens, *OMF*, p. 782.

Dark Moods

Body/mind coaction is manifested in different ways during hangovers. If David Copperfield finds it difficult to say where body ends and thought begins, before eventually re-establishing a relatively stable sense of self, the 'bad child' has made an enemy of his body of which he no longer seems to be in control. Broadly speaking, however, each ought to be able to give a fairly clear account of his reasons for feeling ashamed and we understand that physical distress is meant to be, at least partly, an index of moral inadequacy. Dickens indicates that the ability to control alcohol use is governed by physiology *and* by the psychological response to 'cultural beliefs and social practices'.[37] However, as we saw in Chapter 4, hangovers can also muddy distinctions between body and mind, right and wrong, and a bad conscience can induce denial as often as penitence, demonstrating the complex range of responses to alcohol consumption to which the study of literature alerts us. In Victorian fiction, that range needs to be seen in the context of developing medical understanding of cognition and the mind.

We saw above that Jenny's father is described not just as trembling and flushed, but 'unnerved' as well as in the 'lowest of low spirits', which suggests something other than somatic symptoms or shame. Equally, when MacNish reflects on the 'nervous irritability' that he often discerned in problem drinkers, was he writing about body, mind or some combination of the two? In the nineteenth century, the relationship of body to mind was a complex business. 'Health', as Pamela Gilbert puts it, 'was not purely a physical affair. As the health of the body could be infected by contagion, the health of the mind could be harmed by negative impressions or "moral contagion"'.[38] William Cullen and John Brown pioneered research into the nervous system at the end of the eighteenth century, exploring the way heavy drinking and other excesses overstimulated or depressed the nerves and so the emotions. It was also the case that older concepts of the interrelation of body and mind were still current and an 'ancient humours-based theory of personality ... combined with more contemporary ideas of mood' and even the 'notion of manic-depression', according to Valerie Pedlar, although the latter term was not yet in 'general use' in the Victorian period.[39]

---

37   Herring *et al* (eds), *Intoxication and Society*, p. 2.
38   Pamela K. Gilbert, *Disease, Desire, and the Body in Victorian Women's Popular Novels* (Cambridge: Cambridge University Press, 1997), p. 53.
39   Valerie Pedlar, *'The Most Dreadful Visitation': Male Madness in Victorian Fiction* (Liverpool: Liverpool University Press, 2006), p. 137.

The health of body and mind were popularly felt to be linked, but those links, often figured through a discourse of 'nervous states' or 'nervous conditions', were, as Victoria Bates argues, a little hazy.[40] Equally, even as the largely somatic accounts of MacNish gave way to psychological studies of drinkers later in the century, there was no real medical consensus on the origins of compulsive drinking habits: although Norman Kerr defined inebriety as 'a diseased state of the brain and nervous centers, characterized by an irresistible impulse to indulge in intoxicating liquors or other narcotics, for the relief which these afford', Alexander Peddie saw alcoholism as a purely mental disease, 'symptomatic of some abnormal cerebral condition'.[41] The notion that mental or nervous disease originated in unnatural and excessive physiological stimulation – of the sort identified by Swift and Davidson – began to be reflected in fictional representations of hangovers from around the middle of the nineteenth century. Such representations also demonstrated that more than a little haziness accompanied contemporary attempts to elucidate the feelings of the morning after when it came to consideration of the drinker's emotional state.

In a straightforward way, alcohol provides a false and unsustainable high, succeeded by later depression of the spirits, as in the American novelist J. H. Ingraham's *Edward Austin* (1842), where the titular character's moodiness is attributed to precipitately sobering up:

> But Edward had not taken any wine since he had left his hotel. The intoxicating influence of that had passed off before he reached the theatre, but not so the effect. It left his mind ... in a dull, heavy humor, depressed and sullen. Cheerfulness was banished, and dark feelings reigned in his thoughts. He was irritable and sad at heart, and precisely in that crisis of temper which is most dangerous to its possessor.[42]

40 Victoria Bates, *Sexual Forensics in Victorian and Edwardian England: Age, Crime and Consent in the Courts* (Basingstoke: Palgrave Macmillan, 2016), p. 143.

41 Norman Kerr, 'President's Inaugural Address', *Proceedings of the Society for the Study and Cure of Inebriety*, 1 (April 1884), n.p.; Alexander Peddie, *The Necessity for Some Legalised Arrangements for the Treatment of Dipsomania ...* (Edinburgh: Sutherland and Knox, 1858), p. 12. MacNish had seen sufficient evidence that 'The mind [of inebriates] is ... sadly depressed, and the proceedings of the previous night are painfully remembered' (MacNish, pp. 23–24), although he was less overtly interested in psychology.

42 J. H. Ingraham, *Edward Austin; or, The Hunting Flask* (Boston, MA: F. Gleason, 1842), p. 53.

Most dangerous because it might lead to increased drunkenness or, as happens in the case of Edward who gets into a violent confrontation, behaviour considered out of character. Ingraham reflects the kind of arguments made by temperance reformers such as his countryman Beecher, who maintained that hangovers resulted not only in 'loss of appetite, nausea at the stomach, disordered bile', but also, 'lassitude and depression and melancholy'.[43] Ordinarily good men like Edward became irritable and prone to bouts of frustration and temper.

'Dark feelings' of lassitude, depression and melancholy were more nebulous and less explicable elements of the hangover experience in Victorian temperance fiction that demonstrated the complex humanity of the drunkard. The negative effect of drinking on mood is delineated, for example, in *Danesbury House* by the inebriate Mr Pratt to Mr St George, as the latter continues to probe for reasons why men lose their ability to control their consumption of alcohol. Pratt's imprecision in describing his hangover demonstrates his inability to grasp the nettle of his bleakness:

> '... You need not reproach me, Mr. St. George: when the dark mood is upon me, I reproach myself keener than anybody else can do.'
> 'What do you mean by the dark mood?'
> 'When I have not got no drink in me, sir. I was brought up, you know, a gentleman – though you may not see much remains of it about me now – and the shame, the remorse, the physical depression that overwhelm me are so great. I must of compulsion drink to drown them, even if the habit were not upon me.[44]

Of course, Wood shows that Pratt's hesitancy belies the rudiments of his inadvertently candid psychological account of the hangover. His reasons to feel so ghastly when hungover are attributed largely to the body, but it is a body that takes on the colour of the mind in the form of a 'physical depression', a variation on the theme of a 'deep sense of breakage'. Unable to speak of mental illness as such, the word 'depression' is a powerful enough clue, along with the nebulous 'dark mood', to suggest the damaging effects of alcohol on the mind and temper. The reasons for shame are not then wholly nebulous, but culturally specific, deriving from loss of caste: Pratt was raised a

---

43   The 'vacuum' left by the hangover could only be replaced by 'the destructive power which made it', leading Beecher to propose a causal link between the hangover and the development of socially unacceptable drinking (Beecher, *Six Sermons*, pp. 11, 14).

44   Wood, *Danesbury House*, p. 137.

gentleman, but alcohol has reduced him to a lower status. Nevertheless, his revelatory self-diagnosis seems *to him* encrypted; Wood shows Pratt's personal failings are founded on the way alcohol has altered his mood or, on a larger scale, temperament: 'I was kind, just, honourable, well-intentioned', but, 'now, it is excitement; now it is despondency; both hard to bear, and both urging sin.'[45] The despondency of the hangover follows the excitement of intoxication: a depiction of the nervous system's condition of 'overdrive' perhaps, but Pratt has lost command of his moods and ability to account for his compulsive behaviour. What Pratt's hangover reveals most clearly is that, despite on one level being straightforward evidence of 'sin', he struggles for a vocabulary that might help him to explain more fully the sensations that drive him back to drink.

In *The Tenant of Wildfell Hall*, Anne Brontë presents a similar, but more extensive and psychologically nuanced, account of an addictive personality in the figure of Lord Lowborough, one of Arthur Huntingdon's drinking companions, who suffers from depressive episodes, exacerbated by hangovers. Lowborough's hangovers enrich our understanding of the complex set of psychological ingredients that contribute to problem drinking and, had Brontë recourse to the word 'hangover', she would surely have liberally peppered her characterisation of Lowborough with it. Lowborough's drinking career is first narrated to Helen by Arthur, explained in terms of a failure of gentlemanly conduct on the part of the former. He spectacularly renounces alcohol during one of the group's 'orgies', declaiming drink as 'hell broth': '"It's rank poison," said he, grasping the bottle by the neck, "and I forswear it!"'[46] For Huntingdon, Lowborough's behaviour is vulgar, foolish and casts a shadow over their decadent evenings at club and gaming-houses. He takes advantage of the bleakness of Lowborough's moods when hungover to tempt him back into the kind of foolish sociability that we saw Lamb's drunkard lament in Chapter 4. 'We meant it in kindness', Huntingdon disingenuously protests to Helen, 'we couldn't bear to see the poor fellow so miserable' as a result of 'last night's debauch'. Lowborough's gloom only lifts occasionally when he is drunk.

Lowborough's attempts to forswear company, and the drinking culture on which it subsists, are undermined, however, by crippling melancholy – what we would undoubtedly now call depression. It is hard to say whether depression precedes or succeeds his drinking, but it is exacerbated during hangovers that cause him to lose his integrity.

45   Wood, *Danesbury House*, p. 138.
46   Brontë, *Tenant*, p. 204.

Fig. 5.1 George
Cruikshank, The
Prince Regent with
a hangover in
William Hone's *The
Queen's Matrimonial
Ladder* (1820).

Give not thy strength unto women, nor thy ways to that which destroyeth kings.
Solomon.

Returning to the club, he initially refuses to drink: 'I'm only come to be
with you awhile, because I can't bear my own thoughts.' Lowborough
cannot overcome his depression, or 'gloomy, abstracted moods', without
alcohol, 'so weary of his own moping, melancholy mind'. Resorting to
a variation on the Withdrawal-Relief theme, he takes increasing doses
of laudanum – opium diluted in alcohol – in private, earning him the
nicknames 'the skeleton' and 'the spectre' from Huntingdon's cronies.[47]
Eventually, to beat the blues, and under the provocation of the other
men, Lowborough drains a bottle of brandy. The ensuing effects are 'an
apoplectic fit followed by a rather severe brain fever', a generic term for
aftershock that Molly Engelhardt tells us was 'coined by the Victorians
to refer to an inflammation of the brain caused by a severe shock to
the nervous system'.[48]

---

47   Brontë, *Tenant*, pp. 149, 150.
48   Brontë, *Tenant*, p. 151; Molly Engelhardt, *Dancing out of Line: Ballrooms, Ballets, and*

Brontë depicts a homosocial drinking collective of the kind we have already seen censured in the Georgian period. This is the period in which the action of the novel, though published in 1848, occurs and was sometimes viewed by the Victorians as a hard-drinking age of immorality, in contrast to their own. This is never more starkly encapsulated than in the illustration of the Prince Regent suffering from a hangover at the time of his marriage to Caroline of Brunswick (Fig. 5.1), by the elder George Cruikshank. However, Brontë complicates social judgements passed on the Georgian age, and with it our understanding of a Traditional-Punishment hangover response, by drawing on her rudimentary understanding of the psychology of addiction, introducing a figure who has evidently lost control of his nerves and mind. Lowborough finds himself in a nightmarish cycle of heavy drinking, followed by worsening depressive episodes. Brontë is unambiguous in showing Lowborough self-medicating to ease anxiety and dejection and she appears to be inching towards a more precise language of the depressive temperament of the sort we start to see entering medical discourse:

> Somehow, Lowborough had not the gift of moderation: if he stumbled a little to one side, he must go down before he could right himself: if he overshot the mark one night, the effects of it rendered him so miserable the next day that he must repeat the offence to mend it; and so on from day to day, till his clamorous conscience brought him to a stand – And then, in his sober moments, he so bothered his friends with his remorse, and his terrors and woes, that they were obliged, in self-defence, to get him to drown his sorrows in wine, or any more potent beverage that came to hand; and when his first scruples of conscience were overcome, he would need no more persuading, he would often grow desperate, and be as great a blackguard as any of them could desire – but only to lament his own unutterable wickedness and degradation the more when the fit was over.[49]

Huntingdon's nonchalant appraisal of Lowborough's depression, his 'terrors' and 'woes', bespeaks a type of self-control around alcohol that the other lacks. But the metaphor is mixed – first applying the 'stumbling' of the drunkard to a figure that, *à la David Copperfield*, suggests the hangover is a ship on the ocean ('he must go down

---

Mobility in Victorian Fiction (Athens: Ohio University Press, 2009), p. 196.
49   Brontë, *Tenant*, p. 208.

before he could right himself') he modulates into an image taken from shooting ('overshot the mark') – and indicates Huntingdon's inability to quite comprehend his friend's depression. Huntingdon's assessment sets Lowborough in opposition to his own pleasures of male country pursuits and his indifference is the first tangible demonstration of his callousness, while Lowborough's desperate need to 'repeat the offence to mend it' underlines the fact that he has lost the ability to control his compulsive actions and explain his darkening moods.

Lowborough marries the unsuitable Annabella Wilmot, with whom Huntingdon later has an affair, but eventually divorces and takes a second wife more befitting his temperament. Brontë describes his recovery from the patterns of addictive behaviour and re-connection with a more stable and socially acceptable self through the reawakening of his Christian faith. Huntingdon's offhand and brash dismissal of Lowborough is crystallised in his recommendation of what he calls 'the media-via, ni jamais-ni-toujours plan'.[50] But the 'middle way' of moderation is simply not an option for Lowborough, because the bleak moods of his hangovers prohibit any emotional self-command.

Brontë highlights the part that the kind of Romantic, objectless dread of the hangover plays in the development of compulsive drinking habits. If Lowborough lacks the 'gift' of moderation, the plot of *Tenant* demonstrates that Huntingdon does too, and that his own self-regard – 'don't think, Helen, that I'm a tippler; I'm nothing of the kind … I see that a man cannot give himself up to drinking without being miserable on half his days and mad the other'[51] – is in fact a form of denial. In hangover literature, denial often co-exists with, or complicates the expression of, remorse as we have seen in examples from novels by F. Scott Fitzgerald and in the correspondence of Robert Burns. In Huntingdon's case, he finds he is miserable on at least half his days, but struggles to account for or, more properly, to admit to the reasons for his loss of emotional equilibrium.

When Huntingdon returns to Grassdale Manor, after his first lengthy drinking binge in London, Helen initially struggles to account for his behaviour: 'Thank heaven, he is come at last! But how altered! – flushed and feverish, listless and languid, his beauty strangely diminished, his vigour and vivacity quite departed.'[52] Almost instinctively, she realises that quizzing Arthur on his debauch will only make matters worse: 'I have not upbraided him by word or look; I

50   Brontë, *Tenant*, p. 207.
51   Brontë, *Tenant*, pp. 207–208.
52   Brontë, *Tenant*, p. 237.

have not even asked him what he has been doing. I have not the heart to do it, for I think he is ashamed of himself.' If the physical symptoms that Helen describes suggest some serious illness, as the day wears on and Huntingdon lazes on the sofa, 'peevish', and 'testy' with the servants and his dogs, it becomes apparent that these result from his hangover.[53]

However, hangovers cloud Huntingdon's mind and impair his judgement as much as his physical constitution. Depression is one of the categories of Penning, McKinney and Verster's measure of hangover severity, and they include other emotional repercussions pertinent to Huntingdon such as Blunted affect, Agitation, Impulsivity and Anger (Fig. 1.2), but these cannot be understood in the abstract. Helen desists from doing anything 'that has a tendency to irritate or disturb' Arthur, confirming the 'nervous irritability' that MacNish diagnoses in topers.[54] Following his second extended debauch in London, this time lasting some four months, Huntingdon begins to drink more frequently at home, meaning that Grassdale becomes a location increasingly defined by his hangovers as the novel progresses. Huntingdon's frustrations within the domestic environment are focalised through hangovers as his ability to tolerate them physically and emotionally deteriorates, disclosing the severity of his drinking problem.

By focusing on the sort of objectless dread we found in Romantic-period hangover literature, Brontë builds up the psychological picture of a drunkard's struggle to admit to the extent of his drinking problem. On his return from London, Huntingdon's hangover lasts at least two days. It is defined by weariness, a great thirst, headache, nausea, but allied to anxiety, irritability, impulsivity and anger. On the second morning, Helen notes that he is 'weary still':

> But at dinner, when, after breakfasting at twelve o'clock on a bottle of soda-water and a cup of strong coffee, and lunching at two on another bottle of soda-water mingled with brandy, he was finding fault with everything on the table and declaring we must change our cook – I thought the time was come.
>
> 'It is the same cook as we had before you went, Arthur,' said I. 'You were generally pretty well satisfied with her then.'
>
> 'You must have been letting her get into slovenly habits then, while I was away. It is enough to poison one – eating such a

53 Brontë, *Tenant*, p. 237.
54 Brontë, *Tenant*, p. 237.

disgusting mess!' And he pettishly pushed away his plate, and leant
back despairingly in his chair.[55]

With impaired appetite and his taste jaded by alcohol, Huntingdon
looks to deflect attention from the physical and emotional effects of his
hangover onto the failings of his household staff and Helen's management
in his absence. His despair manifests itself in a great physical thirst and
feelings of heat that he cannot control: 'for I have an infernal fire in
my veins, that all the waters of the ocean cannot quench'.[56] He turns
from water to brandy and wine in an attempt to reassert control over
his body, but he cannot control his moods and becomes irritated to
distraction by the behaviour of his servant, Benson, overcome by audio-
sensitivity when the latter drops a plate: 'have done with that infernal
clatter'. The impairment of Huntingdon's mood goes further than the
earlier peevishness, as his frustration causes him to lash out at Benson:
'Arthur turned furiously around upon him, and swore at him with savage
coarseness.' He then declines into self-pity – a confirmed character trait
in Huntingdon, but exacerbated by the hangover into a state approaching
paranoia – accusing Helen of conspiring with Benson: 'What *could* you
mean, Helen, by taking the servant's part against me.'[57]

Searching for an explanation for his foul temper, it is noticeable
that Helen and Arthur both resort to the contemporary medical
vocabulary of the nerves: 'do you think that I could stop to consider
the feelings of an insensate brute like [Benson], when my own nerves
were racked and torn to pieces by his confounded blunders?' Helen
responds: 'I never heard you complain of your nerves before.'[58] Arthur
Huntingdon's nerves are in that 'unbalanced "overdrive" state' that
characterises the hangover, just as Lowborough's were earlier, but
Brontë is primarily concerned to demonstrate the self-doubt, denial
and mental torment that follow heavy drinking. Huntingdon bewails
his inability to deal with Helen's reproaches due to the extent of
his nervous upheaval and tachycardia: 'If you knew how my heart
throbbed, and how every nerve thrilled through me while you spoke,
you would spare me. You can pity a dolt of a servant for breaking
a dish; but you have no compassion for *me*, when my head is split
in two and all on fire with this consuming fever.'[59] Once again,

55   Brontë, *Tenant*, p. 265.
56   Brontë, *Tenant*, p. 265.
57   Brontë, *Tenant*, p. 266.
58   Brontë, *Tenant*, p. 266.
59   Brontë, *Tenant*, p. 267.

Huntingdon's self-diagnosis is revelatory of the psychological precision of the hangover that we find in Victorian fiction. Yet, through his confused discourse of the body, the nervous system, his mind and emotions, Brontë depicts his inability to properly rationalise and exert control over the situation, or to admit to the extent of his drinking problem, reflecting the elements of uncertainty that prevent complete articulation of his unhappiness.

Huntingdon slips into a state of lassitude, punctuated by the katzen-jammers of his sighs and groans, and demands silence. There is a kind of reciprocity of mind and body at work: Huntingdon's inability to control the effects of the hangover on the body is, of course, partially responsible for his degree of anxiety or gloom, but that bad temper also seems to exacerbate his physical suffering. The discourse of 'shattered nerves' helps to medically label Huntingdon, but Brontë demonstrates its usage plays a part in throwing a veil of imprecision over the dark, nebulous forebodings of the hangover that belong to the mind.[60] Brontë explores the impact of the emotional uncertainties of the hangover on the formation of compulsive drinking habits. For Huntingdon, the hangover entrenches his callousness but, as in other fiction with temperance themes, does not provide the ordinary check on his drinking and he eventually suffers an episode of *delirium tremens* that brings about his early death.

Denial and Diminishment

The victims of hangovers that I have discussed so far in this chapter are faced with uncomfortable symptoms but also moral judgements, which is what we would expect of a morally sensitive age. Hangovers enable the reappraisal of a culture's prevailing ideologies and so, when they are not drunk, Jenny Wren's father feels shame for his failure to fulfil his parental role, and is berated by his daughter for it, and Robert Danesbury is ashamed at his inability to dedicate himself to work like his brother Arthur. The hangover of Dickens's David Copperfield demonstrates that assignable symptoms are part of an awareness of social or cultural failings. These hangover descriptions add to our knowledge of the ways in which alcohol use is determined by both physiology and environment.

---

60   For use of this term, see Janet Oppenheim, *Shattered Nerves: Doctors, Patients, and Depression in Victorian England* (New York and Oxford: Oxford University Press, 1991).

In that regard it is important to note that hangovers in Victorian fiction, as in the literature of earlier centuries, are sometimes periods of straightforward condemnation and comeuppance. In *Nicholas Nickleby* (1839), Dickens uses a hangover scene to pass moral judgement on the villains Lord Frederick Verisopht and Sir Mulberry Hawk as they conspire to seduce Kate Nickleby. They are surrounded by clutter that reveals the activities of the previous night:

> A couple of billiard balls, all mud and dirt, two battered hats, a champagne bottle with a soiled glove twisted round the neck, to allow of its being grasped more surely in its capacity of an offensive weapon; a broken cane; a card-case without the top; an empty purse; a watch-guard snapped asunder; a handful of silver, mingled with fragments of half-smoked cigars, and their stale and crumbled ashes; – these, and many other tokens of riot and disorder, hinted very intelligibly at the nature of last night's gentlemanly frolics.[61]

The inanimate objects hint very intelligibly at the gentlemen's moral status too. Likewise, in Anthony Trollope's *The Way We Live Now* (1875), Lord Felix Carbury's seduction of Ruby Ruggles is met with reprisal as he is beaten by her other suitor, John Crumb, and confined to his rooms; the hangover of his 'good times' is a just reprisal for his callousness.[62]

Yet, as we have seen, Victorian writers were not just in the habit of passing moral judgement or in reflecting prevailing ideologies. They were preserving the complex humanity of the drunkard by teasing out the psychological realities of a hangover. Victorian novelists drew attention to the socio-cultural variables that contributed to the potentially damaging psychological condition of a hangover, as is the case in my two final examples, Eliot's *Janet's Repentance* – which provides a rare opportunity to analyse the hangover of a female drinker in the century – and, taken from the end of the Victorian age, Hardy's *Jude the Obscure*. Both writers demonstrate that the drinker's psychological complexity is often revealed through hangovers that show loss of status and a crisis of self-worth.

Heavy drinking blights the marriage of the middle-class Robert and Janet Dempster in the provincial English town of Milby and the novella is notable for its insights into the cocktail of shameful ingredients that make up the hangovers of a middle-class couple. Robert Dempster, at first

61   Charles Dickens, *Nicholas Nickleby*, intro. Tim Cook (Ware: Wordsworth, 1995), pp. 312–13.
62   Anthony Trollope, *The Way We Live Now*, ed. John Sutherland (Oxford: Oxford University Press, 1982), p. 240.

a successful lawyer, finds that the local community, held together by a web of gossip and hearsay, much as Eliot's later *Middlemarch* would be, can work against, as well as for, him. Happy to exploit and embellish his reputation for good living, iron constitution and a sound business head, the first chapter of the novel sees Dempster hold court on the subject of the arrival in Milby of the new Methodist preacher, Mr Tryan. His forthright views impress the regulars at the *Red Lion*, but his standing in the community is mainly based on his legendary tolerance for drink as the awed Tomlinson asserts: 'I never see Dempster's equal ... Why he's drunk the best part of a bottle o' brandy since we've been sitting, and I'll bet a guinea, when he's got to Trower's his head'll be as clear as mine.'[63] Indeed, Dempster's professional accomplishment is popularly linked to his capacity and tolerance for drink, to the admiration of the farmers of Milby:

> He's a long-headed feller, Dempster; why, it shows yer what a headpiece Dempster has, as he can drink a bottle o' brandy at a sittin', an' yit see further through a stone wall when he's done, than other folks 'll see through a glass winder'.

Dempster thrives on balancing hard living and long working hours, his heedlessness symbolised by the way in which he drives his carriage through town, 'flogging his galloping horse like a madman'.[64] The notion that Dempster can 'carry his liquor like old Nick'[65] ensures his public standing within the community of Milby, but his inability to control his violent temper when drunk leads him to beat his wife, who herself turns to drink to numb the physical pain and injustice. These scenes were particularly shocking as domestic abuse was popularly considered to be a problem of the working classes and, as Leslie Bruce notes, the Victorians 'typically imagined the middle-class family as a violence-free domain'.[66] Dempster's initial public success in mobilising a protest mob against Tryan soon unravels as his professional standing takes a hit when he loses one of his wealthiest clients, the retired corn-factor Mr Jerome. Trapped in a vicious circle, it is hard to tell whether his business fails as the effects of his drinking worsen, or whether his

---

63   George Eliot, *Janet's Repentance*, in *Scenes of Clerical Life*, ed. Thomas A. Noble (Oxford: Oxford University Press, repr. 2009), p. 173.

64   Eliot, *Janet's Repentance*, pp. 177, 189.

65   Eliot, *Janet's Repentance*, p. 198.

66   Leslie Jeanine Bruce, *Outlaw Mothers: Marital Conflict, Family Law, and Women's Novels in Victorian England* (unpublished PhD thesis, University of Southern California, 2007), p. 78.

drinking worsens due to the failure of his business. In either case, what becomes clear is that his worsening hangovers indicate loss of control over not only his body and his profession, but also the equally precarious self-image to which they have contributed, engendered in the crucible of Milby gossip. The 'man whose law-business and liver are both beginning to show unpleasant symptoms', as Eliot wittily phrases it, discovers that his standing makes him the subject of provincial hearsay over which he is unable to assert control. Moreover, he is in 'a constant state of irritated excitement' and 'too much harassed' to be able to do anything about it.[67]

The narrator confirms that the 'various symptoms that things were getting worse with the Dempsters afforded Milby gossip'.[68] These symptoms all implicate alcohol and specifically the decreased ability to withstand its aftershocks. Hence, Dempster's decision to change his known habits and quit driving his carriage: his impaired reactions raise the risks of such an activity. The doctor, Mr Pratt, jokes to his professional rival, Mr Pilgrim, that Dempster 'won't end with a broken neck after all. You'll have a case of meningitis and delirium tremens instead.'[69] Simultaneously, the worsening of Janet's hangovers makes her the focus of much of the female gossips – both good-natured and malicious – of Milby. The likes of Mrs Pettifer and the Misses Pratt and Linnet delight in remarking her loss of social status, from 'the most promising young woman of my acquaintance', as Pettifer puts it. They debate the rumours of Dempster's drunken fits of temper, Janet's denial – 'She will never admit to anybody that he's not a good husband' – and her own apparent drinking: 'it's enough to make her drink something to blunt her feelings'. The hangover is only gestured at – signalling the taboo subject of a middle-class woman's drinking – when Pettifer notes that 'She comes to me sometimes, poor thing, looking so strange.'[70] But that strangeness gradually corroborates her private reliance on alcohol:

> Mrs Dempster, every one remarked, looked more miserable than ever, though she kept up the old pretence of being happy and satisfied. She was scarcely ever seen, as she used to be, going about on her good-natured errands; and even old Mrs Crewe, who had always been wilfully blind to anything wrong in her favourite Janet, was obliged to admit that she had not seemed like herself

67   Eliot, *Janet's Repentance*, p. 227
68   Eliot, *Janet's Repentance*, p. 240.
69   Eliot, *Janet's Repentance* p. 241.
70   Eliot, *Janet's Repentance*, pp. 190–91.

lately. 'The poor thing's out of health,' said the kind little old lady, in answer to all gossip about Janet; 'her headaches always were bad, and I know what headaches are; why, they make one quite delirious sometimes.' Mrs Phipps, for her part, declared she would never accept an invitation to Dempster's again; it was getting so very disagreeable to go there, Mrs Dempster was often 'so strange'.[71]

The passage is indicative of the ways in which hearsay – 'every one remarked' – dominates the operations through which information is relayed to the reader and against which – 'in answer to all gossip' – benevolent figures like Mrs Crewe react. As Patricia Meyer Spacks has argued, the novel's generic operations are deeply invested in a mode of communication that insists on the 'minute awareness of human behavior in all its bearings' and of 'manipulations of power relations'.[72] This is the euphemistic language of gossip – 'out of health', 'so strange' – which testifies to the fact that Janet's reputation is undermined just as surely as is her constitution by her increased susceptibility to hangovers.

Dempster's own humiliation is confirmed as the story reaches its crescendo and, while drunk, he barbarously attacks Janet before flinging her out into the street from where she seeks asylum from her abusive husband at Mrs Pettifer's. The following morning witnesses two hangovers: Janet's is marked by contrition for her own drinking problems and, escaping the shadow of Dempster, she is able to repent, invoking the novel's title, turning to the preacher Tryan who enables her to take the first steps towards a new domestic life. Dempster, on the other hand, wakes with the kind of dismissive attitude and denial of responsibility that so often characterises the hangovers of the dissolute men of Victorian temperance narratives:

> WHEN Dempster awoke in the morning, he was at no loss to account to himself for the fact that Janet was not by his side. His hours of drunkenness were not cut off from his other hours by any blank wall of oblivion; he remembered what Janet had done to offend him the evening before, he remembered what he had done to her at midnight, just as he would have remembered if he had been consulted about a right of road.
>
> The remembrance gave him a definite ground for the extra ill-humour which had attended his waking every morning this

---

71   Eliot, *Janet's Repentance*, pp. 240–41.
72   Patricia Meyer Spacks, *Gossip* (Chicago, IL and London: University of Chicago Press, 1986), p. 20.

week, but he would not admit to himself that it cost him any anxiety. 'Pooh,' he said inwardly, 'she would go straight to her mother's. She's as timid as a hare; and she'll never let anybody know about it. She'll be back again before night.'

But it would be as well for the servants not to know anything of the affair: so he collected the clothes she had taken off the night before, and threw them into a fire-proof closet of which he always kept the key in his pocket. When he went down-stairs he said to the housemaid, 'Mrs Dempster is gone to her mother's; bring in the breakfast.'[73]

It is notable that Dempster's first thoughts are not for any physical suffering but for his status. His actions demonstrate the attempt to cover up his guilt, leading him to lie to the housemaid and are all motivated by denial, an unwillingness to admit to any consequences more serious than Janet spending the night at her mother's. Assignable causes can bring clarity if not comfort, and Dempster's abusive behaviour gives him 'definite ground' on which to base his less easily defined dark feelings ordinarily manifested in less quantifiable frustration and 'ill-humour'. His equilibrium is, perhaps, more disturbed than equivalent scenes involving Arthur Huntingdon, but he nonetheless attempts to brave it out. Eliot presents a close study of the psychology of deflection.

Despite the degree of Dempster's denial, even at this moment of personal crisis, the hangover will, however, have the final say as his increased susceptibility to its punishing effects leads directly to his early death. Growing frustrated at being held up by his horseman Dawes, on the morning following Janet's departure, and, waiting impatiently for his carriage, he takes his 'accustomed glass of brandy' to stave off the jitters. The narrator records that 'ill-humour got the better of prudence' and Dempster furiously berates Dawes for his dilatoriness before lashing out with his horsewhip and cutting the man across the face.[74] In a rage, Dempster recommences driving his own carriage, but is thrown from his gig, which leads to an apoplexy and a fever. Like Arthur Huntingdon, he declines into the horrors of *delirium tremens*, as predicted by Mr Pratt, and fails to recover.

The growing stresses on Dempster due to his persistent drinking are manifested in his short temper and inability to control the impulses of rage. It is not just his body and business that has slipped out of his control, but his ability to mentally and emotionally withstand the psychosocial

---

73   Eliot, *Janet's Repentance*, pp. 253–54.
74   Eliot, *Janet's Repentance*, p. 254.

pressures of diminishment in a provincial town where reputation is everything. Janet loses her reputation for refinement and generosity, just as Robert loses his for tolerance. The same farmers and labourers who venerated Dempster at the beginning of the novel turn against him as his celebrated prowess declines: 'he was losing that physical power of supporting excess which had long been the admiration of such fine spirits as Mr Tomlinson'. The once confident Dempster, conscious of his diminished social standing, becomes wracked with self-doubt during his hangovers – 'some new distrust for himself' – which sets in motion the train of events that lead to his accident and death.[75]

Robert Dempster is representative of the Victorian male who discovers that an image based on the cultural configurations of social drinking is put in jeopardy by the corresponding hangover. Janet's concurrent shame is more overtly attached to the home and her inability to control, and soothe, the temper of her husband, but the judgements of the Milby gossips emphasise the outward facing nature of the private disgrace that she tries to conceal. Eliot shows us that denial and justification are part of psychological defences against perceived diminishment in the eyes of others that cannot be wholly explained outside the specific social and cultural environment of the two drinkers. Janet shows herself capable of re-connecting with acceptable social values during her hangovers, but Robert Dempster, fashioning an image that he can no longer physically and emotionally support, does not.

Hardy's Jude Fawley may not, by way of contrast, be a problem drinker, but drinking, and its aftermath, undoubtedly demonstrates similar psychological problems concerning diminishment and loss of standing. Jude's first hangover comes during his courtship of the manipulative Arabella Donn. Hardy explores the intense psychology of shame that Jude experiences when facing up to the fact that he has made a foolish match with a woman much more sexually and morally liberated than himself. He attends church where everything seems to exacerbate his feelings of social and sexual inadequacy:

> In the dim light and the baffling glare of the clerestory windows he could discern the opposite worshippers indistinctly only, but he saw that Sue was among them. He had not long discovered the exact seat that she occupied when the chanting of the 119th Psalm in which the choir was engaged reached its second part, *In quo corriget*, the organ changing to a pathetic Gregorian tune as the singers gave forth:

75 Eliot, *Janet's Repentance*, p. 240.

Wherewithal shall a young man cleanse his way?

It was the very question that was engaging Jude's attention at this moment. What a wicked worthless fellow he had been to give vent as he had done to an animal passion for a woman, and allow it to lead to such disastrous consequences; then to think of putting an end to himself; then to go recklessly and get drunk. The great waves of pedal music tumbled round the choir, and, nursed on the supernatural as he had been, it is not wonderful that he could hardly believe that the psalm was not specially set by some regardful Providence for this moment of his first entry into the solemn building. And yet it was the ordinary psalm for the twenty-fourth evening of the month.[76]

Hardy shows the psychological formation of a Traditional-Punishment reaction at work as the organ and choir – reminiscent of Burns's ticking clock or Wordsworth's 'pealing organ' we saw in Chapter 4 – provide a censorious accompaniment to the waves of self-reproach that wash over Jude. The hangover emphasises the moral inflexibility of the church and the institution of marriage along with the obstacles that lie in the way of the working man who aspires to greater things. Hardy links Jude's moral sensitivity to the fact that he has been 'nursed on the supernatural', suggesting his self-destructive behaviour is a result of feeling unable to match social expectations.

Social expectations can lead to feelings of diminishment, and this is one of the major factors in Eliot's account of Robert Dempster's habits of deflection and denial. However, Dempster attempts to reassert authority in a different way from Jude, and rather than turning his frustrations on himself, projects them outward through his psychological abuse of Janet. The difference between the two characters may be partly explained by variations in levels of shame-proneness, but these are tied to social contexts and issues of class. Loss of status preoccupies both men and the self-image they construct leads to negative self-evaluation in terms of specific social values. Hence, Jude's second experience with alcohol leads to a hangover that is informed by his feelings of social diminishment. Feeling enraged by the inequities he witnesses in the University of Christminster, Jude drinks recklessly and loses control of his bodily and mental faculties. In a city pub, he defiantly recites the Nicene Creed to a group of locals before breaking out into a rage. His speech is clear, but the body bears witness to the fact that he has lost

---

76   Thomas Hardy, *Jude the Obscure*, intro. Terry Eagleton, notes P. N. Furbank (London: Macmillan, 1975), pp. 114–15.

his judgement. He stumbles off to find Sue Bridehead and confesses his misery. Awaking the next day, he demonstrates physical hangover symptoms but mostly an acute degree of shame-proneness, deriving from his upbringing.

Rather than remain and face Sue, Jude flees her rooms, and indeed Christminster, deciding to return to his home, Marygreen. Overwhelmed by distress at the thought that his ambitions for a place at the university have demonstrated his foolishness at attempting to rise beyond his station, it is noticeable that his body does not just endure a physical reaction but also becomes a site of self-flagellation. As Jude embarks on the punishing 20-mile walk to the Wessex hamlet of his birth, the narrator tells us 'he had ample time to complete the sobering process begun in him', and this self-inflicted punishment works to purge Jude of the taints of his drunken experience the previous night, returning him, physically and symbolically, to an earlier time:

> At some hour of the evening he reached Alfredston. Here he pawned his waistcoat, and having gone out of the town a mile or two, slept under a rick that night. At dawn he rose, shook off the hayseeds and stems from his clothes, and started again, breasting the long white road up the hill to the downs, which had been visible to him a long way off, and passing the milestone at the top, whereon he had carved his hopes years ago.
>
> He reached the ancient hamlet while the people were at breakfast. Weary and mud-bespattered, but quite possessed of his ordinary clearness of brain, he sat down by the well, thinking as he did so what a poor Christ he made.[77]

I have previously observed that hangovers distort perception of the body. Here, Hardy depicts Jude's attempts to reassert control by forcing his body through an act of physical endurance. Through his physical suffering Jude pays spiritual penance and seems to arrive at Marygreen restored to feelings of wholeness. This is a journey back to the values of his youth, a time before the complexity and frustrations of academic ambition intruded, and a recognition of humility: 'what a poor Christ he made'. Control over unsettling psychosocial issues concerning lack of self-respect and wounded pride is reasserted through physical exertion. Jude's trek becomes a way of making spiritual and social atonement for shame; it is a type of atonement that other more problematic drinkers of Victorian fiction find much harder to realise.

77 Hardy, *Jude*, p. 144.

'The inebriate is ever the most quarrelsome in the hours of depression and gloom that follow the false spirits, which he has borrowed from the wine-cup' according to J. H. Ingraham.[78] In the Victorian fiction that I have analysed in this chapter, those hours of depression and gloom are shown to be a product of a complex interplay of physical and psychosocial effects that deepen our understanding of hangovers. Patterns of acceptance and displacement, guilt and excuse, suggest a loss of capacity to regulate or manage the impact of excessive alcohol consumption. Identifying and understanding the corroborating signs of the hangover enabled Victorian novelists to explore more fruitfully the kinds of etiology of drinking problems and the status of problem drinkers that were occupying medical research and the authors of temperance tracts in the nineteenth century. If, on the one hand, Victorian fiction, particularly temperance narratives, passed moral judgement on compulsive drinkers, the depictions of hangovers were nevertheless a key site in exploring the complex humanity of the drunkard. Hangover literature relayed the psychosocial dimensions that contributed to the development of compulsive drinking habits.

78   Ingraham, *Edward Austin*, p. 53.

Chapter 6

The Hangover and the Outsider: Self-fashioning, Shame and Defiance in Twentieth- and Twenty-first-century Fiction

Introduction

Throughout this book I have primarily been concerned to demonstrate that the hangover is a socio-cultural as well as a physiological phenomenon. I have explored what hangover literature can tell us about the relationship between an individual drinker and their environment, particularly the way that cultural beliefs are expressed through reactions to alcohol use. In the seventeenth and eighteenth centuries, we discovered cultural contexts in which Traditional-Punishment and Withdrawal-Relief hangover responses developed and, from the end of the eighteenth century, have explored the literary representation of hangover consciousness that often demonstrates the complex psychological manoeuvres involved in processing moral judgement. My chronological account of hangovers in Western literature and culture has now reached the twentieth and twenty-first centuries where, as I explained in Chapter 1, the word 'hangover' is current, and we find out just how hard-working it is.

The chief point to note about drinking literature in the twentieth century is that it is dominated by defiance and the figure of the 'Romantic outsider', who Steven Earnshaw argues emerges in 'reaction to the imperatives of "society," "family" and "duty"',[1] contesting their hitherto largely unquestioned authority. We find this kind of figure in Charles Bukowski's poem 'Hangover and Sick Leave', where his speaker claims to 'know very little' (1).[2] It is an ironic reference to memory loss, but

---

1   Steven Earnshaw, 'Drink, Dissolution, Antibiography: The Existential Drinker', in *Biographies of Drink: A Case Study Approach to our Historical Relationship with Alcohol*, ed. Mark Hailwood and Deborah Toner (Newcastle-upon-Tyne: Cambridge Scholars, 2015), p. 204 (pp. 204–22).

2   Charles Bukowski, 'Hangover and Sick Leave', *The Rooming House Madrigals: Early Selected Poems, 1946–1966* (Los Angeles, CA: Black Sparrow Press, 1988).

equally a dismissive attitude to adult life. He initially claims to 'fear' the reprisals of an 'angry wife', 'landlord', 'psychiatrist', 'police' and 'priest' (12–16), representing domestic responsibility, work, emotional and physical wellbeing, the law and religion, but his actions suggest otherwise. Bukowski's speaker is tired, but otherwise indifferent to both physical symptoms and the judgements and values of conventional American life. Instead of becoming anxious he exudes a self-sufficient resilience:

> there is nothing to
> prove
> and I raise the covers
> to the ears of my empty head
> and breathe in and out. (27–31)

The statement 'I stay in bed' (8) hardly constitutes a grand act of defiance, but therein lies its force. It is the power of the shrug, rather than the bellow.

'Hangover and Sick Leave' partakes of a tradition of drinking narratives – usually novels – that dominate writing about alcohol in the twentieth century and more recently, wherein the habitual drunkard, male and female, often 'prone to glorify the seamy' side of life, guides readers to places 'where standard values are questioned'.[3] The theme runs throughout what Richard Bradford calls the tradition of 'the drunken monologue'[4] – confessional narratives such as Jack London's *John Barleycorn: Alcoholic Memoirs* (1913), Bukowski's *Post Office* (1971) and *Factotum* (1978), Helen Fielding's *Bridget Jones's Diary* (1996) and A. L. Kennedy's *Paradise* (2004) – but also typifies the behaviour of character drunkards found in novels by the likes of Patrick Hamilton and Alan Sillitoe. In such drinking narratives, society is usually viewed, as in 'Hangover and Sick Leave', as a hollow performance of conventional roles against which the habitual drinker 'seeks', according to Earnshaw, 'to define an authentic self in the process of being repeatedly or continuously drunk'.[5]

Writers like Bukowski have played a large part in weaving a mystique around rebellious outsider figures who captivate because of blatant disregard for socially acceptable standards of behaviour. Such a drinker

---

3   Neeli Cherkovski, 'Introduction' to Charles Bukowski, *Factotum* (London: Virgin Books, 2009), pp. v–vi.

4   Richard Bradford, *The Novel Now: Contemporary British Fiction* (Oxford: Blackwell, 2009), p. 137.

5   Earnshaw, 'Drink, Dissolution, Antibiography', p. 206.

gives the impression of being more liberated and apparently enlightened than in earlier periods, when, as we have seen, the hangover was often represented as a moral curb and period of personal reappraisal and where expressions of defiance were generally underpinned by the 'hair of the dog'. However, continuities with earlier times remain and it is difficult to be 'repeatedly or continuously drunk' without suffering from a hangover. Even amongst the most defiant of the twentieth-century's drunken outsiders the self-assertion we find in 'Hangover and Sick Leave' is rare. As we will see in the examples of hangover literature in this chapter, far from being exempt from moral accountability, these drinkers find hangovers weaken their resistance of 'standard values' showing continuities with earlier hangover literature. In fact, it is, perhaps, in the overtly self-aware, and boldly defiant, outsiders of twentieth- and twenty-first-century literature and culture, purporting to be at liberty from the kind of moral judgements that preoccupied earlier ages, that we discover most about the way that hangovers play host to negative affect – guilt, shame and humiliation – which complicates the fashioning of an authentic outsider self. More often than not, these novels tend to feature hangovers during which the most assertively independent drinker is revealed to be psychologically regulated, as Foucault has it, by 'systems of thoughts composed of ideas, attitudes, courses of action, beliefs and practices'.[6]

I began this book with some close analysis of hangovers experienced by characters in twentieth-century fiction in order to establish their social and cultural as well as physical dimensions, to show that some of the most interesting aspects of hangovers lie in individual and collective acts of perception, but this chapter gives a more extensive, themed account of the way that, despite often exploring emancipation from the values represented by Bukowski's angry wife, psychiatrist, police and priest, modern fiction reveals the precarity of a defiant self-image built upon heavy drinking. It shows that such precarity derives variously from the persistence of social codes, intergenerational clashes, gender norms that reveal hostility towards sexual promiscuity, particularly in women, and class. The chapter considers each of these issues in turn, demonstrating that the hangovers we find in drinkers of twentieth- and twenty-first-century fiction are complex organisms that play host to not only the customary painful knot of bodily sensations, but also a conflicting set of moral and cultural values over which an individual's identity and self-esteem are fought for, around which feelings that we

---

6   Iara Lessa, 'Discursive Struggles Within Social Welfare: Restaging Teen Motherhood', *British Journal of Social Work*, 36.2 (2006), p. 285 (pp. 283–98).

commonly associate with the morning after, such as shame and guilt, continue to orbit. To draw the strands of this book's argument into a conclusion, the final section of the chapter probes the issue of memory loss as perhaps the ultimate example of the hangover's abstract, impenetrable superstructure that defies articulation.

Mythopoesis or the Cult of the Drunken Individual

Matt Treeby and Raimondo Bruno argue that affective reactions to drunkenness such as guilt and shame occur when individuals feel in breach of 'internalized moral principles'.[7] Drunkenness may give the illusion of autonomy from conventional social values, but hangover literature generally reveals, as Emile Durkheim argued, that the behaviour of drinkers is policed by 'social facts', or 'sacred values'.[8] Bukowksi's speaker is, perhaps, the exception that proves the rule.

David Nash and Anne-Marie Kilday elaborate on Durkheim's propositions, arguing that guilt 'describes a collection of psychological tools possessed by an individual which persuades them to form their own personal deterrent, policing agent and judicial mechanism'.[9] This is the process often called 'internalisation' that, for Durkheim, generates the illusory 'cult of the individual'. But J. P. Tangney and R. L. Dearing argue that negative emotional states 'lead to notably different motivational and self-regulatory outcomes' depending on specific psychosocial contexts. Temperament can also play a part and the recent research of Beth Marsh suggests that shy people are more likely to suffer from hangxiety.[10] We have already seen writers like Frances Burney and Thomas Hardy explore shame-proneness through hangovers. I have previously stated that I am not attempting to differentiate precisely between types of negative affect in this book – partly because I have argued throughout that the hangover is an experience where emotions can overlap confusingly – but

---

7   Matt Treeby and Raimondo Bruno, 'Shame and Guilt-Proneness: Divergent Implications for Problematic Alcohol Use and Drinking to Cope with Anxiety and Depression Symptomatology', *Personal and Individual Differences*, 53.4 (2012), p. 613 (pp. 613–17).

8   See Emile Durkheim, *Sociology and Philosophy*, trans. D. F. Pocock ([1953] London: Taylor and Francis, 2009).

9   David Nash and Anne-Marie Kilday, *Cultures of Shame: Exploring Crime and Morality in Britain 1600–1990* (London: Palgrave, 2010), p. 6.

10   Beth Marsh *et al*, 'Shyness, Alcohol Use Disorders and "Hangxiety": A Naturalistic Study of Social Drinkers, *Personality and Individual Differences*, 139.3 (2019), pp. 13–18.

the way in which outsiders arrive at self-regulatory outcomes, the ways in which they may be causally related to identifiable actions, even as they appear to float free of cause and effect, is particularly evident in hangovers of twentieth-century fiction.

Before we can get further into these issues, however, we need to account for the establishment of the myth of the drunken Romantic outsider. For Earnshaw, the text that is foundational in depicting this 'existential' figure is London's semi-autobiographical *John Barleycorn*.[11] In this drinker's 'memoir', London presents a drinker who is 'an ongoing project', who confronts 'what it is to exist by making a commitment to drink large amounts of alcohol'.[12] Given this billing, it is interesting to note that London's self-diagnosed 'alcoholic' explicitly refers to his hangovers as a purely physical, rather than emotional, experience. He repeatedly describes a 'physical loathing for alcohol', but 'manfully hid[es] all such symptoms of dislike' because 'Drink was the badge of manhood.'[13] Forceful masculinity dominates the adventures of the 'Oyster Pirates' in the unnamed narrator-protagonist's native Oakland, California. He has a terrific tolerance for alcohol and owns a 'stomach that would digest scrap-iron', although this does not spare him from other severe physical repercussions.[14] Boasting an ability to drink his fellow seamen under the table by the age of 16, on one wild night the narrator-protagonist drives his skiff into a muddy bank from where he 'pitched headforemost into the ooze' of the estuary injuring himself against the barnacle-covered stakes. 'I knew I was drunk', he claims, 'but what of it?' Noticeably the next morning's hangover does not negate his defiance, despite the significant somatic aftershocks:

> I paid for it. I was sick for a couple of days, meanly sick, and my arms were painfully poisoned from the barnacle scratches. For a

11 See Earnshaw, 'Drink, Dissolution, Antibiography'. According to the editors of *Intoxication and Society*, the rebellious drunken individual fascinated writers from the nineteenth century onwards because of the cultural revolution that occurred whereby alcohol and drugs came to be viewed as 'social problems'. It 'demanded high levels of self-control, individualism and accountability to the demands of a capitalist economy, all of which were found incompatible with certain patterns of heavy alcohol use'. Jonathan Herring, Ciaran Regan, Darin Weinburg and Phil Withington, 'Starting the Conversation', in Herring *et al* (eds), *Intoxication and Society: Problematic Pleasures of Drugs and Alcohol* (Basingstoke: Palgrave Macmillan, 2013), p. 12 (pp. 1–30).

12 Steven Earnshaw, *The Existential Drinker* (Manchester: Manchester University Press, 2018), p. 1.

13 Jack London, *John Barleycorn: Alcoholic Memoirs*, ed. John Sutherland (Oxford: World's Classics, 2009), pp. 28–29.

14 London, *Barleycorn*, p. 32.

week I could not use them, and it was a torture to put on and take off my clothes.

I swore, 'Never again!' The game wasn't worth it. The price was too stiff. I had no moral qualms. My revulsion was purely physical.[15]

The physical price alone, which includes some self-inflicted injuries amongst the other assignable symptoms, does not corrupt the homosocial ideal represented by the unorthodox lifestyle of the Oyster Pirates, built on the 'warm-glowing camaraderie' of saloons like the *Last Chance*. Unwilling to submit to the 'petty routine' of work, drunkenness, including its after-effects, is fundamental to the 'spirit of revolt, of adventure, of romance, of the things forbidden and done defiantly' with which London conjures and through which he fashions his protagonist's identity.[16] The cycle of drunkenness and hangovers affirms the outsider's oppositional stance: 'Here I was', he narrates, 'thirsting for the wild life of adventure, and the only way for me to win it was through John Barleycorn's mediation.'[17]

The narrator-protagonist's reputation for consuming large quantities of alcohol first enables him to escape, and set himself symbolically against, the 'killing machine-toil' of work in a cannery, bringing him into association with men who 'flouted restrictions and the law, who carried their lives and their liberty in their hands'.[18] As with Herman Melville and Joseph Conrad, London's depiction of the lives of physically hardened sailors living on the fringes of society smacks of mythopoesis. Taking work as a deep-sea sealer in Japan, regular hangovers unambiguously mark the stages in the alcoholic's progress as an alpha male in an aggressively masculine world: 'I was learning what it was to get up shaky in the morning, with a stomach that quivered, with fingers touched with palsy, and to know the drinker's need for a stiff glass of whisky neat in order to brace up.'[19] Withdrawal-Relief is adopted as a form of self-medication, but London continually ascribes this to a susceptibility to physical factors rather than shame. Even when his narrator wakes up in the Bonin Islands after a wild night singing sea shanties to find he has been robbed by a group of apprentice English sailors, the essential commitment to a life of adventure is undiminished:

15 London, *Barleycorn*, p. 34.
16 London, *Barleycorn*, pp. 39–40.
17 London, *Barleycorn*, p. 65.
18 London, *Barleycorn*, pp. 43, 39.
19 London, *Barleycorn*, p. 78.

And next, after the blackness, I open my eyes in the early dawn to see a Japanese woman, solicitously anxious, bending over me. She is the port-pilot's wife, and I am lying in her doorway. I am chilled and shivering, sick with after sickness of debauch. And I feel lightly clad. Those rascals of run-away apprentices! They have acquired the habit of running away. They have run away with my possessions. My watch is gone. My few dollars are gone. My coat is gone. So is my belt. And yes, my shoes.[20]

In this example of hangover consciousness, the present tense captures the befuddled mind that links together feelings of cold and lightness before registering that something is amiss. But at this point London's alcoholic is only bereft of money and possessions: he admits to no sense of personal diminishment or embarrassment and the word 'rascals' lacks the bite that might turn into shame or self-reproach.

The narrator-protagonist freely admits that 'John Barleycorn' – a personification of alcohol – 'inhibits morality', leading him to buy rounds of drinks rather than, for example, send money home to his impoverished mother. But, on sailing the following morning, 'broke' and 'poisoned', he feels nonetheless 'contented': 'I had no regrets. I was proud.'[21] Physical injuries, near-death drunken experiences, debt and even an aborted suicide attempt, become stories for the water-front gossips, part of 'a giggle and laugh and another drink' rather than a source of shame.[22] They do not lead to introspection and the desire to mend his ways that are consistent with what we know of the normative Traditional-Punishment response to hangovers. Even the suicide attempt, in which the alcoholic recounts nearly drowning, is put down to a 'maniacal trick' played by John Barleycorn, 'when my nerves and brain were fearfully poisoned' and judgement, and sense of self, impaired.[23] The hangover establishes the mythopoetic key of the work because it apparently hosts none of Durkheim's 'sacred' values that might disturb the psyche by conflicting with those defiantly asserted through drunkenness.

Only when London's narrator-protagonist recounts his later domestic life, fatherhood and writing career in the second half of the novel – when, put simply, his more conventional social position is at stake – are the values that he espouses sacralised and behaviour regulated by the emotional content of his hangovers: 'I still believed in many things – in

20 London, *Barleycorn*, p. 94.
21 London, *Barleycorn*, pp. 53, 66.
22 London, *Barleycorn*, p. 67.
23 London, *Barleycorn*, p. 71.

the love of all men and women in the matter of man woman love; in fatherhood; in human justice; in art.'[24] Faith in these values gradually diminishes as drink undermines his capacity to work leading to the embarrassment of delivering a public lecture hungover – 'a day of wretchedness'. Disenchantment induces, according to London's alcoholic, 'a mental need, a nerve need, a good-spirits need' for alcohol, even as he claims that his constitution remains largely unimpaired by excessive drinking.[25] Attempting to cheat his physical hangovers during a sea cruise, which he takes as a rest cure, he maintains a 'canny self-intoxication', carefully avoiding the 'nausea of over-drinking, the after-effect of over-drinking, the helplessness and loss of pride of over-drinking'.

London's discourse begins to reveal, despite his alcoholic's claims to be 'beating the game', that years of drunkenness 'must ultimately be paid for, and with interest'.[26] When sobering up, payment manifests itself in a type of nihilism that he calls a 'cosmic sadness' or, elsewhere, 'a Nietzsche sickness': severe depression, in more commonplace terms, attributable to disenchantment.[27] Moreover, the more frequent adoption of a Withdrawal-Relief model of recovery signals the alcoholic's inability to support the rebellious spirit he earlier established. 'I was suffering from the morning sickness of the steady, heavy drinker', he admits. 'What I needed was a pick-me-up, a bracer ... So it was a drink before breakfast to put me right for breakfast.'[28] The need for a 'bracer' to overcome the physical symptoms of nausea and loss of appetite is no longer attributable purely to the body; attempts to offset the cosmic sadness – an example of the kind of abstract dread or 'deep sense of breakage' we have previously seen in self-evaluation during hangovers – dismantles the writer's faith in the essential decency of human nature.

John Barleycorn is indeed foundational in establishing the lineaments of the romanticised drunken outsider. It is also foundational in disclosing that the hangover undoes the myths of drunken self-determination. Noticeably, as a greater degree of free-floating misery arises out of social pressures to conform, hangovers become more problematic. The latter is something that the 'angry young man' of the 1950s, another manifestation of the self-mythologising rebel, also discovers. In Alan Sillitoe's *Saturday Night and Sunday Morning* (1958), Arthur Seaton represents post-war,

---

24   London, *Barleycorn*, p. 135.
25   London, *Barleycorn*, p. 159.
26   London, *Barleycorn*, p. 176.
27   See Per Serritsev Petersen, 'Jack London's Dialectical Philosophy Between Nietzsche's Radical Nihilism and Jules de Gaultier's Bovarysme', *Partial Answers*, 9.1 (2011), p. 67 (pp. 65–77); London, *Barleycorn*, p. 189.
28   London, *Barleycorn*, p. 183.

working-class disenfranchised youth, flouting restrictions and the law. Although willing to submit to the routine of work during the week, he requires compensation through Saturday nights filled with drink and sex and the occasional fist fight. The opening of the novel sees Seaton victorious in a drinking competition with a loudmouth sailor, but it is a 'violent preamble to a prostrate Sabbath'.[29] In a semi-comatose state, cautionary voices of conventional moral wisdom run through Seaton's head, but are easily dismissed: '"Couldn't care less, couldn't care less, couldn't care less" – in answer to the questions that came into his mind regarding sleeping with a woman who had a husband and two kids, getting blind drunk on seven gins and umpteen pints, falling down a flight of stairs, and being sick over a man and a woman.'[30] However, if *Saturday Night and Sunday Morning* contains examples of hangovers that punctuate heavy nights out, it is perhaps most notable as an example of the hangover as a generational motif and, as Seaton gets increasingly cocky and reckless, seeing three women, two of them married, the voices echo in his head more compellingly.

The hangover, or Sunday morning, gradually becomes more significant than the carnivalesque abandon of Saturday night. Seaton fashions an identity in contrast to his father, who spends his weekends glued to the television, and Jack, depicted as the average grafting husband and father. 'Factories sweat you to death', Seaton protests, 'labour exchanges talk you to death, insurance and income tax offices milk money from your wage packets and rob you to death.'[31] First and foremost, he declaims against the conventional course of marriage and fears 'courting' Doreen more than an outraged husband's reprisals: 'he realized that, by going out with a single girl he may one day – unwittingly and of course disastrously – find himself on the dizzy and undesired brink of the hell that older men called marriage, an even more unattractive prospect than coming one day face to face with some husband's irate and poised fist'.[32] Eventually, however, the latter leads to the former when he is beaten up by a couple of squaddies on the instigation of the husband of Winnie, Brenda's sister, and Jack.

Seaton endures a mammoth hangover, taking to his bed for a week to recover from his binge and his injuries: 'he lay there for days on end like a dead dog .... He heard the rattle of plates and cups from

29   Alan Sillitoe, *Saturday Night and Sunday Morning* (London: Harper Collins, 1995), p. 9.
30   Sillitoe, *Saturday Night*, p. 17.
31   Sillitoe, *Saturday Night*, p. 202.
32   Sillitoe, *Saturday Night*, p. 156.

downstairs, the dull thumping of factory turbines ... He only vaguely noticed the combined pandemonium rolling over the black cloud of his melancholy.'[33] The factory and what it represents of conventional working life exerts its power over Seaton. More than just physical violence, the hiding that Seaton receives symbolises the retaliation of hegemonic social forces, work and conventional married life, against which he previously rebelled and, despite his defiant prediction that 'that's not for me. Me, I'll have a good life: plenty of work and plenty of booze and a piece of skirt every month till I'm ninety', Seaton recognises that 'it was no use fighting against the cold weight of his nameless malady'.[34]

Sillitoe encapsulates the manner in which the impenetrable 'black cloud' of Seaton's malady gradually lifts with the realisation that he needs to 'grow up' and face the consequences for transgressing acceptable social standards. Seaton attempts to deflect his own 'Nietzsche sickness' onto physical symptoms – 'I don't feel well. I've got a bad back again, and my guts are terrible' he tells his mother. However, new anxieties and fears – 'No place existed in the world that could be called safe' – see him accept the comfort of a more conservative life with Doreen. The 'friendly forbearing voice' of Jack, who advises Seaton to 'knuckle under', wins out over Seaton's defiance as he endures 'life's penance at the lathe' and even begins to relish the prospect of adult responsibility: 'he would be the man of the house'.[35] More than the physical injuries he suffers, Seaton's ultimate failure to sustain an authentic outsider status through being repeatedly drunk is due to his gradual assimilation into conventional mid-century, working-class British life. Looking ahead towards marriage with Doreen he feels 'good in his heart about it, easy and confident, making for better ground than he had ever trodden before'. 'I must be drunk, he thought. No I'm not. I'm stone cold sober.'[36] But Sillitoe is clear that this altered sober outlook is a product of Seaton's hangover. He organises his narrative around the transition from drunkenness to sobriety, from Saturday night to the working week, but paramount in physical, psychosocial and symbolic terms is the impact of Sunday morning.

33   Sillitoe, *Saturday Night*, p. 179.
34   Sillitoe, *Saturday Night*, pp. 183, 180.
35   Sillitoe, *Saturday Night*, pp. 182–83, 190, 203, 217.
36   Sillitoe, *Saturday Night*, pp. 214–15.

Sacred Values and Intergenerational Conflict

The myth of the invincible, drunken outsider is firmly established by the likes of London and Sillitoe, but, as they link hangovers to their drunkards' greater awareness of 'sacred' values, the defiance they represent diminishes and the myth dissolves. London's alcoholic and Arthur Seaton convincingly set themselves against hegemonic forces, but these eventually speak through them in their vulnerable, hungover condition. A set of sacred values emerge out of personal confusion and the hangovers of both figures are shown to mark a 'stage' in their gradual assimilation into more orthodox social roles. Arthur Seaton seeks 'to construct a uniquely personal set of rules and beliefs as a way of resisting absorption' by mainstream cultural values.[37] That last quotation applies not, however, to Sillitoe, but to a later iteration of the rebellious young man who defies social norms through a commitment to heavy drinking: Charles Bukowski's Henry Chinaski. Less angry than Arthur Seaton, Chinaski accepts his hangovers in novels such as *Post Office* and *Factotum* with a type of stoicism, as a fundamental condition of his oppositional stance to the values espoused by his father and working-class, conservative America in the 1940s. Nevertheless, Chinaski is vulnerable to what we could call an intergenerational conflict of values concerning work, family and self-care.

In *Post Office*, Chinaski works as a mailman, downtrodden and driven to rebel against the exertion of arbitrary power by a series of pedantic bosses. His postal deliveries have the flavour of an interminable, Bunyanesque, marathon across the streets of suburban Los Angeles, due to his chronic hangovers. In winter he is dashed by rain and snow. In summer, the physical discomfort has the potential to signify penance –'The whiskey and beer ran out of me, fountained from my armpits, and I drove along with this load on my back like a cross, puffing out magazines, delivering thousands of letters, staggering, welded to the side of the sun'[38] – but Bukowski, as working-class Christ, instead makes delivering mail symbolic of non-conformity. For Chinaski, punishment as a consequence of drinking is ideological as much as physical, a 'defence', as Neeli Cherkovski puts it, 'against the status quo'.

By accepting 'defeat' and humiliation he discovers a 'jumping-off' point for an alternative lifestyle.[39] Endurance and toil are motifs of a quest

---

37   Niall Griffiths, 'Introduction' to Charles Bukowski, *Post Office* (London: Virgin Books, 2009), p. ix.
38   Bukowski, *Post Office*, p. 26.
39   Cherkovski, 'Introduction' to *Factotum*, pp. vi–vii.

for self-definition within a world where demeaning manual work cannot, like London's narrator-protagonist, be avoided, but equally it cannot be undertaken without the numbness that comes with strenuous drinking and its consequences. Withstanding the hangover is a daily event that proves Chinaski's ability to do enough to keep a job that will allow him to spend his nights drinking and having sex in defiance of conservative American family values. As Niall Griffiths explains: 'The post office, or any world of work, is only one institutionalised system of control', in Bukowski's fiction, 'that is designed to beat people, to condition them into accepting that humiliation and failure is the norm.'[40] To treat the postal service as anything other than a route to money for extra-curricular pleasures would be to admit such humiliation and defeat.

Even so, as Cherkovski reminds us, the 'literary rebel in Bukowski cannot quite shake off those classic American values' of home and work as he suggested he was able to in 'Hangover and Sick Leave'.[41] In *Factotum* – the title referring to Chinaski's inability to hold down any regular employment, drifting from one manual job to the next – he explores the pull of these values through the judgements that Chinaski is forced to bear during his hangovers. As Sarah Maddison argues, 'Intergenerational guilt involves our individual and collective choices about what we do in response to our knowledge' of the past.[42] Family life features prominently as impoverishment forces Chinaski to return to his parents' Los Angeles home. He returns with drinking habits that clash with his father's principles and, after a series of binges, the latter attempts to shame his son into sobering up and finding work:

> 'Where do you get the money to drink? You don't have any money!'
> 'I'll get a job.'
> *'You're drunk! You're drunk! My Son is a Drunk! My Son is a God Damned No-Good Drunk!'*
> The hair on my father's head was standing up in crazy tufts. His eyebrows were wild, his face puffed and flushed with sleep.
> 'You act as if I had murdered somebody.'
> *'It's just as bad!'*
> '… ooh, shit …'

40   Griffiths, 'Introduction' to *Post Office*, p. viii.
41   Cherkovski, 'Introduction' to *Factotum*, p. vii.
42   Sarah Maddison, *Beyond White Guilt: The Real Challenge for Black-White Relations in Australia* (Sydney: Allen & Unwin, 2011), pp. 7–8. See also the discussion of intergenerational continuities and discontinuities in proneness to shame and guilt in June Price Tangney and Ronda L. Dearing, *Shame and Guilt* (New York and London: Guilford Press, 2002), pp. 148–49.

Suddenly I vomited on their Persian *Tree of Life* rug. My mother screamed. My father lunged toward me.

'Do you know what we do to a dog when he shits on the rug?'

'Yes.'

He grabbed the back of my neck. He pressed down, forcing me to bend at the waist. He was trying to force me to my knees.

'I'll show you.'

'Don't ...'

My face was almost in it.

'I'll show you what we do to dogs!'[43]

Chinaski's war of values means confronting open frustration, violence and rage. Fathers, and figures of authority more generally in *Factotum*, are threatening and sinister, but uphold a clear set of values that the son contests through drunkenness. The scene in which Chinaski throws up on the expensive rug bearing the image of the Tree of Life wittily encapsulates the theme of sacrilege, but the violation of sacred, middle-class principles also informs the father's language of God, damnation and family: *'My Son is a Drunk!'*

During his hangover, Chinaski wavers between remorse – as he scours the 'Help Wanted' section of the local newspaper and takes aspirin – and defiance, eventually embracing the latter by turning to the comfort of a barroom. Arrested the following night for being drunk and disorderly, his father collects Chinaski from gaol and upbraids him: 'You've disgraced your mother and myself.' Driving down Broadway, Chinaski can only respond: 'Let's go in and catch a drink.'[44] The subject of Withdrawal-Relief focuses Bukowski on the theme of intergenerational discord, appalling the father and providing the son with an escape route. The confinement of the car physically represents Chinaski's moral claustrophobia.

As in 'Hangover and Sick Leave', indifference is the weapon of youth. But the stakes are raised further by the spectre of war. Chinaski avoids the draft, claiming 'The shrink said I was unfit',[45] but hangovers repeatedly place him in situations where not only is his commitment to the values of his parents questioned but also his patriotism. His father's accusations about failing to serve his country return, for example, during the period in which he takes lodgings in St Louis with the efficient landlady Mrs Downing and wholesome girls Gertrude and

43   Bukowksi, *Factotum*, p. 15.
44   Bukowski, *Factotum*, pp. 18–19.
45   Bukowski, *Factotum*, p. 19.

Hilda. Hangovers highlight the degree to which Chinaski's lifestyle destabilises his status as an outsider. Physical debility usually combines with questions about his integrity, as on the morning after his first night in the lodging house:

> When I awakened in the morning it was very cold. I was shivering uncontrollably. I got up and found that one of the windows was open. I closed the window and went back to bed. I began to feel nauseated. I managed to sleep another hour, then awakened. I got up, dressed, barely made it to the hall bathroom and vomited. I undressed and got back into bed. Soon there was a knock on the door. I didn't answer.[46]

The assignable symptoms of a hangover soon yield to psychosocial ones. Bukowski mines a rich comic vein as Chinaski is unable to prevent Hilda, Gertrude and Mrs Downing – bearing nourishing soup – into his room. Their polite, or naïve, questioning – 'We heard you in the bathroom. Are you sick?' – and inability to understand the reasons why a healthy young man should not be at work or fighting the Nazis, puncture Chinaski's already physically traumatised sense of self:

> 'You're not in the army?'
> 'No.'
> 'What do you do?'
> 'Nothing.'
> 'No work?'
> 'No work.'
> 'Yes,' said Gertrude to Hilda, 'look at his hands. He has the most beautiful hands. You can see that he has never worked.'[47]

Trapped in a domestic farce, Chinaski's need to assert his autonomy through a lifestyle of heavy drinking and draft dodging, to avoid absorption by orthodox value systems, is undermined by the generosity of others and Bukowski is alert to the irony that there is more charm and comfort in the conventional domestic values that Mrs Downing embodies.

Chinaski fights his intergenerational conflict during his hangovers, which establish the rhythm of his life as a factotum, ironically removed from the most significant event of the twentieth century:

46   Bukowski, *Factotum*, pp. 34–35.
47   Bukowski, *Factotum*, p. 35.

At some point during one of our hellish nights World War II ended. The war had always been at best a vague reality to me, but now it was over. And the jobs that had always been difficult to get became more so. I got up each morning and went to all the public employment agencies starting with the Farm Labor Market. I struggled up at 4.30a.m., hungover, and was usually back before noon. I walked back and forth between the agencies, endlessly ... there was very little money and we fell further and further behind with the rent. But we kept the wine bottles lined up bravely, made love, fought, and waited.[48]

Chinaski's war is fought elsewhere: on the streets, in cheap lodgings and at racetracks amidst dictatorial time-servers, truculent toadies, sexually insatiable women and endless bottles of alcohol while he temporises in the absence of anything better. There is no denying that Chinaski works – a lot – and subsisting on low pay takes a high level of resolution. But the nature of his resistance becomes more difficult to define under the duress of hangovers as the novel progresses. Disturbed by less quantifiable emotional aspects of the hangover he becomes more existential, as we have seen happen to London's alcoholic and Arthur Seaton. He wonders aloud 'What kind of man am I? ... My father told me I'd end up like this!'[49] Chinaski, impoverished, gambles uncontrollably, becomes violent and sexually aggressive with women, indulging in paranoid fantasies of punishment and imprisonment whilst shirking in a job at a warehouse packing bicycle parts:

A man with a hangover should never lay flat on his back looking up at the roof of a warehouse. The wooden girders finally get to you; and the skylights – you can see the chicken wire in the glass skylights – that wire somehow reminds a man of jail. Then there's the heaviness of the eyes, the longing for just one drink, and then the sound of people moving about, you hear them, you know your hour is up, somehow you have to get on your feet and walk around and fill and pack orders.[50]

Bukowski's claustrophobic vision of imprisonment in an urban hell captures Chinaski's nervous anxiety, the stress that alcohol places on the optic nerves, and vertigo, which Penning, McKinney and Verster

48   Bukowski, *Factotum*, pp. 74–75.
49   Bukowski, *Factotum*, p. 73.
50   Bukowski, *Factotum*, p. 63.

include in their list of hangover symptoms. (In *Post Office*, Chinaski has an equivalent period of dizzy spells.) Physical causes modulate into symbolic ones, however, in Bukowski's choice of imagery. The hangover cannot, unlike the speaker of 'Hangover and Sick Leave', be indulged due to the unrelenting pressure of work.

Despite unflinching honesty, assertions of independence and contrariety for its own sake, all qualities that typify drunken outsiders, Chinaski is not spared the hangover's emotional aspects. When, for instance, the tempestuous Jan abandons him he loses a job installing fluorescent lights and his hangover results in a crisis in self-determination:

> I got my first paycheck and moved out of Jan's place and into an apartment of my own. When I came home one night, she had moved in with me. What the fuck, I told her, my land is your land. Shortly thereafter, we had our worst fight. She left and I got drunk for three days and three nights. When I sobered up I knew my job was gone. I never went back. I decided to clean up the apartment. I vacuumed the floors, scrubbed the window ledges, scoured the bathtub and sink, waxed the kitchen floor, killed all the spiders and roaches, emptied and washed the ashtrays, washed the dishes, scrubbed the kitchen sink, hung up clean towels and installed a new roll of toilet paper. I must be turning fag, I thought.[51]

Chinaski's frantic cleaning spree appears to externalise his feelings of abjection and self-disgust. Bukowski presents another version of a Traditional-Punishment hangover reaction. The violation done to Chinaski's integrity through such out-of-character actions cannot be owned and so he dismisses them as the behaviour of a 'fag', but the hangover unmistakably instils the need to heal or rebuild identity through judicial mechanisms manifested in a desperate search for cleanliness.

'With home in my head I can't bear to be awake': The Stigmatised Female Drinker

Chinaski's hangovers are the psychosocial battleground on which, following Durkheim, Treeby and Bruno and Tangney and Dearing, the war of values that his parents represent is harrowingly fought. Shame at the violation of family values is a prominent theme in twentieth-century

51 Bukowski, *Factotum*, p. 107.

fiction, but is found as frequently in female as in male outsider figures. The figure of the hungover woman, and the female drinker generally, is a rarity and even taboo in earlier periods, but in the twentieth century more writers have tackled the subject.

Two periods are particularly notable for the fictional representation of women drinkers and these will occupy me here. Following the First World War and, particularly, the US's emergence from the prohibition era, drunken women become much more conspicuous in literature than they had previously been, particularly in novels set in the bohemian, ex-patriate, cultural centres of Europe. They include Ernest Hemingway's Lady Brett Ashley in *Fiesta: The Sun Also Rises* (1926), Christopher Isherwood's Sally Bowles in *Goodbye to Berlin* (1939), Jean Rhys's Sasha Jensen in *Good Morning, Midnight* (1939) and Patrick Hamilton's Netta Longdon in *Hangover Square* (1941). Each of these women is notable for their mixture of charisma, defiance and emotional volatility or vulnerability, so we might expect hangovers to feature alongside descriptions of their drunkenness. Later in the century, an equally significant cultural shift in women's drinking habits occurs with the rise of the 'ladette' and 'post-ladette' phenomena of the 1990s and 2000s that we find in Fielding's *Bridget Jones's Diary* and Kennedy's *Paradise*. Although ladettes often proclaim the ability to throw off earlier gender norms, generally through adopting behaviours conventionally associated with male drinkers, we will see that hangovers indicate the persistent presence of the sort of gendered judgements and social anxieties that are attached to the brash 'flappers' – usually associated with drinking, smoking and casual attitudes to sex – of the interwar years.

The links between these periods is found in the transgression of normative constructions of femininity, or what Alison Rolfe, Jim Orford and Sue Dalton call the 'stigmatizing subject positions' of women drinkers, which come to define their psychological states.[52] Moira Plant notes that women's drinking has, until recent times, conventionally been hidden from view within the home, making women drinkers natural outsiders, and that conspicuous public consumption of alcohol by women often carries negative connotations and punitive reactions.[53] These include judgements about sexual impropriety and availability, lack of self-control and allegations of what Rolfe, Orford and Dalton call

---

52   Alison Rolfe, Jim Orford and Sue Dalton, 'Women, Alcohol and Femininity: A Discourse Analysis of Women Heavy Drinkers' Accounts', *Journal of Health Psychology*, 14.2 (2009) p. 329 (pp. 326–35).

53   Moira Plant, *Women and Alcohol: Contemporary and Historical Perspectives* (London: Free Association Books, 1997).

'unfeminine, immoral, unrespectable' behaviour.[54] Patsy Staddon believes
that 'Women suffer disproportionately from shame when attempting to
deal with alcohol issues', which is often due to a perceived 'failure to
live up to accepted norms of femininity and their iconic position as being
central to family sustainability'.[55] Yet, these discourses often provide the
main 'resources' that 'women draw upon, modify or resist' in attempting
to cope with and explain the feeling that alcohol dependency causes the
'spoiling or forfeiting of feminine identities'.[56]

As a result, Rolfe, Orford and Dalton maintain that it is a challenge
for women drinkers 'not to be positioned as manly, sexually promiscuous
or lacking respectability', but that 'Women negotiate this challenge in a
number of different ways', by, for example, 'taking up a "lad" identity;
preserving a feminine identity through adhering to gendered ways of
drinking; and direct resistance of these gendered subject positions.'[57]
At times these categories overlap, which is true of Hemingway's Brett
Ashley. A sexually promiscuous woman, she self-consciously adopts
male drinking habits and associated discourses in order to fit within
male drinking environments; as a 'modern girl' she cuts her hair short,
dresses in a masculine way and her refrain is 'I say, give a chap a
brandy and soda.'[58] Each aspect of her self-fashioning allows her to evade
criticism concerning sexual impropriety that might be associated with her
drunkenness. Likewise, Hamilton's Netta Longdon manipulates the male
figures who vie for her attention, oscillating between highly feminine,
flirtatious performances and the adoption of male forms of drinking
parlance. This enables her strategically to resist a stable, feminine
subject position and take on a more fluid sexual one in relation to her
suitor George Harvey Bone, whom she despises, usually addressing him
disparagingly by his surname in the manner of a public-school bully.[59]

Drunken resistance of traditional female subject positions is, however,
weakened during hangovers, which is something we find in the case
of Sally Bowles, perhaps the most compelling example of the interwar

---

54   Rolfe *et al*, 'Women, Alcohol and Femininity', p. 327. Sheila B. Blume similarly
      notes that women's drinking is usually accompanied by a 'culturally ingrained
      expectation of hypersexuality and sexual promiscuity' ('Sexuality and Stigma:
      The Alcoholic Woman', *Alcohol Health and Research World*, 15.2 [1991], p. 139
      [pp. 139–48]).

55   Patsy Staddon, 'Improving Support for Women with Alcohol Issues', *Folk.
      us-PenCLAHRC Awarded Study* (22 September 2013), pp. 5–6.

56   Rolfe *et al*, 'Women, Alcohol and Femininity', p. 333.

57   Rolfe *et al*, 'Women, Alcohol and Femininity', p. 330.

58   Ernest Hemingway, *Fiesta: The Sun Also Rises* (London: Arrow Books, 2004), p. 18.

59   Patrick Hamilton, *Hangover Square* (London: Penguin, 2001), p. 36.

phenomenon of the liberated girl with a drink problem. In *Goodbye to Berlin*, Isherwood introduces Bowles, a cabaret artist who asserts her independence through excessive drinking and casual sex; she is a female counterpart to London's mythologised Romantic outsider who establishes a parallel mythology of the defiant female drinker. Bowles was such a compelling mixture of glamour, sophistication, and desultoriness, that she outgrew Isherwood's novel to take centre stage in adaptations for theatre – John Van Druten's *I am a Camera* (1955) on which Kander, Ebb and Masteroff's Broadway musical *Cabaret* (1966) was based – and the screen – Bob Fosse's 1972 *Cabaret* starring Liza Minnelli. Van Druten's Bowles does not differ markedly from Isherwood's character, but the outcome of her actions is altered in quite significant ways and comparison between the two versions of the story shows how hangovers host Bowles's misgivings about her sexual impropriety and the 'spoiling or forfeiting' of normative feminine identities.

In *Goodbye to Berlin*, Bowles flaunts her promiscuity, first introduced making a phone call to 'the man I slept with last night ... He makes love marvellously.'[60] Her cabaret act at the Lady Windermere night club is only described briefly, and Isherwood, the first-person narrator, focuses instead on her off-stage performances at their lodgings at Frl. Schroeder's. She is often tired but buoyant in the morning and, while Isherwood unenthusiastically consumes Fritz's coffee, Bowles mixes Prairie Oyster cocktails: 'They're about all I can afford.'[61] Late nights with Klaus Linke, a pianist, leave her 'looking tired but very pleased with herself', as Isherwood, seemingly captivated against his will, and Frl. Schroeder, more wholeheartedly enchanted, prepare her breakfasts and make her bed. When Klaus abandons her, Bowles is philosophical and her relationship with Isherwood focuses around their shared dreams of fame and fortune as 'Curled up on the sofa in the big dingy room, she smoked, drank Prairie Oysters, talked endlessly of the future.'[62]

However, the physical strain of her liberty starts to show during her relationship with the hard-drinking American, Clive: 'She was drinking nearly as much whisky as Clive himself. It never seemed to make her really drunk, but sometimes her eyes looked awful, as though they had been boiled. Every day the layer of make-up on her face seemed to get thicker.'[63] As Bowles's physical hangovers worsen, she is also abandoned

---

60   Christopher Isherwood, *Goodbye to Berlin* (London: Triad/Panther, repr. 1986), p. 32.
61   Isherwood, *Goodbye*, p. 36.
62   Isherwood, *Goodbye*, pp. 45–46, 51.
63   Isherwood, *Goodbye*, pp. 53–54.

by Clive and drinks heavily, but graver consequences are in store: 'Next morning, Sally felt very ill. We both put it down to the drink. She stayed in bed the whole morning and when she got up fainted. I wanted her to see a doctor straight away, but she wouldn't.'[64] Pregnant with Klaus's child, Bowles chooses a termination and continues to embrace a life of hedonism. As their relationship develops, Isherwood grows to see Bowles's brazen outbursts as a product of nervousness and shyness: '[Y]ou've got into this trick of trying to bounce [strangers] into approving or disapproving of you, violently.' Her impulsive nature, and the seemingly consequence-free backdrop of Weimar Berlin, is, however, emphasised by her engagement to a young man posing as a theatrical agent who subsequently steals her savings after they spend a night in a hotel. Telling the story, she 'giggled a little, like a naughty child which has intentionally succeeded in amusing the grown-ups'.[65] She departs for Paris at the end of the story, vivacity undiminished, despite the manifest signs of ageing to which Isherwood draws the reader's attention, and he never sees her again.

Isherwood's juxtaposition of Sally's shamelessness and her vulnerability becomes increasingly poignant following the abortion when she imagines what it would have been like to have the baby: 'Do you know, last night, I sat here for a long time by myself and held this cushion in my arms and imagined it was my baby?'[66] The emotional, rather than physical toll, of Sally's lifestyle and her ability to tolerate its repercussions and resist the 'iconic position' of motherhood is jeopardised by the episode, but she remains largely a riddle to Isherwood, which is also true of Van Druten's adaptation, although for different reasons.

In *I am a Camera*, the Sally Bowles character endures the same turmoil as in *Goodbye to Berlin*, but Van Druten is more interested in developing feelings of uncertainty and self-division through her scenes of hangover. Van Druten's Bowles shares with Isherwood's the desire for freedom, which means social and sexual liberty, revelling in her sensuality: '[Klaus] made me feel like a marvellous nymph, miles away from anywhere.'[67] At such points, monochrome Berlin fades into the background behind Sally's colourful imagination. Bowles sarcastically promises to behave respectably – 'ladylike' – in front of Chris's tutee, Natalia, and her nauseous mornings are comic to begin with. When

64   Isherwood, *Goodbye*, p. 58.
65   Isherwood, *Goodbye*, pp. 41, 80.
66   Isherwood, *Goodbye*, p. 62.
67   John Van Druten, *I am a Camera*, in *Famous Plays of 1954* (London: Victor Gollancz Ltd., 1954), p. 25.

Natalia discusses her phthisis, Sally interjects 'Do you mind not going on about it? I think I am going to be sick.'[68] But through the pregnancy plot, Van Druten highlights Bowles's uncertainty, not only about her body but about her values: 'It's like finding out that all the old rules are true, after all.' Chris advises drinking to forget, but the play suggests he is wrong in his view that 'you can duck', 'the facts of life'. Only semi-ironically Bowles wonders 'Do you think I could be a nun, Chris?', and reflects 'I can see now why people say operations like this are wrong.'[69]

Van Druten amplifies the emotional uncertainty of Sally Bowles and she internalises a punitive reaction to her sexual transgression. Hangovers force her back into the kind of stigmatising subject position identified by Rolfe *et al* that her drinking momentarily allowed her to escape. The reprehensible Clive, who leaves Bowles and Isherwood to travel around the world, demonstrates that real freedom depends on having a private income. Van Druten teases out the different consequences of an outsider identity based on drinking for men and women: as Chris reflects on his life in Berlin – 'I don't regret the time I've spent here. I wouldn't have missed a single hangover of it'[70] – Sally is the character shown to have been deeply wounded and she internalises a Traditional-Punishment response before turning to the Withdrawal-Relief recovery method. Initially her drinking problem worsens. She starts consuming alcohol before breakfast, which is the only occasion at which Chris expresses shock at her behaviour. Together they indulge in a new fantasy, but not this time about freedom so much as conformity. 'We're going to be good', declares Bowles, acknowledging her failure to hitherto adopt acceptable standards of femininity. The attraction of a respectable life is one without hangovers: 'And think how we'll feel in the mornings. Imagine what it will be like to wake up without coughing, or feeling even the least bit sick.'[71]

The biggest change that Van Druten makes to Isherwood's original plot is the arrival of Bowles's mother in Berlin after a 'drunk and sentimental' phone call. Her view that '[t]he old things are still the best' persuades Bowles – at her most vulnerable to self-doubt while nursing a hangover – to return home to England, but she is not so much leaving Berlin as abandoning a way of life.[72] Chris recognises this when he defiantly drinks brandy in front of Mrs Watson and laments to Sally:

68 Van Druten, *Camera*, pp. 27, 29.
69 Van Druten, *Camera*, pp. 48, 54, 57.
70 Van Druten, *Cameria*, p. 115.
71 Van Druten, *Camera*, p. 86.
72 Van Druten, *Camera*, pp. 91, 101.

'You're disappearing, right in front of my eyes.'[73] Rather than leave for Paris at the end of the play, Bowles is bundled off home by her mother and, in acquiescing, yields to the feelings of shame that pursue her after the abortion and, publicly at least, accepts the sacred values that she has earlier so passionately and stylishly defied.

Paris forms the backdrop for the story of Rhys's Sasha Jensen, another female drinker who seems in danger of disappearing before the reader's eyes due to being forced to confront her 'failure to live up to accepted norms of femininity'. Through the narrative of Sasha's trauma following the death of her new-born child and the breakdown of her marriage, Rhys takes readers to areas 'where standard values are questioned', but hangovers disclose a woman unable to detach herself from 'self-regulatory outcomes' through drunkenness. According to Rolfe, Orford and Dalton, social expectations surrounding alcohol consumption force women into habits of 'self-surveillance',[74] which is an accurate description of Sasha's mental state as she tarries in cafés and bars, riddled with feelings of self-doubt, mistrust and despair, haunted by her losses and anticipating the next drink. In Sasha's case self-surveillance manifests in obsessive checking, cataloguing and scheduling time, which is designed to prove that, otherwise adrift in her thoughts, her drinking does not prompt her to lose control, physically, sexually and, above all, emotionally.

Sasha's opening account of herself sets the novel's tone: 'I have been here five days. I have decided on a place to eat at midday, a place to eat in at night, a place to have my drink after dinner. I have arranged my little life. The place to have my drink in after dinner … Wait, I must be careful about that.'[75] In an obsessive-compulsive manner, Sasha continually checks her emotional state while drunk and hungover against an internalised set of values, which involve maintaining a façade of equanimity. Prompted to cry in a café when a woman hums the jazz number *Gloomy Sunday* – nicknamed the Hungarian Suicide song – Sasha characteristically upbraids herself, labelling the experience a 'catastrophe'. The woman's response – 'Sometimes I'm just as unhappy as you are. But that's not to say I let everyone see it'[76] – frames the embarrassment of Sasha's hangovers, which revolve around her concern that she has let herself down. The scene haunts the hungover Sasha, mixing with her other memories of the money she borrowed to take the Paris trip: 'I lie awake, thinking about it, and about the money

73   Van Druten, *Camera*, p. 109.
74   Rolfe *et al*, 'Women, Alcohol and Femininity', p. 332.
75   Jean Rhys, *Good Morning, Midnight* (London: Penguin, 1967), p. 9.
76   Rhys, *Good Morning, Midnight*, p. 10.

Sidonie lent me and the way she said: "I can't bear to see you like this." Half-shutting her eyes and smiling the smile which means: "She's getting to look old. She drinks."'[77] The generosity of Sidonie is, however, presented as an intrusion and stalls Sasha's recovery, prompting her to inspect her situation relentlessly through the judgements of another: 'I can't sleep. Rolling from side to side ...'

> I put the light on. The bottle of Evian on the bedtable, the tube of luminal, the two books, the clock ticking on the ledge, the red curtains ... I can see Sidonie carefully looking round an hotel just like this one. She imagines its my atmosphere. God, it's an insult when you think about it! More dark rooms, more red curtains ...
> But one mustn't put everything on the same plane. That's her great phrase. And one mustn't put everybody on the same plane, either. Of course not. And this is my plane ... Quatrième à gauche, and mind you don't trip over the hole in the carpet. That's me.[78]

Luminal was a drug used to control seizures and was taken as a general sedative during the 1930s. Sasha adopts her friend's judgements about slovenliness but, in her weariness, is unable to negate, with anything but forced irony, the words of her advice. The apartment oscillates between sanctuary and prison in Sasha's tormented, hungover hours, but the prison is as much a set of values as it is a physical place.

Sasha interprets her hypersensitivity as a feminine weakness, attempting to avoid the stigmatising position that women's drinking is 'a means of coping with emotional pain'.[79] For Rolfe, Orford and Dalton, this is fed by the commonly accepted belief that there is a gendered division in drinking problems, a 'binary division of men as strong (and therefore able to cope with day-to-day life) and women as more emotional and in need of "something to lean on"'.[80] Hence, the strain and vulnerability Sasha experiences when hungover leads her into routines of self-surveillance designed to prevent emotional outpourings:

> But careful, careful! Don't get excited. You know what happens when you get excited and exalted don't you? ... Yes. ... And then, you know how you collapse like a pricked balloon, don't you? Having no staying power. ... Yes, exactly. ... So, no excitement.

77 Rhys, *Good Morning, Midnight*, p. 11.
78 Rhys, *Good Morning, Midnight*, pp. 11–12.
79 Rolfe *et al*, 'Women, Alcohol and Femininity', p. 329.
80 Rolfe *et al*, 'Women, Alcohol and Femininity', p. 329.

> This is going to be a quiet, sane fortnight. Not too much drinking, avoidance of certain cafés, of certain streets, of certain spots, and everything will go off beautifully.[81]

Sasha avoids areas of the city that she associates with earlier, happier times, just as she avoids her own thoughts through self-medicating with alcohol and taking luminal at night. Her sexual liaison with the gigolo, René, is distressing rather than celebratory and accompanied by self-recrimination and the fear that he has robbed her: 'You've had dinner with a beautiful young man and he kissed you and you've paid a thousand francs for it. Dirt cheap at the price.'[82] It is slim consolation to discover that René has not in fact taken the money.

Rhys takes us into the mind-set of a woman whose attempts to outwardly adopt the sophisticated behaviour and demeanour of a sexually liberated, modern girl are undermined by her inability to deal with trauma without reliance on alcohol. The hangover is a dark shadow that is similarly cast over the likes of Brett Ashley and Sally Bowles, although the self-assertion of the latter two far outstrips that of Sasha Jensen and it is the outsider's defiance despite psychological injuries that remains fascinating. The other part of Bowles's fascination lies in the way she mimics sexual behaviour that is more readily condoned in men (just as do Brett Ashley and Netta Longdon). As Linda Mizejewski argues, Bowles is part of a complex mixture of anxieties about sexual fluidity and the rise of fascism depicted throughout *Goodbye to Berlin*, elements of which we also find present in *Good Morning, Midnight*.[83] In the 1990s, the post-feminist 'ladette' phenomenon disclosed similar alarm about the link between female alcohol consumption and sexual abandon.[84] Rickards *et al* note that there was a marked increase of alcohol consumption amongst young women in the 1990s.[85] The term 'ladette' was coined by the British media to describe 'A young woman characterized by her enjoyment of social drinking, sport, and other activities typically considered to be male-oriented, and often by attitudes or behaviour regarded as irresponsible or brash' (*OED*). As Alison Mackiewicz argues: '"Ladettes"

---

81   Rhys, *Good Morning, Midnight*, p. 14.
82   Rhys, *Good Morning, Midnight*, p. 154.
83   Linda Mizejewski, *Divine Decadence: Fascism, Female Spectacle, and the Makings of Sally Bowles* (Princeton, NJ: Princeton University Press, 1992), p. 35.
84   The moral panic of the two periods has been linked by Carolyn Jackson and Penny Tinkler in '"Ladettes" and "Modern Girls": "Troublesome" Young Femininities', *Sociological Review*, 55.2 (2007), pp. 251–72.
85   L. Rickards *et al*, 'Living in Britain, no. 31. Results from the 2002 General Household Survey' (London: Stationery Office, 2004).

were troublesome; not only because they occupied space outside the
traditional feminine (indoor) domestic sphere, but also, more importantly,
because they were presented as vying for space once reserved for men
only – public drinking.'[86] The mirroring of male drinking behaviour is,
however, shown to only operate at a surface level by hangovers that
differentiate the kind of social judgements passed on male and female
drinking in a text such as *Bridget Jones's Diary*.

Bridget Jones may not qualify as a ladette in all regards, but her
ability to navigate life as a single woman in the mid-1990s involves
her engaging with conflicting social judgements about female drinking,
and mixed messages, that lead her to transgress her internalised moral
principles. While on the one hand her self-assertive friend, Shazzer,
proclaims the pair represent a 'pioneer' generation of women 'daring to
refuse to compromise in love and relying on our own economic power',
on the other Bridget feels the pressure from her overbearing mother
to marry and have children and so conform to the 'iconic position' of
motherhood. A self-confessed regular drinker, it is during her hangovers
that Bridget voices anxieties about her incapacity to meet acceptable
standards of female conduct. The novel opens with a list of New Year's
resolutions through which Bridget fashions a self-image based on a
set of respectable personality traits that include cultivating a cool and
conventional exterior, not broadcasting her need for a partner, giving up
smoking and cutting back on alcohol. Much of the comedy of the novel
comes from her failure to live up to this initial set of standards, her
susceptibility to the charms of the philandering Daniel Cleaver and her
reluctance to form an engagement with the more suitable Mark Darcy
(her mother's favoured choice).

Invited to a turkey buffet at the house of her parents' friends, the
Alconburys, on New Year's Day, her mother attempts to set her up
with Darcy: 'Being set up with a man against your will is one level
of humiliation, but being literally dragged into it by Una Alconbury
whilst caring for an acidic hangover, watched by an entire roomful
of friends of your parents, is on another plane altogether.'[87] Alcohol
helps Bridget to surmount social embarrassment of this sort and to
silence her inner critic and she resists the prospect of becoming a
'Smug Married', but her hangovers are full of self-recrimination – 'Oh

---

86   Alison Mackiewicz, 'Alcohol, Young Women's Culture and Gender Hierarchies',
       in Patsy Staddon (ed.), *Women and Alcohol: Social Perspectives* (Bristol and Chicago,
       IL: Policy Press, 2015), p. 70.
87   Helen Fielding, *Bridget Jones's Diary* (London: Picador, repr. 2001), p. 13.

why am I so unattractive? Why?'[88] – based around negative evaluation of body image and personality that she attributes to contemporary representation of women in the media: 'Wise people will say Daniel should like me just as I am, but I am a child of Cosmopolitan culture, have been traumatized by super-models and too many quizzes and know that neither my personality nor my body is up to it if left to its own devices.' Her self-loathing is compounded by her physical suffering:

> 8 a.m. Ugh. Wish was dead. Am never, ever going to drink again for the rest of life.
> 8.30 a.m. Oooh. Could really fancy some chips.
> 11.30 a.m. Badly need water but seems better to keep eyes closed and head stationary on pillow so as not to disturb bits of machinery and pheasants in head.[89]

Bridget's mother reminds her, 'There's nothing worse than a woman drunk, darling', but Bridget's hangovers show the real paucity of options to middle-class conformity. Hence, she worries when fighting off the sexual attentions of Cleaver that 'I may have been right, but my reward, I know, will be to end up all alone, half-eaten by an Alsatian.' Shazzer represents female defiance, bemoaning Bridget's assimilation: 'Even the most outrageous minxes lose their nerve, wrestling with the first twinges of existential angst: fears of dying alone ... Stereotypical notions of shelves, spinning wheels and sexual scrapheaps.'[90] But during hangovers, a cocktail of reasons for self-loathing that derive from the late twentieth century undermine Bridget's ability to follow the independent course advocated by the more dominant Shazzer.

In her depiction of the hangovers of Hannah Luckraft in *Paradise*, A. L. Kennedy updates the motif of the post-feminist hangover for the twenty-first century with more extreme examples of the kind of physical and emotional suffering that Bridget Jones undergoes. Hannah deliberately styles herself as an outsider – though lacking the principles of a Shazzer – defined by incipient alcoholism, sexual promiscuity and disregard for health, both mental and physical. Her shocking behaviour and defiance may suggest at times that she feels morally unaccountable, as with the speaker of 'Hangover and Sick Leave', and has outgrown the shame-proneness of a Sasha Jensen or Bridget Jones. However, Kennedy

88   Fielding, *Bridget Jones*, p. 16.
89   Fielding, *Bridget Jones*, p. 68.
90   Fielding, *Bridget Jones*, pp. 34, 33, 20.

opens the novel with a hangover scene that establishes the manner in which Hannah hosts not only the physical repercussions of drinking, but also a conflicting set of gendered values that damage her self-image and integrity.

Waking in a hotel to a 'generalised sting of yellow light', with little memory of how she got there – a stolen credit card and unwelcome evidence of a sexual encounter are the only clues as to the previous night's events – Hannah is unable to establish from the clock whether it is 8.42 in the morning or evening. Kennedy's deadpan humour characterises the outsider, evoking the offhand beat of Raymond Chandler: 'Either way, from what I can already see, I would rather not be involved in this too far beyond 8.43.'[91] It is, in fact, morning and downstairs breakfast is being served. Thirsty, racked by headache and nausea, Hannah quaffs large quantities of apple juice at the buffet, but finds that antagonists lie in wait both within and without; the former embodied by her spinning head and volatile stomach, the latter by an English family with whom she is forced to share a table. Hannah dismisses the father – 'Mr Wispy' – for his gingery, problem hair and conventionality: 'the type to have hobbies: sad ones that he'll want to talk about'. His children are intractable and unreceptive: 'The girl glowers with some vehemence' across the table.[92]

The hotel is a deliberate pastiche of low horizons and the mundane, but it is the body that delivers the first significant blow, as we have often seen before. Hannah eyes 'a woman shovelling out what could be eggs': 'I can see them shudder and slide. They unnerve me in a way they should not – because eggs ought to have no particular power over me – and I realise that I'm about to have a feeling, something unpleasant, an episode.' The shuddering and sliding are equally attributable to Hannah's physiological and emotional states: Kennedy reminds us of the way hangovers blur distinctions between body and mind. Hannah struggles to interpret sensations, slipping between acceptance and defiance: in this case the rational mind dismisses the manipulative influence of eggs, but the stomach has other ideas. Kennedy describes the sudden emotional hyperbole, paranoia and sickness, that crowd upon Hannah – 'I may cry, or become unsteady, or find myself vomiting' – who realises for certain that she is about to lose control of her body and the contents of her stomach.[93]

Nevertheless, the breakfast with Mr Wispy is not really about a physical reaction as Kennedy uses the hangover to express Hannah's

---

91   A. L. Kennedy, *Paradise* (London: Vintage, 2015), p. 3.
92   Kennedy, *Paradise*, pp. 4, 10.
93   Kennedy, *Paradise*, p. 12.

deeply internalised feelings of self-disgust. Surrounded by images of conventional British family life, these derive from Hannah's own past and undermine her self-fashioning as a promiscuous single woman and prospect of escaping conventional family values. Hannah first strives to conceal her hangover from the family: 'Trying to balance myself at the top of my neck, not picturing my personality starting to slop out over my sides, running down to my chin.'[94] The image grotesquely figures her feelings of abjection. More than just indicating a coaction of body and mind, the hangover makes the self vulnerable; private life threatens to spill shamefully into public view. Second, she has to endure the 'queasily rising box' that is the hotel lift: the somatic effects of the hangover appear to pervade and be attributable to the physical world, although they arise in and belong to the self. That self is compromised and splintered by the multiple reflective surfaces of the lift in which Hannah endures a nightmarish sense of *mise-en-abyme*. Her degraded physical image presents itself 'from a few especially disastrous angles my right selves and my left selves reflect each other unrelentingly'.[95] Not 'sides' but 'selves': Kennedy's choice of language denotes the way that reflection captures the damaged emotional, as much as physical, life through the hangover's relentlessness. The mirror is the perfect image for an experience that distorts body consciousness.

Under extreme physical and emotional duress, Hannah's qualified observation, 'I'm home. Perhaps', has much in common with Sally Bowles's mother announcing, 'I'm taking Sally home'.[96] As Hannah confesses, during the hangover that prompts her brother Simon to send her to dry out in a Canadian sanatorium, 'with home in my head I can't bear to be awake'.[97] Throughout the novel Hannah's hangovers play host to signs of gendered conflict in more personally damaging ways than is the case for Bridget Jones. As memories gradually return it becomes apparent that she ended up in this hotel having escaped from the sanatorium, flying to London, via a drunken interlude in Budapest with an unidentified man called Kussbachek. Fictions of Kussbachek lead to some sardonic reflections on Hannah's temperamental differences from her mother: 'Kussbachek – if my mother had been meeting a Kussbachek … she would have brought a little present with her. She would have paid her visit properly. In Hungary, I didn't do what she taught me. This is the way with me – I was brought up well, but the details of that

94   Kennedy, *Paradise*, p. 13.
95   Kennedy, *Paradise*, p. 13.
96   Van Druten, *Camera*, p. 109.
97   Kennedy, *Paradise*, p. 146.

don't always show.' If Hannah deflects the significance of being out of step with family values onto trivialities, such as her inability to wrap presents as neatly as her mother, Kennedy places great weight on her conclusion 'my mother gets it right'.[98] Reassurance that '[t]here is no current cause for gloom, or maudlin recollections of the family home and how handy my mother might have been with fancy paper and adhesive tape' is denial.[99] Her composure proves unsustainable because Hannah cannot unequivocally negate her mother's rectitude and, in so doing, extrapolate herself from the shame at her difference from conventional middle-class parents, her brother's successful marriage and professional life as a doctor, and an idyllic childhood to which she returns obsessively during the lonely, haunted hours of her mornings. Her hangovers suggest an inability to cope with transgression, particularly of a sexual variety, despite her distinctive candidness on the subject: 'I do feel remorse for every sin. Inside, I am mostly built out of remorse.'[100]

The only option from hereon in is flat disavowal. '[T]he idea of my mother and father has to be strictly controlled for the sake of my health', she announces. 'I will cast up little childhood scenes, seek out the clean and early times and dream above them nicely, but beyond that, I'm taking no risks.'[101] Seeking out cleanliness is more than just metaphoric, as the final suppressed memory of her drunken escapade – the shock recollection that her sexual partner of the night before was actually the physically repellent Mr Wispy – returns in cruel and comic fashion. A shower becomes a scene of ritual washing, an overt example of a Traditional-Punishment response, reminiscent of Henry Chinaski's cleaning spree in *Factotum*, which showcases Hannah's feelings of being penetrated, both sexually, but also ideologically, by all that Mr Wispy symbolises of her fears about the hypocrisies of family life:

> The best move I can make is to have a shower ... I'm healing right now, if I think about it, rebuilding whatever is amiss.
> I don't even mind that the soap smells of dog, or that the drain is looking nastily clogged. That's really – it's not what you'd want near your feet – a grubby, perforated plate that's matted with hairs which are clearly not mine, clearly moving in the flow of water, reddish yellow, some of them definitely pubic, others more wispy: wispy would be the only word to describe them.

---

98   Kennedy, *Paradise*, p. 29.
99   Kennedy, *Paradise*, p. 30.
100 Kennedy, *Paradise*, p. 217.
101 Kennedy, *Paradise*, p. 217.

>The only word to make the shower curtain crawl along my side
>and cling, the only word to make the water blind me, the only word
>to show me elbowing open my bedroom door in the grey stumble
>of last night, last early morning and Wispy trying open-mouthed
>kisses and missing, thumping like a wet, cupped hand against my
>chin, my cheek – I am already ducking him, but I am also letting
>him in and seeing his damp struggle out of his jacket and his shirt
>and he can't take off the ginger hair across his stomach.[102]

Kennedy fills Hannah's idle indifference to her surroundings with
a wonderful sense of foreboding. The ensuing rush of association is
reminiscent of so many previous hangovers we have seen, from Dickens's
David Copperfield to Amis's Jim Dixon. Red hair clogging the plughole
prompts total recall, unlocking memory just as Hannah recalls unlocking
her door to let Wispy into her hotel bedroom. The grotesque contents of
the clogged-up drain – 'grubby', 'matted', 'wispy' and the unwelcomely
affirmative, 'definitely pubic' – suddenly intrude on the self from which
they can no longer be distinguished. The shower curtain, which crawls
and clings to Hannah's body, makes that process all the more visceral.
Her memories of administering oral sex – 'I did. I really did' – are banal
rather than appalled, but nevertheless she resolves to 'stay under the
shower longer and scrub the way he must have done' before he returned
to his wife.[103] It would be an oversimplification to say that her subsequent
forthright dismissal of shame and acknowledgement of the indiscretion
– 'I have a need that isn't thirsty' – is undone by these initial feelings
of revulsion and by her self-exoneration that in drink 'I am not myself',
but the dual movement of assignment and deflection characteristic of the
hangover is noticeably only offset by Withdrawal-Relief, which provides
forgetfulness if not genuine healing: 'if I now go down to the bar I
can have another drink and that will make me feel not grisly at all ...
my condition does indeed mean that I am ruined without drink'.[104] Traces of
medicalisation accompany the word 'condition', which plays its part in
deflecting attention from the acknowledgement of responsibility that the
emotional crisis otherwise signifies.

Kennedy underlines the complex mingling of acceptance and
deflection, insight and wilful blindness, that characterise Hannah's
hangovers. She returns to the grooves of thought that implicate family
and childhood: 'Once I've scraped myself thoroughly clean I can go

102 Kennedy, *Paradise*, pp. 31–32.
103 Kennedy, *Paradise*, p. 32.
104 Kennedy, *Paradise*, p. 33.

downstairs and melt my unease down to a whisper with half a gill. And it's not even Mr Wispy that's upsetting me, in any case. I'm mildly troubled because, for some, reason, I keep hearing my younger voice ask my mother why she couldn't give flowers.'[105] Despite her confused affirmations to the contrary, Hannah's actions, and recurrent obsessions, vocalise shame in the face of a clash of values concerning acceptable female behaviour. And, despite her apparent empowerment through sexual promiscuity that at first seems to mark her out from the flappers of the 1920s and 1930s and the ladettes of the 1990s, these are deeply embedded values and seldom fail to frame her hangovers. 'Negative reinforcement', which is the need to escape from 'aversive states such as withdrawal or stress', maintains her reliance on alcohol.[106] Combined memories of Wispy and her mother's generosity collude in an unwelcome fashion that disturbs Hannah sufficiently enough to prompt the need to adopt the Withdrawal-Relief method of recovery – the method that Treeby and Bruno associate with highly developed moral sensibility and shame, but also with proneness to alcohol addiction.

Humiliation and Class Consciousness

In the period of the hangover a sense of identity, framed by specific cultural assumptions, is prone to suffer damage. The psychosocial pathways of negative affect represented in twentieth-century hangover literature often arise in injuries to self-esteem and feelings of humiliation that may result in pride, denial, contrariety and resentment, but also substantiation and admission. If these issues are often gendered for drunken outsiders, as I have argued, then they also frequently necessitate addressing related beliefs about class and social status. We have already seen the results of feelings of loss of standing on the hungover individual in the Victorian fiction I analysed in Chapter 5, but Patrick Hamilton's *Twenty Thousand Streets Under The Sky* (1935) showcases the continuing impact of class consciousness on male and female drinkers of the twentieth century and on the prospect of admission and denial. Hamilton forensically inspects the hangover as a painful period of social embarrassment and shattered dreams for those who attempted to exert their individuality through drunkenness in inter-bellum London.

---

105 Kennedy, *Paradise*, p. 33.
106 Karen D. Ersche, 'Intoxicants and Compulsive Behaviour: A Neuroscientific Perspective', in Herring *et al* (eds), *Intoxication and Society*, p. 214 (pp. 210–31).

In *Twenty Thousand Streets Under The Sky* – a series of three shorter novels that were first published between 1929 and 1935 and that say more about the social dynamics of hangovers than the more famous *Hangover Square* – Hamilton vividly captures the way that class consciousness leads to self-reproach in the hangovers of Bob, bar waiter at the London pub *The Midnight Bell*, and Jenny Maple, servant turned prostitute, whom he meets and falls in love with while waiting tables. Hamilton first tells the tale of Bob's infatuation with Jenny and the latter's seemingly callous manipulation of his devotion in order to extort money, before relating Jenny's own back story through her first encounter with alcohol and the glitz of London night life. Bob's collusion in his downfall is measured by his loss of money as he gradually exhausts his £80 savings in the forlorn attempt to persuade Jenny to take on more respectable employment and marry him. Bob's inability to impose his will on Jenny and raise her status or 'save' her is marked not by her forthright character, but by the kind of shrug that I earlier identified as a constituent of the outsider in Bukowski's 'Hangover and Sick Leave'. Characteristically failing to rendezvous with Bob at agreed times – 'Any time you like, dear', is her customary, noncommittal refrain – being inexplicably uncontactable by telephone, or unexpectedly disappearing from her lodgings, Bob stalks her through the streets of Piccadilly in order to secure meetings. 'Her inconsequence was awful', the narrator remarks.[107]

When Jenny fails to show up at Victoria station for a holiday in Brighton, Bob, having given her £20 to 'buy' her from an assignation with a client who had promised her the same amount, embarks on a bender, during which he is robbed of his final savings and awakes in a doss house, after being deposited there by another prostitute. The morning brings acute physiological distress – his 'mouth resembles sandpaper', his 'ears are singing', he dare not move 'for fear of being sick' – followed by the particular torment of humiliation, knowledge of the extent of his self-delusion about Jenny and a desire for penance or punishment, proportionate to his shattered sense of integrity, manifested in many shades of self-pity:

> Hoping obscurely (and he knew not why) for the dawn, Bob maintained one position, put his hands to his head – as though praying – as though indicted by life for his sins and folly – and submitted to the passing of an hour ... Tears of sorrow and dissipation filled Bob's eyes .... Reading his own fate in the sky,

107 Patrick Hamilton, *Twenty Thousand Streets Under the Sky* (London: Vintage, 2004), pp. 147–48.

he sensed something too vast, profound, and inconsolable to be malignant; and the tears, half of self pity, half of dissipation, flowed.

What now? He could go to 'The Midnight Bell', he supposed. They would always welcome him there. Ella, the Governor, the Governor's Wife. They had always been so good and friendly, and he had played them so false. With his inner passion, his secret life, he had thought to deceive them – but they would take him back. He would have to get the governor to advance him some money. There was no doubt that he'd get it. If possible, he would start work again at once ....

What story could he tell them – how account for his return? He would have to tell them something near the truth. The thought gave him relief. He so sorely needed confession. 'I'm afraid I've got in with a bad lot lately,' he would say, and they would forgive and understand.[108]

Bob's waking moments are dominated by cathartic feelings of guilt and remorse that signal constructed emotion. Prayer is almost an automatic, bodily reaction; 'indicted' establishes a vocabulary of crime, trial and punishment and a sense of submission in the face of his actions sets a *mea culpa* tone. He expresses desire for correction or penalty, characteristic of the Traditional-Punishment model of hangover response, slipping into an extensive period of self-regard for his folly in pursuing a prostitute who never loved him.

Through the kind of penitent's rhetoric with which we are familiar from earlier chapters, Bob conjures a scene of repentance and 'confession' featuring his employers and Ella, barmaid at *The Midnight Bell*. However, Bob's sin is specific to his historical moment. Hamilton shows transgression of class values: Bob has consorted with, and had the hubris to believe he could tame, Jenny, flying in the face of Ella's warnings. His sense of deception and secrecy arise from hiding the facts of his courtship of Jenny. Even then, the psychological process implicates an attempt to rebuild his damaged self-image as he contemplates how to tell his story and how much to reveal, before the guilt of the hangover forces his hand, preparing him for full confession. Bob, even in acute physical and emotional distress, attempts to reconstruct a more socially acceptable identity by establishing a hierarchy of values with Jenny cast as outsider and Ella and his employers as insiders. Parents may be absent from the equation, but Bob constructs a surrogate family at the pub from whom he can seek reparation. Tallying exactly

---

108 Hamilton, *Twenty Thousand Streets*, pp. 216–18.

with the expression of Hannah Luckraft, Bob sees his abjection as 'a healing thought'.[109] The process of healing is an endorsement of orthodox standards of morality: the wholesome sexual propriety of Ella as opposed to the shameless promiscuity of Jenny.

Jenny's role as the authentic outcast – Bob only temporarily performs this part – and antagonist is confirmed by Bob's conclusion that he had 'never disturbed, for one instant, the calm equability of her degradation'.[110] It is dually a sign of his humiliation at being tricked and a projection of judgement on Jenny, establishing her as morally and emotionally tainted, rendered incapable of feeling due to her profession and sexual proclivities. In the twentieth century, the female hangover often stages a response to perceived sexual aberration as we have seen in the case of Hannah Luckraft, and, in the second story, Hamilton uses a hangover to allow the reader to enter and gain understanding of Jenny's own complex milieu as an outsider, disclosing patterns of behaviour that differ somewhat from those of Bob, even while her breach of acceptable values savours of the same kind of regard for social status.

Jenny's first night of drunkenness leads her to reject her usual suitor, the pale and consumptive Tom, and to despise her role as maidservant to 'two old fossils' in Chiswick. 'I don't want your dirty jobs' she tells Tom, who reminds her that she has to be at work in the morning: 'You thought you was dealing with a skivvy – didn't you?'[111] Unfortunately this elevated sense of status leads her into a drunken escapade with a couple of pick-up artists, and a drink-driving incident in which a man on a bicycle is knocked down and killed. The morning after, Jenny awakes partially clothed in an alien bed with no memory of how she got there, experiencing a colossal feeling of humiliation, proportionate to her earlier sense of headiness at being repeatedly flattered for her beauty (one of her suitors even offers her a job as a department store model). The transgression of class values and the judgement of authority figures haunt Jenny during a hangover that puts her firmly back in her place as a working-class woman. Hamilton indicates that, once the clouds of uncertainty disperse, punishment is causally linked to her own earlier feelings of superiority:

> Where was she? She had got to do some thinking – some quick thinking. She was so sick and giddy she could hardly think. She

109 Hamilton, *Twenty Thousand Streets*, p. 220.
110 Hamilton, *Twenty Thousand Streets*, p. 220.
111 Hamilton, *Twenty Thousand Streets*, pp. 289, 298.

had got to get out of here. She must think. Sitting up in bed, staring at the window, her teeth chattering, Jenny thought.

She had got to get out. The door was behind her. She would have to go out and see where she was. Not yet. She was too cold.

Oh – what had God done to her? This was God's doing. She had been 'bad', and now she was stricken. This was her punishment. Why had she not listened? The very darkness of the day bespoke God's wrath and gloom against her.

Would she ever be forgiven now? What had she done that was so terrible? The accident! – that was it – she had almost forgotten in her panic. They had killed a man. He must have been killed. Remembering Violet's screams she could not doubt it.

Somewhere, under this awful sky, that man lay dead. It was no dream. Somewhere, at this moment a crowd of people knew of the crime and were clamouring for knowledge of the guilty party. Had they already succeeded in finding it? Would they succeed? What would aid them? The police! By now it was in the hands of the police! The police were after her! Oh, worse than God – the police! She wished she was dead.[112]

Hangover consciousness involves elevated levels of anxiety, bordering on paranoia, as Jenny's memories of the accident coalesce out of her initial physical and mental confusion. The amplification of negative affect that typifies penitent's rhetoric means, however, that the hangover contains its unassignable or elusive elements too, and Jenny's plea for forgiveness is only partially tethered to the specific incident: surprisingly, 'she had almost forgotten it in her panic'. Jenny envisages a hellish scene of spiritual torment with Calvinist overtones. 'Bad' – its force emphasised by the inverted commas – could be a judgement from any number of ambiguous authority figures, but this crystallises into the specific threat of the police. The church and law, which we saw casually dismissed by Bukowski in 'Hangover and Sick Leave', here police Jenny through a Traditional-Punishment fantasy. The image of a 'crowd' or mob of people baying for vengeance – evoking the skimmington that I discussed in Chapter 3 – gives extra anxious impetus to the short clauses and heavily punctuated thoughts. Jenny performs the part of criminal and outcast in her fantasy of punishment.

Where she differs from Bob is in the degree to which she adheres to class principles: wishing she were dead, Jenny is unable to believe that she can be forgiven for transgressing social norms and this eventually

---

112 Hamilton, *Twenty Thousand Streets*, p. 307.

leads her, unlike Bob, to develop a drinking problem. Her feelings of humiliation are given teeth by the richly comic circumstances when awaking in a house in Richmond Park, with one of the men from the previous night, whom she immediately identifies as a 'gentleman'. There is no hint of sexual violation or threat, despite Jenny's feelings of vulnerability and inability to find her dress. In fact, Jenny finds herself in much greater danger of condescension. In a scene of mundane culture clash – the opposite of Jenny's visions of damnation – her 'gentleman's' apparent indifference is contrasted with her own paranoia and obsessive rehearsal of potential excuses for lateness:

> Who was he – this casual male? So this was his flat. He was a 'gentleman' obviously. She could tell that from his voice and looks. In other circumstances she might have been flattered by the acquaintanceship. Why didn't he come? He didn't care. He was a 'gentleman' – he had no work to go to – no job to go to.
>
> How long did it take to get from Richmond to Chiswick? Half an hour – it shouldn't take more. What excuse could she make if she was late? If she could only think of a good excuse.[113]

Jenny finds herself, not unlike Hannah Luckraft, in a farcically decorous situation as the gentleman first runs her a bath and then begins to prepare breakfast, shuffling in his 'loose carpet slippers', with no hint of urgency. As his 'blasted skivvy's down with flu', Jenny ends up running his bath and then preparing the boiled eggs herself.[114] There is a bitter irony in Jenny waiting on the man of higher class, considering she spent the previous evening drunkenly protesting her position as a 'skivvy'. As with Luckraft, Jenny's inability to hurry things along or excuse herself from the ritual of breakfast – even though the eggs turn her stomach – is due to the enactment of propriety in which both collude.

Thoughts of the injured Tom torment her: 'If only she were with Tom now – instead of this hard, cold-mannered "gentleman." She hated him and his class.' Hamilton is unambiguous in demonstrating that Jenny's hangover is a tragedy of social status. Announcing 'I'm a servant', is more than coming clean. It is part of her adoption of a Traditional-Punishment ethic as she burns 'with humiliation' and recalls the folly of 'her castles-in-the-air of the night before'.[115] Having fantasised in her cups about dating a man with a car, she finds herself stuck in a nightmarish

113 Hamilton, *Twenty Thousand Streets*, p. 310.
114 Hamilton, *Twenty Thousand Streets*, p. 313.
115 Hamilton, *Twenty Thousand Streets*, p. 318.

inversion of that vision as her gentleman eventually drives her into town: 'She saw a few people on the pavement glancing at them as they passed – but without interest. She might have been a "lady" taking a drive. If they only knew how far she was from that.'[116] Reality exposes her delusion, but also the social boundaries that her hangover makes abundantly clear she is unable to surmount. Attempting to get to work – a world of work that separates her from her idle companion – the car journey symbolises the desire to return to respectable and civilised values not unlike the walk that Jude Fawley takes to Marygreen discussed in Chapter 5. However, unlike the repentant Jude, Jenny fails to complete her literal and figurative ride. Late beyond any explanation, she allows herself to be taken to another pub and drinks whisky. A 'brisk medicining', changes the entire dynamic of the situation as she numbs her conscience and nerves with more alcohol. Alcohol lifts her from what she now calls an 'absurd depression': 'the mists had disappeared now simply vanished like magic!'[117] It is only a short step from this to spending the entire day with her new 'gentleman friend' and turning her back on the respectable employment of washing dishes, making beds and cooking.

Hamilton uses the hangover to expose the paucity of choices for a working-class woman in the 1930s. As the narrator informs us, the episode constitutes 'the turning point of her life', which eventually leads Jenny to petty theft and prostitution.[118] As with Hannah Luckraft, the hangover also provides a commentary on inflexible gender roles: the former's family is replaced by the latter's service, but both women can only define themselves against socially acceptable behaviour through drunken, sexual promiscuity that they later regret. It is only with alcohol flowing through her veins that Jenny genuinely defies social reprisals.

'A Deep Sense of Breakage': Omission and Memory Loss

In this book's introduction, I quoted Kingsley Amis's belief that writers on the hangover often 'omit the psychological, moral, emotional, spiritual aspects: all that vast, vague, awful, shimmering metaphysical superstructure'. Without neglecting the body, I have tried to return these aspects to the discussion of hangovers and, in so doing, identify examples of constructed emotion, the shifting socio-cultural

116 Hamilton, *Twenty Thousand Streets*, p. 322.
117 Hamilton, *Twenty Thousand Streets*, pp. 327, 330.
118 Hamilton, *Twenty Thousand Streets*, p. 329.

explanations for negative affect that exist alongside, and emerge from, Laing's 'deep sense of breakage' or Don Birnam's 'state of mortal apprehension'.[119] There are many different ingredients – physiological and socio-cultural – that can constitute a Traditional-Punishment response. So far in this chapter, as in earlier ones, I have explored some of the psychosocial pathways that can be pursued to untangle the whys and wherefores of the nebulous apprehensions of misery and dread that contribute to our understanding of what it is to suffer from a hangover. This has necessitated discussion of emancipation from social values, gender, class and intergenerational conflict. Omission itself is another matter, but one that I want to focus on to conclude this chapter as it allows me to return to that observation of Amis with which I began and draw the remaining threads of this book's argument together.

Memory loss has particular pertinence for understanding the outsider who fashions an identity through drunkenness. In TV and film, omission is often used as an organisational trope, mainly in comedy. In the sitcom *Black Books* (2000–04), the hard-drinking oddball, Bernard Black, portrayed by Dylan Moran, wakes to find he has accidentally offered a job to Manny (Bill Bailey) who he spends much of the remainder of the series trying to get rid of. Both characters often drink to oblivion. In the episode called 'The Black Out' (2000), Bernard wakes with an almighty hangover and no memory of why his friend has disowned him; searching out 'fizzygoodmakesyoufeelnice', or Alka-Seltzer, he attempts to reconstruct his movements of the night before, eventually recalling that he defecated in a wicker chair at a dinner party. In the episode 'Drunk' (2012) from *Not Going Out* (2006–19), Lee (Lee Mack) and Lucy (Sally Bretton) wake in bed together believing they made a sex tape, and the plot revolves around them trying to recover the tape from Lucy's parents' house. Likewise, the plot of Todd Phillips's *The Hangover* (2009) concerns a stag-night gone wrong in which husband-to-be Doug goes missing after a night at Caesars Palace in Las Vegas. The rest of the party wake in the morning to discover Doug has been replaced by a tiger, a chicken and a baby in the wardrobe. It transpires Stu married a stripper named Jade, the mother of the baby, before the group accidentally took Rohypnol – explaining their collective memory loss – had a run-in with a naked Chinese gangster, Mike Tyson (owner of the tiger) and the police. Doug is finally discovered on the roof of the hotel, heavily sunburned, where the others had left him as a prank the previous night.

---

119 Charles Jackson, *The Lost Weekend* (London: Penguin, 1989), p. 162.

When memory loss features in the plots of twentieth-century drinking narratives, however, there is a more postmodern emphasis in the issues it raises about the limits that the hangover places on articulation of the self that invites further scrutiny of the drunkard's 'deep sense of breakage'. Hannah Luckraft, for instance, takes comfort in her blackouts because they indicate abnegation of responsibility for behaviour while drunk, a way 'to free your personality from events'.[120] Memory loss is, perhaps, the ultimate challenge to the notion of the 'stable self' I discussed in Chapter 5; that is, the self embedded in conventional values, the sort with which Earnshaw has argued transgressive drinkers are usually forced to re-connect. It is also the ultimate example of the way that hangovers muddy distinctions between perception and sensation, the way they sustain ambiguous impressions of dread or prompt existential crises of articulation, which we have seen is so central a component of the subject from at least the literature of the Romantic period onwards.

In *The Long Goodbye* (1954), for example, Raymond Chandler tackles the notion that the hangover blackout is a modern, existential phenomenon. The hangovers of Philip Marlowe, Chandler's hard-drinking private investigator, are deliberately depicted as routine. They are equally a feature of the lowlife bar flies and the over-privileged idle rich of California. Marlowe negotiates the hangover in businesslike fashion:

> I opened my eyes and saw the crown of a tree moving gently against a hazed blue sky. I rolled over and leather touched my cheek. An axe split my head. I sat up. There was a rug over me. I threw that off and got to my feet on the floor. I scowled at a clock. The clock said a minute short of six-thirty.
>
> I got up on my feet and it took character. It took will power. It took a lot out of me, and there wasn't as much to spare as there once had been. The hard, heavy years worked me over.
>
> I ploughed across to the half-bath and stripped off my tie and shirt and sloshed cold water in my face with both hands and sloshed it on my head. When I was dripping wet I toweled myself off savagely.[121]

Chandler emphasises Marlowe's numb, stoical brand of heroism, inured to and yet wearied by the familiar physical sensations of the hangover. Washing and towelling are actions undertaken 'savagely', without any

120 Kennedy, *Paradise*, p. 19.
121 Raymond Chandler, *The Long Goodbye* (Harmondsworth: Penguin, 1959), p. 181.

exploration of emotional content. Marlowe meets the hangover with a defiant scowl.

The hangover that becomes the key to unravelling the link between the seemingly unconnected murder of Terry Lennox and apparent suicide of novelist Roger Wade is contrasted to this one. Wade's particular problem is his drunken blackouts and Marlowe is assigned by Wade's publisher to keep his client out of trouble. The reasons for Wade's drinking are unclear – he is, like Don Birnam, an evasive drunkard – but Marlowe links them to frustrated creativity. His hangovers are full of self-indulgence, pity and introspection, deliberately juxtaposed to those of Marlowe: 'they wonder what I'm running away from. Some Freudian bastard has made that a commonplace.'[122] The notion that Wade harbours a guilty, unnamable secret is noticeably fuelled by the concerns of his wife, Eileen, who initially enlists Marlowe's help in finding Wade who has booked himself into a sanatorium in an attempt to dry out. Eileen bemoans: 'He can't stand much more of it, Mr Marlowe. It will kill him. The intervals are getting shorter … I'm scared … Roger was always a drinker, but not a psychopathic drinker.'[123]

Marlowe discovers that Wade has a history of drunken violence to his wife but, following a night of intoxication when Wade attempts suicide, explodes the myth of the self-tormented Romantic drunkard, unable to unearth his buried trauma, by providing his own, more accurate diagnosis of events. Wade's 'secret' is, as Marlowe has already ascertained, 'just his excuse':

> He thinks he has a secret buried in his mind and he can't get at it. It may be a guilty secret about himself, it may be about someone else. He thinks that's what makes him drink, because he can't get at this thing. He probably thinks that whatever happened, happened while he was drunk and he ought to find it wherever people go when they're drunk – really bad drunk, the way he gets.[124]

Wade's real trouble derives from a more recent date, as he mistakenly believes he has murdered Terry Lennox during one of his periods of violent blackout. Marlowe's short shrift with psychiatric diagnosis – and the myth of the drunken Romantic outsider – enables him to see that Wade is being exploited by Eileen, who maliciously exaggerates her husband's 'problem', driving him towards a mental breakdown, to

---

122 Chandler, *Long Goodbye*, p. 148.
123 Chandler, *Long Goodbye*, p. 90.
124 Chandler, *Long Goodbye*, p. 155.

disguise the fact that she – as she believes – murdered Lennox, her first husband who returns unexpectedly having supposedly been killed during the Second World War. For Marlowe, Wade's problem was that he was 'an egotistical drunk and he hated his own guts', that his self-loathing arose from the fact that 'he was just a mercenary hack'.[125] Wade's credulity and egotism allow him to fool himself into believing that his failures as a writer derive from a special, complex psychological problem. The detective trumps the psychiatrist. Believing his wife's lies, Wade attempts to end his own life, but his failure prompts Eileen to kill him herself. Lennox eventually resurfaces at the end of the novel to reveal he escaped to Mexico rather than face the scandal.

The contrast between the attitudes of Wade and Marlowe when hungover is used by Chandler to query the drunken search for self-knowledge of the romanticised outsider that always carries with it the dangers of maudlin self-indulgence that we saw in the Romantic period and in Anne Brontë's *The Tenant of Wildfell Hall*. So, when Marlowe, having had his drink spiked at the Wade's, returns to his flat with a raging hangover and feels the temptation of self-pity – 'I was brooding and mean and irritable and over-sensitive' – he draws himself back from the brink with a curt note to self: 'Phooey. I was looking at life through the mists of a hangover.'[126] Chandler makes it clear that Marlowe's attitude to the hangover is not just a way of life, but also a means of survival in a world where privilege is blackened by crime. Chandler, who acknowledged his own greater similarities to the character of Wade, lauds the more admirable Marlowe for refusing to yield to nagging self-doubt.[127]

Chandler demonstrates that the hangover is an excellent vehicle for detective fiction precisely because memory lapses create blanks that require filling. This is also the observation of Martin Amis in *The Information* (1995), who remarks 'Every hangover, after all, is a mystery; every hangover is a whodunnit.'[128] In Adam Hobhouse's *The Hangover Murders* (1935), the whodunnit concerns the shooting of Jack Huling, part of a group of nouveau riche drinkers reminiscent of the swell guys of Chandler's Idle Valley, and close friend of narrator Tony Milburn.[129] The story opens at Huling's house with the graphic

125 Chandler, *Long Goodbye*, pp. 239, 259.
126 Chandler, *Long Goodbye*, p. 186.
127 See Leonard Cassuto, 'Raymond Chandler', in *The Cambridge Companion to American Novelists*, ed. Timothy Parrish (Cambridge: Cambridge University Press, 2013), p. 176 (pp. 168–78).
128 Martin Amis, *The Information* (London: Vintage, 2008), p. 271.
129 Adam Hobhouse, *The Hangover Murders* (New York: Alfred A. Knopf, 1935).

hangovers of Tony and his wife Carlotta. 'When I opened my eyes', narrates Tony, 'I was sure they were going to fall out of my head and start rolling across the floor like a couple of marbles. The pillow felt as if it had been cooked in butter.' As so often, the hangover's elusive aspects prompt verbal inventiveness. Carlotta is 'like a fly flying around in a milk-bottle'; Tony is 'a green bubble'.[130] It quickly becomes apparent that the experience is not an unusual one for the couple – they drink highballs as a remedy – and their hazy memories disturb them less than their shared impression of a bad dream. However, the discovery of Jack's body throws more urgency on the situation as they attempt, with the help of the gumshoe detective, Danny Harrison, to piece together their movements on the fateful night and those of the well-to-do crowd with whom they associate. Suspicion falls on each character in turn, particularly Tony who, it transpires, had fallen out with Jack at an inn and threatened to stab him. Following two more murders the mystery is solved by Danny, when Carlotta's memory returns and she recalls that the party went night swimming. It is Carlotta's recollection of Cecile Whitridge's mismatched bathing suit that proves the Whitridges had also been part of the company and that Jake Whitridge had murdered Jack in a disagreement about money.

Hobhouse's detective plot is constructed entirely around the hangover as mutual suspicion threatens the friends and evidence is gradually pieced together. But lost memory is more than just a way of staging narrative for Hobhouse; it is also social commentary and raises psychological questions. Memory loss is a fundamental characteristic of the otherwise carefree group of socialites, ordinarily unburdened by consequences for their drunken behaviour, protected by their status and wealth: wealth that means never having to remember what you did the night before. But in the scene in which John Henry Hampton Jones, a psychiatrist specialising in mechanical hypnosis, examines each character in turn, hangovers turn out to be more than just instrumental in the plot. Suddenly having to face the worst sort of consequence, lost alcoholic memories are a point of vulnerability, the route to a self that is perhaps best kept hidden, as Tony realises when about to go under:

> Somebody had to go into that dark room and give up his mind to John, give up your mind and let him handle it and pry into it until he found out anything, everything he might want to know about it. You would have to give away your mind in that dark

room, let John know all its secrets, even those of its secrets you
didn't know yourself.[131]

The issue here is not just the revelation of the incidents surrounding
Jack's death but the possibility of exposure, of the revelation of human
nature: 'Now we know. Now we know everything.'[132] Hobhouse, through
the mouthpiece of the professional man, establishes the kind of complex
relationship between agency and its loss that calls into question, just as
does Chandler, the pampered lifestyles of the hedonistic rich. Moreover,
memory loss functions as a way to pose questions about the psychological
reasons for drinking to forget:

> 'As a general thing, partial loss of memory, even in drunkenness,
> indicates a desire to lose memory,' he said, 'or if not that, at least
> indifference to retain it. To be more exact, if a drunken person
> loses part of his memory it means either that he has spent a dull
> evening and has no wish to remember it, or else that he has seen
> or done something shameful or disgusting or terrifying and wishes
> to forget it completely. The drunken man never remembers his
> rages, his pugnacity, or his attempted rapes.'[133]

Drinking to forget is one thing, but blackouts also present a fundamental
obstruction to self-fashioning through drunkenness, which is a type of
willed freedom, but in a postmodern sense a way of cheating the notion
of a stable, and narratable, self.

The Milburn's crowd evades responsibility through drinking beyond
memory. But, in the tradition of the drunken outsider of the twentieth
century, the memory loss of a hangover that instills abstract feelings of
dread and hangxiety may well turn out to be, despite suggesting loss of
agency, the definitive act of defiant self-assertion. As Earnshaw remarks,
the drunken confessional of the twentieth century often presents 'the
alternation of the social self that is meant to adhere to its identity as
self-narrating autobiography, and the self that is a not-self, that has
no memory, and hence cannot narrate itself and provide its self with
identity'.[134]

In Martin Amis's *Money* (1984), for example, John Self experiences
blackouts that affect the narration of the story in a postmodern way. His

---

131 Hobhouse, *Hangover Murders*, p. 53.
132 Hobhouse, *Hangover Murders*, p. 53.
133 Hobhouse, *Hangover Murders*, p. 55.
134 Earnshaw, 'Drink, Dissolution, Antibiography', p. 213.

unreliable memory, warped by alcohol, invites attention to the processes of telling in his frequent use of second-person narration: 'Oh yeah, and while I remember – I haven't briefed you about that mystery caller of mine yet, have I? Or have I? Oh that's right, I filled you in on the whole thing. That's right. Some whacko. No big deal ... Wait a minute, I tell a lie. I haven't *briefed* you about it. I would have remembered.'[135] More than just make Self an unreliable narrator, or indicate bouts of self-doubt, Self's memory problems occlude his ability to probe into the heart of his emotional problems *à la* Roger Wade. Having been assaulted by his tormentor, Fielding Goodney, while drunk he wakes in a hedge 'full of nettles, crushed cigarette packs, used condoms and empty beercans' to find his back lacerated 'as if I'd slept on a bed of nails', 'a grey swelling over my left eye', with no memory of the fight. His body tells a cryptic tale: 'My back, my great white back was scored with thirty or forty sharp red welts, regularly patterned, as if I'd slept on a bed of nails.'[136] Although the mystery is later pieced together – the marks were from the high heel shoes Goodney wore when disguised as a barroom tart – Self's hangover moves into the territory of Chandler's Wade, Charles Lamb's drunkard, Jackson's Birnam and many other drunkards who risk accusations of egotism, suggesting some deep and insoluble problem lies at the heart of his drinking:

> It was now eight thirty. I bathed my face with water and felt hot fingers beginning to tickle my back. For ten minutes I vomited elaborately, with steamhammer back convulsions that I had no strength to resist or contain. Then for twice that long I sat twitching on the shower's deck, the silver snout tuned to full heat and heft but doing nothing much to wash off my rot. I must be *very unhappy*. That's the only way I can explain my behaviour. Oh man, I must be so depressed. I must be fucking suicidal. And I wish I knew *why*.[137]

It is telling that Self's focus journeys away from the source of his physical scars to speculate on the origins of his emotional ones – the vague, awful shimmering superstructure, or deep sense of breakage, of the hangover. His shower follows a pattern that we have already seen in *Post Office* and *Paradise*, but the 'rot' is so much a part of his character that it is unclear whether it is physical grime or a moral judgement. The hangover is very physical – particularly Amis's description of vomiting – but takes

135 Martin Amis, *Money: A Suicide Note* (London: Vintage, repr. 2005), p. 27.
136 Amis, *Money*, p. 122.
137 Amis, *Money*, p. 123.

its primary interest from the admission of emotional vulnerability that is somehow both candid and vague at the same time. The vagueness is crucial as it adds an impenetrable dimension to Self's character that, even as the plot unwinds, means he retains a level of unintelligibility to himself and the reader.

Memory loss places limits on how candid the hungover Self – and we might say more generally the drunken outsider – can ever be as the revelation of Goodney's sadistic manipulation fails to explain Self's own 'Nietzsche sickness'. Amis leaves options open for the reader's condemnation and excuse of Self's behaviour, but the omissions in his story impress the postmodern feeling of fragmentation *per se*. Self stands outside orthodox social values, pushing them to the limit in fact, with unrecoverable lost time and actions meaning that, *contra* the fear of Tony Milburn under the gaze of the psychiatrist, the totality of his character avoids scrutiny. As Hannah Luckraft explains in *Paradise*, it is not just a case of loss but actually a type of liberation that even, potentially, offers the profoundest way out of the problem of moral acquiescence or defiance that we have seen haunt so many outsider figures during their hangovers. Hence, Hannah turns her own omissions into the ultimate form of defiance, even if this is simultaneously a type of denial. Attempting to recall the events of her evening with Kussbachek she draws a typical blank and ponders on the time lost through alcoholic oblivion:

> Because once you've begun to have blackouts, you'll never stop and so before and after don't exist – you've mastered the art of escaping from linear time. The jumps and jolts take a bit of getting used to – driving is particularly tricky, guessing what gear you're in, or if you're trying to overtake – but this keeps you bright and springy, alert. And there is nothing unnatural about it, nothing dreadful: some level of blacking out is what lets people survive.[138]

Ordinary habits of denial do not suit Hannah who turns memory loss into a way 'to free your personality from events' that might otherwise instil a Traditional-Punishment response.[139] The process is complicated by the continual recall of family values, as I earlier argued, but she makes a postmodern gambit for seeing hangovers as a way of coupling the inscrutability of her problems to her avoidance of conformity. And so, Hannah re-invents a self that is always provisional:

---

138 Kennedy, *Paradise*, pp. 18–19.
139 Kennedy, *Paradise*, p. 19.

Beyond that there's nothing until 8.42 this morning – only a soft, neutral space within which I would like to suggest that a meeting occurred between myself and Kussbachek with a passing-on of thanks, or greetings, or messages from family and friends, or some other communications of importance. Also M. H. Virginas must, at some point, have responded to my conviviality by placing his or her credit card in my wallet, or by lending the card to me, but neglecting to give me a note of the necessary return address. I don't know.[140]

Not knowing involves the act of rescripting the self in order to tell her story, a feature of Hannah's hangovers that acts as a commentary on the entire novel. The question becomes not how much Hannah is prepared to tell but how much she is able to tell whilst hungover. The socio-cultural dimensions often revealed by hangover sensations here remain shrouded in mystery. The insight that this liberates her from the tainted relationship with social orthodoxies that her family, particularly mother, represent is purposely left unconfirmed by Kennedy.

Hangovers give Hannah Luckraft the (partial) chance to begin anew, or at least hold out that promise in her estimation. Whether or not they sustain this function in moral terms is dubious but, as far as narrative goes, they always signal doubt about telling. Perhaps the wish is stronger than the reality for Hannah as she establishes Mr Hitt, a fellow patient in the Canadian sanatorium, as a figure of aspiration. Hannah tells us that 'Hitt suffers from Korsakoff's syndrome – alcohol-induced dementia – so he begins each day as himself, but with many key events and circumstances missing.' The fact that he will 'accept anyone's explanations for why he has turned out as he is' allows Hannah to cadge him for a fake debt that gives her the funds to escape back to Britain.[141] More than this, Hitt is the ultimate example, the mythological apex perhaps, of the drunken outsider, mentally detached from his past, adrift from himself. What Hitt lacks, however, and something that Hannah misses, is his own agency in telling his story as his life is actually scripted by others, including Hannah. 'We are old friends', he remarks, 'I knew your father', but can go no further. 'That's right', Hannah responds, 'You worked together, in the university ... He is continuing your research. It's going well.'[142] The drunkard's ego is not quite prepared to forsake agency in

140 Kennedy, *Paradise*, p. 29.
141 Kennedy, *Paradise*, p. 190.
142 Kennedy, *Paradise*, pp. 191–92.

this way. If the stories of Mr Hitt really do just peter out, Hannah's keep advancing and unravelling, her hangovers suggesting that her outsider status will always, tragically in her own eyes, keep her yoked to linear time and unable to wholly occupy the kind of soft, 'neutral space' that might take us all the way back to Bukowski's 'Hangover and Sick Leave' with which I started. Then again, even that momentary glimpse of self-sufficiency proves unsustainable in Bukowski's prose fiction, as I have argued.

***

In fiction of the twentieth and twenty-first centuries, hangovers often host a war of cultural values, that can variously be sourced to issues of class, gender and intergenerational pressures, which induce responses ranging from pride and defiance to humiliation, shame and guilt. These lead variously to Traditional-Punishment or Withdrawal-Relief responses, which my literary-cultural study of the hangover has enabled me to describe in greater depth than the psychobiological studies from where the terms derive. Many enlightened, self-aware outsiders of twentieth-century fiction suggest that they successfully eschew conventional social values, generally through the regular consumption of alcohol, but the hangover usually says otherwise. Indeed, it tends to reveal that those individuals who seem most flamboyantly dismissive of social and cultural judgement, such as the Arthur Seatons, John Selfs and Hannah Luckrafts, host the biggest crises in self-determination.

As so often throughout this book, we have seen that there is much to be gained from examining physical descriptions of hangovers, but only when they are viewed as part of a larger, more complex, interpersonal and cultural phenomenon that forces a reappraisal of the individual, sees the body as part of a moral discourse, and invites understanding of the overlap between sensation, emotion and cognition. The example of Mr Hitt, whose medical condition lies outside the concerns of this study, also reminds us that the insights into character that are revealed during the hangover are themselves provisional on the processes of telling, or expressing feeling, and that sometimes this involves the retention of the nebulous and inexplicable. The drunken outsider's ability to construct an identity free from the shackles of social norms involves, at its furthest extent, an obliteration of memory and the self; but twentieth-century hangover literature shows that this is hard to sustain for any length of time.

As this book has shown, by attending to the psychological and culturally inflected dimensions of hangover literature at different periods, we increase the likelihood of our understanding something of the vast, vague, awful shimmering superstructure to which they often belong and the multiple variations that exist within categories of response, such as Traditional-Punishment and Withdrawal-Relief, which psychological research has provided. Hangover literature enables analysis of the changing perceptions of the symptoms that science uses to pathologise hangovers. While analysis of representations of drunkenness reveals many types of social concerns, it is in literary depictions of the morning after that the psychological impact of the ideological requirements that regulate attitudes and courses of action, can be analysed in most detail. This literary-cultural account of hangovers has developed our critical understanding of how alcohol use is governed by physiology, but also cultural beliefs and social practices.

Bibliography

Primary

Adams, John, *A Sermon Preached at White-hall on Sunday, the 17th of February* ... (London: printed by Benj. Motte, 1695)

Allestree, Richard, *The Practice of Christian Graces, or, The Whole Duty of Man* (London: D. Maxwell for T. Garthwait, 1658)

————, *The Gentleman's Calling* (London: printed for T. Garthwait, 1660)

————, *Eighteen Sermons Whereof Fifteen Preached the King, the Rest Upon Publick Occasions* (London: printed by Tho. Roycroft for James Allestry, St Paul's Church-yard, 1669)

————, *Forty Sermons Whereof Twenty One Are Now First Published* (Oxford and London: printed for R. Scott, G. Wells, T. Sawbridge, R. Bentley, 1684)

Ames, Richard, *Fatal Friendship, or, The Drunkard's Misery being a Satyr against Hard Drinking* (London: printed for Randal Taylor, 1693)

Amis, Kingsley, *Lucky Jim* ([1953] Harmondsworth: Penguin, 1961)

————, 'The Hangover' (1972), in *Everyday Drinking: The Distilled Kingsley Amis*, intro. Christopher Hitchens (London: Bloomsbury, 2010)

Amis, Martin, *Money: A Suicide Note* ([1981] London: Vintage, 2005)

————, *The Information* ([1995] London: Vintage, 2008)

Anon., *The Abdicated Prince, or, the Adventures of Four Years* (London: John Carterson, 1690)

————, *A Modest Defence of Chastity* (London: A. Bettesworth, 1726)

————, *A Dissertation Upon Drunkenness. Shewing to What an Intolerable Pitch that Vice is Arriv'd at in the Kingdom* (London: printed for T. Warner, 1727)

Arthur, T. S., *Ten Nights in a Bar-Room and What I Saw There* (Bedford, MA: Applewood Books, 2010)

Austen, Jane, *Persuasion* (London: Penguin, 1994)

————, *Jane Austen's Letters*, ed. Deirdre Le Faye, 4th edn. (Oxford: Oxford University Press, 2011)

Baker, Thomas, *Tunbridge Walks: or, The Yeoman of Kent* (Dublin: printed for William Smith, repr. 1758)

Barrow, Isaac, *Sermons Preached Upon Several Occasions* (London: printed for Brabazon Aylmer, Cornhill, 1679)

B. E., *A New Dictionary of the Canting Crew* ... (London: printed for W. Hawes, P. Gilbourne and W. Davis, 1699)

Beecher, Lyman, *Six Sermons on the Nature, Occasions, Signs, Evils, and Remedy of Intemperance* (New York: The American Tract Society, 1827)

Behn, Aphra *The Debauchee; or, the Credulous Cuckold* (London: printed for John Amery, 1677)

Bishop-Stall, Shaughnessy, *Hungover: The Morning After and One Man's Quest for a Cure* (New York: Penguin, 2018)

Bold, Henry, *Poems lyrique, macaronique, heroique, &c.* (London: printed for Henry Brome, 1664)

Bourne, Reuben, *The Contented Cuckold, or, The Woman's Advocate* (London: printed by Randall Taylor, 1692)

'Bow Wow', *Punch* (31 May 1884), p. 264

Brackett, Charles and Billy Wilder, *The Lost Weekend* (Berkeley, Los Angeles, London: University of California Press, 2000)

Brome, Alexander, *Songs and Other Poems* (London: printed for Henry Brome, 1664)

Brontë, Anne, *The Tenant of Wildfell Hall*, ed. G. D. Hargreaves (Harmondsworth: Penguin, 1979)

Brooke, Humphrey, *Ugieine, or A Conservatory of Health* (London: R. W. for G. Whittington, 1650)

Bukowski, Charles, *Post Office* ([1971] London: Virgin Books, 2009)

————, *Factotum*, intro. Neeli Cherkovski ([1978] London: Virgin Books, 2009)

————, *The Rooming House Madrigals: Early Selected Poems, 1946–1966* (Los Angeles, CA: Black Sparrow Press, 1988)

Bunyan, John, *The Barren Fig Tree, or, the Doom and Downfall of the Fruitless Professor* ([1673] London: printed for J. Robinson, St Paul's Church-yard, 1688)

————, *Grace Abounding & The Life and Death of Mr. Badman* ([1680] London: J. M. Dent & Sons Ltd., repr. 1953)

Burney, Frances, *Evelina*, ed. Susan Kubica Howard (Toronto: Broadview, 2000)

Burns, Robert, *Poems Songs and Letters Being the Complete Works of Robert Burns*, ed. Alexander Smith (London: MacMillan and Co., 1868)

————, *The Poems and Songs of Robert Burns*, ed. James Kinsley, 3 vols (Oxford: Clarendon Press, 1968)

————, *Robert Burns' Commonplace Book*, ed. Raymond Lamont Brown (Wakefield: S. R. Publishers Ltd, 1969)

————, *The Letters of Robert Burns*, ed. G. Ross Roy, 3 vols (Oxford: Clarendon Press, 1985)

Burrell, Sophia, *Poems. Dedicated to the Right Honourable the Earl of Mansfield* (London: J. Cooper, Bow Street, Covent Garden, 1793)

Byron, George Gordon, Lord, *The Letters and Journals of Lord Byron*, ed. Leslie A. Marchand, 12 vols (London: John Murray, 1973–82)

————, *The Complete Poetical Works*, ed. Jerome J. McGann, 7 vols (Oxford: Clarendon Press, 1980–93)

Carpenter, Richard, *The Downfall of Anti-Christ* (London: John Stafford, 1644)

Chaloner, Thomas, *The Merriest Poet in Christendom: Or, Chaloner's Miscellany, Being a Salve for Every Sore* (London: George Lee, 1732)

Chandler, Raymond, *The Long Goodbye* (Harmondsworth: Penguin, 1959)

Charleton, Walter, *Enquiries into Human Nature* (London: printed for M. White by Robert Boulter, 1680)

Coleridge, Samuel Taylor, *Unpublished Letters of Samuel Taylor Coleridge*, ed. E. L. Griggs, 2 vols (New Haven, CT: Yale University Press, 1933)

————, *The Collected Letters*, ed. Earl Leslie Griggs, 6 vols (Oxford: Clarendon Press, 1957–71)

————, *The Complete Poems*, ed. William Keach (London: Penguin, 2004)

Colvill, Robert, *Britain, a Poem in Three Books* (Edinburgh: Wal. Ruddiman, Jr. & Co., 1747)

Coventry, Francis, *The History of Pompey the Little: or, the Life and Adventures of a Lap-Dog* (London: printed for M. Cooper, 1751)

Cowley, Abraham, *Abraham Cowley: Poetry and Prose*, ed. L. C. Martin (Oxford: Oxford University Press, 1949)

Cowper, William, *The Task and Other Selected Poems*, ed. James Sambrook (London and New York: Routledge, 2013)

Darby, Charles, *Bacchanalia, or, A Description of a Drunken Club* (London: printed for Robert Boulter, 1680)

Defoe, Daniel, *Giving Alms No Charity*, in *The Shortest Way with Dissenters and Other Pamphlets* ([1704] Oxford: Blackwell, 1927)

————, *Colonel Jack*, ed. Gabriel Cervantes and Geoffrey Sill ([1722] Ontario: Broadview, 2015)

————, *Roxana*, ed. David Blewitt ([1724] Harmondsworth: Penguin, 1987)

————, *A Brief Case of the Distillers and the Distilling Trade* (London: printed for T. Warner, 1726)

————, *Augusta Triumphans: Or, the Way to Make London the Most Flourishing City in the Universe* (London: J. Roberts, 1728)

Dennis, John, *The Triumvirate: or, The Battle*, in *Poems in Burlesque* (London: printed for the Booksellers of London and Westminster, 1692)

Dickens, Charles, *Nicholas Nickleby*, intro. Tim Cook ([1839] Ware: Wordsworth, 1995)

————, *David Copperfield*, ed. Jerome H. Buckley ([1850] New York and London: Norton, 1990)

————, *Our Mutual Friend*, ed. Stephen Gill ([1865] Harmondsworth: Penguin, repr. 1977)

Dryden, John, *The Works of John Dryden*, ed. Vinton A. Dearing and H. T. Swedenberg, 20 vols (Berkeley and Los Angeles, London: University of California Press, 1962–74)

D'Urfey, Thomas, *Trick for Trick, or, The Debauch'd Hypocrite* (London: printed for Langley Curtis, 1678)

Eliot, George, *Janet's Repentance*, in *Scenes of Clerical Life*, ed. Thomas A. Noble (Oxford: Oxford University Press, repr. 2009)

Farquhar, George, *The Beaux' Stratagem*, in *Restoration Drama: An Anthology*, ed. David Womersley (Oxford: Blackwell, 2000)

Fielding, Helen, *Bridget Jones's Diary* (London: Picador, repr. 2001)

Fielding, Henry, *Amelia*, ed. Martin C. Battestin ([1751] Oxford: Clarendon Press, 1983)

—————, *An Enquiry into the Causes of the Late Increase of Robbers and Related Writings*, ed. Malvin R. Zirker ([1751] Oxford: Clarendon Press, 1988)

Finch, Anne, Countess of Winchilsea, *Miscellany Poems, on Several Occasions* (London: W. Taylor, 1713)

—————, *Selected Poems of Anne Finch, Countess of Winchilsea*, ed. Katharine M. Rogers (New York: Ungar, 1987)

Fitzgerald, F. Scott, *This Side of Paradise*, ed. James L. W. West III ([1920] Cambridge: Cambridge University Press, 1995)

—————, *Tender is the Night* ([1934] London: Harper Collins, 2011)

Fosse, Bob (dir.), *Cabaret* (Allied Artists, 1972)

Freud, Sigmund, *The Standard Edition of the Complete Psychological Works of Sigmund Freud*, trans. James Strachey, 24 vols (London: Hogarth Press, repr. 1963)

Gay, John, *Poetry and Prose*, ed. Vinton A. Dearing and Charles E. Beckwith, 2 vols (Oxford: Clarendon Press, 1974)

Gould, Robert, *Love Given Over: Or, a Satire Against the Pride, Lust, and Inconstancy, &c. of Woman with Sylvia's Revenge, or a Satyr Against Man, in Answer to the Satyr Against Woman* (London: H. Hills, 1709)

Greene, Edward Burnaby, *The Satires of Persius Paraphrastically Imitated, and Adapted to the Times* (London: T. Spilsbury for J. Dodsley, 1779)

Hall, Thomas, *The Beauty of Holiness* (London: printed by Evan Tyler for John Browne, St Paul's Church-yard, 1653)

Hamilton, Patrick, *Twenty Thousand Streets Under the Sky* ([1929–35] London: Vintage, 2004)

—————, *Hangover Square* ([1941] London: Penguin, 2001)

Hardy, Thomas, *Jude the Obscure*, intro. Terry Eagleton, notes P. N. Furbank (London: Macmillan, 1975)

Harrold, Edmund, *The Diary of Edmund Harrold, Wigmaker of Manchester 1712–15*, ed. Craig Horner (Aldershot: Ashgate, 2008)

Hemingway, Ernest, *Fiesta: The Sun Also Rises* (London: Arrow Books, 2004)

Herrick, Robert, *The Poetical Works of Robert Herrick*, ed. L. C. Martin (Oxford: Clarendon Press, 1956)

Heywood, Thomas, *Philocothonista, or, The Drunkard, Opened, Dissected, and Anatomized* (London: Robert Raworth, 1635)

Hilton, George, *The Rake's Diary: The Journal of George Hilton*, ed. Anne Hillman (Berwick-upon-Tweed: Curwen Archives Trust, 1994)

Hobhouse, Adam, *The Hangover Murders* (New York: Alfred A. Knopf, 1935)

Hone, William, *The Queen's Matrimonial Ladder, a National Toy with Fourteen Step Scenes*, 15th edn. (London: William Hone, 1820)

Ingraham, J. H., *Edward Austin; or, The Hunting Flask* (Boston, MA: F. Gleason, 1842)

Isherwood, Christopher, *Goodbye to Berlin* (London: Triad/Panther, repr. 1986)

Jackson, Charles, *The Lost Weekend* (London: Penguin, 1989)

Jerrold, Douglas, *Punch's Letters to His Son, Corrected and Edited from the Mss. in the Alsatian Library* (London: Wm. S. Orr & Co., 1843)

Johnson, Samuel, *A Dictionary of the English Language...*, 2 vols (London: W. Strahan, 1755)

Jonson, Ben, *The Cambridge Edition of the Works of Ben Jonson*, ed. David Bevington, Martin Butler and Ian Donaldson, 7 vols (Cambridge: Cambridge University Press, 2012)

Keats, John, *Keats's Poetry and Prose*, ed. Jeffrey N. Cox (New York and London: Norton, 2009)

Kennedy, A. L., *Paradise* (London: Vintage, 2015)

Kerr, Norman, 'President's Inaugural Address', *Proceedings of the Society for the Study and Cure of Inebriety*, 1 (April 1884)

Lamb, Charles, *The Essays of Elia* (London: Grant Richards, 1901)

————, *The Letters of Charles and Mary Lamb: Letters of Charles Lamb, 1796–1801*, ed. Edwin Wilson Marrs, 3 vols (Ithaca, NY and London: Cornell University Press, 1975)

————, *Selected Writings*, ed. J. E. Morpurgo (New York: Routledge, 2003)

Leslie, Charles Robert, *Autobiographical Recollections*, 2 vols (London: John Murray, 1860)

Lloyd, Robert, *The Poetical Works* (London: printed for T. Evans, 1774)

London, Jack, *John Barleycorn: Alcoholic Memoirs*, ed. John Sutherland (Oxford: World's Classics, 2009)

Lovelace, Richard, *The Poems of Richard Lovelace*, ed. C. H. Wilkinson (Oxford: Clarendon Press, repr. 1963)

Lund, John, *Collection of Oddities* (Doncaster: C. Plummbe, 1780?)

MacNish, Robert, *The Anatomy of Drunkenness* (New York: Appleton, 1827)

Mayhew, Henry, *London Labour and the London Poor*, 4 vols (London: Charles Griffin and Co., 1865)

Milton, John, *Il Penseroso, Complete Shorter Poems*, ed. John Carey (London: Longman, 1971)

Peddie, Alexander, *The Necessity for Some Legalised Arrangements for the Treatment of Dipsomania ...* (Edinburgh: Sutherland and Knox, 1858)

'Philanthropos', *The Trial of the Spirits: Or, Some Considerations Upon the pernicious Consequences of the Gin Trade to Great Britain* (London: printed for T. Cooper, 1736)

Phillips, Todd (dir.), *The Hangover* (Warner Bros., 2009)

Pope, Alexander, *The Rape of the Lock*, in *Selected Poetry*, ed. Pat Rogers (Oxford and New York: Oxford University Press, 1996)

Reynolds, Sir Joshua, *A Discourse Delivered to the Students of the Royal Academy on the Distribution of Prizes, December 11, 1769, by the President* (London: Thomas Davies, 1769)

Rhys, Jean, *Good Morning, Midnight* (London: Penguin, 1967)

Rochester, John Wilmot, Earl of, *Complete Poems and Plays*, ed. Paddy Lyons (London: Everyman, 1993)

————, *The Works of John Wilmot, Earl of Rochester*, ed. Harold Love (Oxford: Oxford University Press, 1999)

Sartre, Jean Paul, *Nausea*, trans. Robert Baldick (London: Penguin, 2000)

Shakespeare, William, *Hamlet*, ed. Philip Edwards ([1600] Cambridge: Cambridge University Press, 1985)

————, *2 Henry IV*, ed. Giorgio Melchiori ([1600] Cambridge: Cambridge University Press, 2007)

————, *The Merry Wives of Windsor*, ed. Giorgio Melchiori ([1600] Walton-on-Thames: Arden, 2000)

Sillitoe, Alan, *Saturday Night and Sunday Morning* (London: Harper Collins, 1995)

Spenser, Edmund, *The Yale Edition of the Shorter Poems of Edmund Spenser*, ed. William A. Oran *et al* (New Haven, CT & London: Yale University Press, 1989)

Stone, Arthur Daniel, *A Practical Treatise on the Diseases of the Stomach and Digestion* (London: Cadell and Davies, 1806)

Swift, Jonathan, *The Complete Poems*, ed. Pat Rogers (New Haven, CT and London: Yale University Press, 1983)

Taylor, John, *Divers Crabtree Lectures Expressing the Severall Languages that Shrews Read to Their Husbands, either at Morning, Noone, or Night* (London: I. Okes for John Sweeting, 1639)

Thackeray, William Makepeace, *Vanity Fair*, ed. Peter Shillingsburg (New York and London: Norton, 1994)

Trollope, Anthony, *The Way We Live Now*, ed. John Sutherland (Oxford: Oxford University Press, 1982)

Van Druten, John, *I am a Camera*, in *Famous Plays of 1954* (London: Victor Gollancz Ltd., 1954)

Verdi, Giuseppe, *Falstaff*, dir. Franco Zeffirelli (Hamburg: Deutsche Grammophon, 2009)

Ward, Edward, *A Satyr Against Wine. With a Poem in Praise of Small Beer* (London: B. Brag, 1705)

————, *The Rambling Fuddle-Caps: or, A Tavern Struggle for a Kiss* (London: B. Bragge, 1706)

Waterland, Daniel, *Advice to a Young Student with a Method of Study for the First Four Years ...* (Oxford: Richard Clements, 1755)

Wodehouse, P. G., *The Mating Season* (London: Penguin, 1999)

Wolfe, Tom, *The Bonfire of the Vanities* (London: Vintage, 2010)

Wood, Mrs Ellen, *Danesbury House*, ed. Curt Herr (Alfred, NY: Whitlock Publishing, 2009)

Wood, Nick (dir.), *Black Books* (Assembly Film and Television, 2000–04)

————, *Not Going Out* (Avalon Television, 2006–19)

Wordsworth, William and Dorothy Wordsworth, *The Early Letters of William and Dorothy Wordsworth*, ed. Ernest de Selincourt, 5 vols (Oxford: Clarendon Press, 1935)

Wordsworth, William, *The Prose Works of William Wordsworth*, ed. W. J. B. Owen and Jane Worthington Smyser, 3 vols (Oxford: Clarendon Press, 1974)

—————, *The Major Works*, ed. Stephen Gill (Oxford: Oxford University Press, repr. 2000)

Wurdz, Gideon, *The Foolish Dictionary* (1904), <http://www.fullbooks.com/The-Foolish-Dictionary.html>

Young, Thomas, *Englands Bane: or, the Description of Drunkennesse* (London: William Jones, 1617)

Secondary

Abel, Ernest L., 'The Gin Epidemic: Much Ado About What?', *Alcohol and Alcoholism*, 36 (2001), pp. 401–405

Achilleos, Stella, 'The Anacreontea and a Tradition of Refined Male Sociability', in Smyth (ed.), *A Pleasing Sinne*, pp. 21–35

Ahern, Stephen, 'Diagnosing Romanticism', *ESC*, 31.2–3 (June/September 2005), pp. 69–76

Amigoni, David, Paul Barlow and Colin Trodd (eds.), *Victorian Literature and the Idea of the Grotesque* (Farnham: Ashgate, 1999)

Barker-Benfield, G. J., *The Culture of Sensibility: Sex and Society in Eighteenth-Century Britain* (Chicago, IL and London: University of Chicago Press, 1996)

Bates, Victoria, *Sexual Forensics in Victorian and Edwardian England: Age, Crime and Consent in the Courts* (Basingstoke: Palgrave Macmillan, 2016)

BBC, 'Drinking Problem: What Did You do Last Night?' <http://news.bbc.co.uk/1/hi/programmes/the_westminster_hour/4109735.stm>

Berridge, Virginia, *Demons: Our Changing Attitudes to Alcohol, Tobacco, and Drugs* (Oxford: Oxford University Press, 2013)

Blocker, Jack S., Ian R. Tyrrell and David M. Fahey (eds), *Alcohol and Temperance in Modern History: An International Encyclopedia* (Santa Barbara, CA, Denver, TX and Oxford: ABC Clio, 2003)

Blume, Sheila B., 'Sexuality and Stigma: The Alcoholic Woman', *Alcohol Health and Research World*, 15.2 (1991), pp. 139–48

Boyle, Peter, Paolo Boffetta, Albert B. Lowenfels, Harry Burns, Otis Brawley, Witold Zatonski and Jürgen Rehm (eds), *Alcohol: Science, Policy, and Public Health* (Oxford: Oxford University Press, 2013)

Bradford, Richard, *The Novel Now: Contemporary British Fiction* (Oxford: Blackwell, 2009)

Bruce, Leslie Jeanine, *Outlaw Mothers: Marital Conflict, Family Law, and Women's Novels in Victorian England* (unpublished PhD thesis, University of Southern California, 2007)

Capp, Bernard, *England's Culture Wars: Puritan Reformation and its Enemies in the Interregnum, 1649–1660* (Oxford: Oxford University Press, 2012)

Cascardi, Anthony, *The Subject of Modernity* (Cambridge: Cambridge University Press, 1992)

Cassuto, Leonard, 'Raymond Chandler', in *The Cambridge Companion to American Novelists*, ed. Timothy Parrish (Cambridge: Cambridge University Press, 2013), pp. 168–78

Clark, Anna, *The Struggle for the Breeches: Gender and the Making of the British Working Class* (Berkeley, Los Angeles, London: University of California Press, 1995)

Clark, Peter, *The English Alehouse: A Social History* (London: Longman, 1983)

Cooke, Michael G., 'De Quincey, Coleridge, and the Formal Uses of Intoxication', *Yale French Studies*, 50 (1974), pp. 26–40

Crofton, John, 'Editorial: Extent and Costs of Alcohol Problems in Employment: A Review of British Data', *Alcohol and Alcoholism*, 22.4 (1987), pp. 321–25

Dillon, Patrick, *Gin: The Much-Lamented Death of Madame Geneva* (Boston, MA: Justin, Charles & Co., 2003)

Dixon, Thomas, '"Emotion": The History of a Keyword in Crisis', *Emotion Review*, 4.4 (Oct. 2012), pp. 338–44

Durkheim, Emile, *Sociology and Philosophy*, trans. D. F. Pocock (London: Taylor and Francis, 2009)

Earnshaw, Steven, *The Pub in Literature: England's Altered States* (Manchester and New York: Manchester University Press, 2000)

————, 'Drink, Dissolution, Antibiography: The Existential Drinker', in *Biographies of Drink: A Case Study Approach to our Historical Relationship with Alcohol*, ed. Mark Hailwood and Deborah Toner (Newcastle-upon-Tyne: Cambridge Scholars, 2015), pp. 204–22

————, *The Existential Drinker* (Manchester: Manchester University Press, 2018)

Engelhardt, Molly, *Dancing out of Line: Ballrooms, Ballets, and Mobility in Victorian Fiction* (Athens: Ohio University Press, 2009)

Enterline, Lynn, *The Tears of Narcissus: Melancholia and Masculinity in Early Modern Writing* (Stanford, CA: Stanford University Press, 1995)

Ersche, Karen D., 'Intoxicants and Compulsive Behaviour: A Neuroscientific Perspective', in Herring *et al* (eds), *Intoxication and Society*, pp. 210–31

Faflak, Joel and Richard C. Sha (eds), *Romanticism and the Emotions* (Cambridge: Cambridge University Press, 2014)

Fairer, David, 'Lyric and Elegy', in David Hopkins and Charles Martindale (eds), *The Oxford History of Classical Reception in English Literature*, 4 vols (Oxford: Oxford University Press, 2012), III, pp. 519–46

Feldman Barrett, Lisa, *How Emotions are Made: The Secret Life of the Brain* (New York: Macmillan, 2017)

Flather, Amanda, *Gender and Space in Early Modern England* (Woodbridge: The Boydell Press, 2007)

Foucault, Michel, *The Archaeology of Knowledge*, trans. A. M. Sheridan Smith (London and New York: Routledge, 2002)

Fowler, Richard Hindle, *Robert Burns* (London: Routledge, 1988)

Garvey, S. P., 'Can Shaming Punishments Educate?', *University of Chicago Law Review*, 65.4 (1988), pp. 733–94

Gately, Iain, *Drink: A Cultural History of Alcohol* (London: Penguin, 2008)

George, M. Dorothy, *London Life in the Eighteenth Century* (Harmondsworth: Penguin, 1925)

Gilbert, Pamela K., *Disease, Desire, and the Body in Victorian Women's Popular Novels* (Cambridge: Cambridge University Press, 1997)

Gilmore, Thomas B., *Equivocal Spirits: Alcoholism and Drinking in Twentieth-Century Literature* (Chapel Hill: University of North Carolina Press, 1987)

Greenfield, Anne, 'Introduction', in *Interpreting Sexual Violence, 1660–1800*, ed. Anne Greenfield (Oxford: Routledge, repr. 2016)

Hailwood, Mark, *Alehouses and Good Fellowship in Early Modern England* (Woodbridge: The Boydell Press, 2014)

Hands, Thora, *Drinking in Victorian and Edwardian Britain: Beyond the Spectre of the Drunkard* (London: Palgrave Macmillan, 2018)

Herring, Jonathan, Ciaran Regan, Darin Weinberg and Phil Withington (eds), *Intoxication and Society: Problematic Pleasures of Drugs and Alcohol* (London: Palgrave Macmillan, 2012)

Institute of Alcohol Studies, *Alcohol in the Workplace Factsheet* (March 2014)

Jackson, Carolyn and Penny Tinkler, '"Ladettes" and "Modern Girls": "Troublesome" Young Femininities', *Sociological Review*, 55.2 (2007), pp. 251–72

Jordan, Sarah, *The Anxieties of Idleness: Idleness in Eighteenth-Century British Literature and Culture* (Lewisburg: Bucknell University Press, 2003)

Kostas, Makras, 'Dickensian Intemperance: The Representation of the Drunkard in "The Drunkard's Death" and *The Pickwick Papers*', *19: Interdisciplinary Studies in the Long Nineteenth Century*, 10 (2010), pp. 1–18

Laing, Olivia, *The Trip to Echo Spring: Why Writers Drink* (Edinburgh and London: Canongate, 2013)

Lessa, Iara, 'Discursive Struggles Within Social Welfare: Restaging Teen Motherhood', *British Journal of Social Work*, 36.2 (2006), pp. 283–98

Levin, Susan M., *The Romantic Art of Confession: De Quincey, Musset, Sand, Lamb, Hogg, Frémy, Soulié, Janin* (Columbia, SC: Camden House, 1998)

Lucas, E. V., *The Life of Charles Lamb* (London: Methuen, 1968)

Ludington, Charles, *The Politics of Wine in Britain: A New Cultural History* (Basingstoke: Palgrave Macmillan, 2013)

Maddison, Sarah, *Beyond White Guilt: The Real Challenge for Black-White Relations in Australia* (Sydney: Allen & Unwin, 2011)

Marcus, Leah S., *The Politics of Mirth: Jonson, Herrick, Milton, Marvell, and the Defense of Old Holiday Pastimes* (Chicago and London: University of Chicago Press, 1986)

Marsh, Beth, Molly Carlyle, Emily Carter, Paige Hughes, Sarah McGahey, Will Lawn, Tobias Stevens, Amy McAndrew and Celia J. A. Morgan, 'Shyness, Alcohol Use Disorders and "Hangxiety": A Naturalistic Study of Social Drinkers', *Personality and Individual Differences*, 139.3 (2019), pp. 13–18

McBride, Charlotte, 'A Natural Drink for an English Man: National Stereotyping in Early Modern Culture', in Smyth (ed.), *A Pleasing Sinne*, pp. 181–92

McGann, Jerome, *Byron and Romanticism*, ed. James Soderholm (Cambridge: Cambridge University Press, 2002)

McIntosh, James R., 'Gin Craze', in *Alcohol and Temperance in Modern History: An International Encyclopedia*, ed. Blocker, Tyrrell and Fahey, pp. 265–67

McKeon, Michael, *The Secret History of Domesticity: Public, Private, and the Division of Knowledge* (Baltimore, MD: Johns Hopkins University Press, 2005)

Mackiewicz, Alison, 'Alcohol, Young Women's Culture and Gender Hierarchies', in Patsy Staddon (ed.), *Women and Alcohol: Social Perspectives* (Bristol and Chicago, IL: Policy Press, 2015)

McShane Jones, Angela, 'Roaring Royalists and Ranting Brewers: The Politicisation of Drink and Drunkenness in Political Broadside Ballads', in Smyth (ed.), *A Pleasing Sinne*, pp. 69–78

Miner, Earl, *The Cavalier Mode from Jonson to Cotton* (Princeton, NJ: Princeton University Press, 1971)

Mizejewski, Linda, *Divine Decadence: Fascism, Female Spectacle, and the Makings of Sally Bowles* (Princeton, NJ: Princeton University Press, 1992)

Monckton, H. A., *A History of the English Public House* (London: Bodley Head, 1969)

Nash, David and Anne Marie Kilday, *Cultures of Shame: Exploring Crime and Morality in Britain, 1600–1900* (London: Palgrave Macmillan, 2010)

Newman, Ian, *The Romantic Tavern: Literature and Conviviality in the Age of Revolution* (Cambridge: Cambridge University Press, 2019)

Nicholls, James, *The Politics of Alcohol: A History of the Drink Question in England* (Manchester and New York: Manchester University Press, 2009)

O'Callaghan, Michelle, 'Tavern Societies, the Inns of Court, and the Culture of Conviviality in Early Seventeenth-Century London', in Smyth (ed.), *A Pleasing Sinne*, pp. 37–54

Oppenheim, Janet, *Shattered Nerves: Doctors, Patients, and Depression in Victorian England* (New York and Oxford: Oxford University Press, 1991)

Paulson, Ronald, *Hogarth: Art and Politics, 1750–1764* (Cambridge: The Lutterworth Press, 1993)

Pedlar, Valerie, *'The Most Dreadful Visitation': Male Madness in Victorian Fiction* (Liverpool: Liverpool University Press, 2006)

Penning, R., A. McKinney and J. Verster, 'Alcohol Hangover Symptoms and Their Contribution to the Overall Hangover Severity', *Alcohol and Alcoholism*, 47.3 (May–June 2012), pp. 248–52

Petersen, Per Serritsev, 'Jack London's Dialectical Philosophy Between Nietzsche's Radical Nihilism and Jules de Gaultier's Bovarysme', *Partial Answers*, 9.1 (2011), pp. 65–77

Phillips, Rod, 'Gin', in *Alcohol and Temperance in Modern History*, ed. Blocker, Tyrrell and Fahey, pp. 263–65

—————, *Alcohol: A History* (Chapel Hill: University of North Carolina Press, 2014)

Plant, Moira, *Women and Alcohol: Contemporary and Historical Perspectives* (London: Free Association Books, 1997)

Porter, Roy, *London: A Social History* (Harmondsworth: Penguin, 2000)

Porter, Roy and Mikuláš Teich, *Drugs and Narcotics in History* (Cambridge: Cambridge University Press, 1995)

Rickards, L., K. Fox, C. Roberts, L. Fletcher and E. Goddard, 'Living in Britain, no. 31. Results from the 2002 General Household Survey' (London: Stationery Office, 2004)

Riede, David G., *Allegories of One's Own Mind: Melancholy in Victorian Poetry* (Columbus: Ohio State University Press, 2005)

Roberts, Helene E. (ed.), *Encyclopedia of Comparative Iconography: Themes Depicted in Works of Art* (Chicago, IL: Fitzroy Dearborn, 1998)

Rohsenow, D. J., J. Howland, S. J. Minsky, J. Greece, A. Almeida and T. A. Roehrs, 'The Acute Hangover Scale: a New Measurement of Immediate Hangover Symptoms', *Addictive Behaviors*, 32.6 (June 2007), pp. 1314–20

————, J. Howland, J. T. Arnedt, A. B. Almeida, J. Greece, S. Minsky, C. S. Kempler and S. Sales, 'Intoxication With Bourbon Versus Vodka: Effects on Hangover, Sleep, and Next-Day Neurocognitive Performance in Young Adults', *Alcoholism, Clinical and Medical Research*, 34.3 (March 2010), pp. 509–18

Rolfe, Alison, Jim Orford and Sue Dalton, 'Women, Alcohol and Femininity: A Discourse Analysis of Women Heavy Drinkers' Accounts', *Journal of Health Psychology*, 14.2 (2009), pp. 326–35

Roth, Marty, *Drunk the Night Before: An Anatomy of Intoxication* (Minneapolis and London: University of Minnesota Press, 2005)

Scodel, Joshua, *Excess and the Mean in Early Modern English Literature* (Princeton, NJ and Oxford: Princeton University Press, 2002)

Shrank, Cathy, 'Beastly Metamorphoses: Losing Control in Early Modern Literary Culture', in *Intoxication and Society: Problematic Pleasures of Drugs and Alcohol*, ed. Jonathan Herring *et al*, pp. 193–209

Slutske, W. S., 'Genetic Influences on Alcohol-related Hangover', *Addiction*, 109.12 (December 2014), pp. 2027–34

Smyth, Adam (ed.), *A Pleasing Sinne: Drink and Conviviality in Seventeenth-Century England* (Cambridge: D. S. Brewer, 2004)

————, '"It were far better to be a *Toad*, or a *Serpant*, then a Drunkart": Writing about Drunkenness', in Smyth (ed.), *A Pleasing Sinne*, pp. 193–210

Snyder, Katherine V., *Bachelors, Manhood and the Novel, 1850–1925* (Cambridge: Cambridge University Press, 2004)

Spacks, Patricia Meyer, *Gossip* (Chicago, IL and London: University of Chicago Press, 1986)

Span, S. A. and M. Earleywine, 'Familial Risk for Alcoholism and Hangover Symptoms', *Addictive Behavior*, 24.1 (Jan–Feb 1999), pp. 121–25

Spurr, John, *England in the 1670s: The Masquerading Age* (Oxford: Blackwell, 2000)

Staddon, Patsy, 'Improving Support for Women with Alcohol Issues', *Folk. us-PenCLAHRC Awarded Study* (22 September 2013)

Stephens, Richard, Jonathan Ling, Thomas M. Heffernan, Nick Heather and Kate Jones, 'A Review of the Literature of Cognitive Effects of Alcohol Hangover', *Alcohol and Alcoholism*, 43.2 (2008), pp. 163–70

Swift, Robert and Deena Davidson, 'Alcohol Hangover: Mechanisms and Mediators', *Alcohol Health and Research World*, 22 (1998), pp. 54–60

Tangney, June Price and Ronda L. Dearing, *Shame and Guilt* (New York and London: Guilford Press, 2002)

Taylor, Anya, *Bacchus in Romantic England: Writers and Drink, 1780–1830* (Houndmills: Macmillan, 1999)

Treeby, Matt and Raimondo Bruno, 'Shame and Guilt-Proneness: Divergent Implications for Problematic Alcohol Use and Drinking to Cope with Anxiety and Depression Symptomatology', *Personal and Individual Differences*, 53.4 (2012), pp. 613–17

Tsai, G., D. R. Gastfriend and J. T. Coyle, 'The Glutamatergic Basis of Human Alcoholism', *American Journal of Psychiatry*, 152.3 (1995), pp. 332–40

Verster, Joris, *et al*, 'The Alcohol Hangover Research Group Consensus Statement on Best Practice in Alcohol Hangover Research', *Current Drug Abuse Reviews*, 3.2 (June 2010), pp. 116–26

———, ECNP conference paper (2015) <https://www.sciencedaily.com/releases/2015/08/150829123815.htm>

Vickery, Amanda, *Behind Closed Doors: At Home in Georgian England* (New Haven, CT & London: Yale University Press, 2009)

Vigarello, Georges, *The Metamorphoses of Fat: A History of Obesity* (New York: Columbia University Press, 2013)

Walton, Stuart, *Out Of It: A Cultural History of Intoxication* (London: Penguin, 2001)

Ward, Arthur, *Death and Eroticism in the Poetry of Keats and Tennyson* (Los Angeles: University of California Press, 1975)

White, Jonathan, 'The "Slow But Sure Poyson": The Representation of Gin and Its Drinkers, 1736–1751', *Journal of British Studies*, 42.1 (2003), pp. 35–64

Withington, Phil, 'Introduction', *Cultures of Intoxication, Past & Present*, 222. Suppl_9 (2014), pp. 9–33

——— and Angela McShane (eds), *Cultures of Intoxication, Past and Present*, 222. Suppl_9 (2014)

———, 'Food and Drink', in *The Ashgate Companion to Popular Culture in Early Modern England*, ed. Andrew Hadfield, Matthew Dimmock and Abigail Shinn (Farnham: Ashgate, 2014), pp. 149–62

Wrightson, Keith, 'Alehouses, Order and Reformation in Rural England, 1590–1660', in Eileen Yeo and Stephen Yeo (eds), *Popular Culture and Class Conflict, 1590–1914: Explorations in the History of Labour and Leisure* (Brighton: Harvester, 1981), pp. 1–27

Wu, S. H., 'Heritability of Usual Alcohol Intoxication and Hangover in Male Twins: The NAS-NRC Twin Registry', *Alcoholism, Clinical and Experimental Research*, 38.8 (August 2014), pp. 2307–13

Yeomans, Henry, *Alcohol and Moral Regulation: Public Attitudes, Spirited Measures and Victorian Hangovers* (Bristol and Chicago, IL: Policy Press, 2014)

Ylikhari, R. H., C. J. P. Eriksson, Matti Huttunen and E. A. Nikkilä, 'Metabolic Studies on the Pathogenesis of Hangover', *European Journal of Clinical Investigation*, 4.2 (April 1974), pp. 93–100

Index

.